Commitment to Sustaina

Ooligan Press is comn
an academic leader in
publishing practices. Using both the
classroom and the business, we will
investigate, promote, and utilize
sustainable products, technologies, and
practices as they relate to the production
and distribution of our books. We hope
to lead and encourage the publishing
community by our example. Making

BOOK

sustainable choices is not only vital to the
future of our industry—it's vital to the future of our world.

OpenBook Series

One component of our sustainability campaign is the OpenBook
Series. *The Wax Bullet War: Chronicles of a Soldier & Artist* is the
sixth book in the series, so named to highlight our commitment
to transparency on our road toward sustainable publishing.
We believe that disclosing the impacts of the choices we make
will not only help us avoid unintentional greenwashing, but
also serve to educate those who are unfamiliar with the choices
available to printers and publishers.

Efforts to produce this series as sustainably as possible focus
on paper and ink sources, design strategies, efficient and safe
manufacturing methods, innovative printing technologies,
supporting local and regional companies, and corporate
responsibility of our contractors.

All titles in the OpenBook Series will have the OpenBook
logo on the front cover and a corresponding OpenBook
Environmental Audit inside, which includes a calculated paper
impact from the Environmental Paper Network.

OpenBook Environmental Audit
The Wax Bullet War: Chronicles of a Soldier & Artist
Figures below are calculated for a print run of 3,000 paperbacks.

	Chemicals	Greenhouse Gases	Energy	Fiber	Waste
Paper[†]					
Cover Paper: 10pt Kallima C1S. 153 lbs. used.	Insufficient data.	428 lbs. carbon dioxide equivalent used in production.[‡] Tembec is committed to being carbon-neutral by 2015.	2 million BTUs used in production[‡] Manufactured by Tembec, in Canada.	Paper produced from approximately two trees.[‡]	147 lbs. of solid waste produced in paper production.[‡]
Text paper: 50-lb. Tembec offset, 30% PCW. 2,982 lbs. used.	Less than 1-lb. reduction of volatile organic compounds; 1-lb. reduction of hazardous air pollutants.[‡]	925-lb. reduction of carbon dioxide equivalent.[‡]	5 million BTU reduction in net energy[§] Manufactured by Tembec.	2-ton reduction in virgin fiber use, the equivalent of about 11 trees.[‡]	336-lb. reduction in solid waste; 5,019-gallon reduction in water consumption.[‡]
Printing & Binding					
34.5" sheets printed on Timsons T32 press by United Graphics Inc in Mattoon, Illinois.	Timsons Quick Make Ready system reduces downtime, and make-ready and bindery waste.	UGI uses Barsol solvents to clean their presses.	Insufficient data.		Lamination reduces damage to books, which reduces the number of unread, returned copies.
Perfect bound with Bostik adhesives. 4.5 lbs. used.					
Cover finished with matte lamination film manufactured by Transilwrap Company, Inc. 1,781 ft. used.					Transilwrap Company, Inc. uses recycling programs to reduce factory waste.
Ink					
Vision Series offset printing ink manufactured by Alden & Ott Printing Inks in the United States.	Vision Series ink are vegetable-based.	Insufficient data.	Insufficient data.	n/a	

This Open Book Audit—performed by Ooligan Press—stems from our commitment to transparency in our efforts to produce a line of books using the most sustainable materials and processes available to us.

All quantities and material specifications supplied by United Graphics Inc.

[†] Environmental impact estimates made using the EPN Paper Calculator tool at http://www.papercalculator.org.

[‡] Compared to paper made with 100% virgin fiber.

Praise for The Wax Bullet War

Sean Davis has opened up the soldier's story wide enough for all of our humanity to emerge—messy, beautiful, chaotic, tender, violent, loving. The territory between soldier and artist is breathtaking.

— Lidia Yuknavitch, author of *The Chronology of Water* and *Dora: A Headcase*

Funny, insightful, literate and poignant—this book will draw equal laughs and tears from its readers. It will stand as one of the best combat memoirs to come out of this new generation of warriors.

— John R. Bruning, author of *The Devil's Sandbox*

The best kind of art breaks, inspires, haunts, and ultimately puts us back together in a slightly altered order so that we may see the world as we have never seen it before. Sean Davis's *The Wax Bullet War* does precisely this—connecting our hearts and minds to the dark and perilous as we follow the author's unflinching and dogged attempt to survive some of the most horrific episodes in recent American history.

— Deborah Reed, author of *Things We Set on Fire*

The Wax Bullet War is not a book about battle and its glories. This is a book about duty and its consequences, about rising up from poverty and overcoming PTSD, and about love and art and picking up the pieces and moving on. Sean Davis's language is pure and poetic and visionary, and his story, one of the finest accounts of the combat veteran's experience you will ever read, is unforgettable from page to tightly-composed page. Every American and every citizen of the world should read this book and learn from its message of peace and forgiveness and human understanding.

— Mike Magnuson, author of *The Right Man for the Job*, *Lummox*, and *Heft on Wheels*

Funny, dark, honest, and sad, Davis' tale of training and combat in Iraq is an important reminder that our politics have consequences.

— David Axe, *War is Boring*

A brutally honest account of an ordinary young man surviving extraordinary situations.

— Danfung Dennis, director of the documentary *Hell and Back Again*

The Wax Bullet War

THE WAX BULLET
WAR

Chronicles of a Soldier & Artist

Sean Davis

Ooligan
PRESS

The Wax Bullet War: Chronicles of a Soldier & Artist
© 2014 Sean Davis
All images © 2014 Sean Davis

ISBN: 978-1-932010-70-1

Ooligan Press
Department of English
Portland State University
P.O. Box 751, Portland, Oregon 97207
503.725.9410; fax 503.725.3561
ooligan@ooliganpress.pdx.edu
www.ooliganpress.pdx.edu

Library of Congress Cataloging-in-Publication Data available by request from the publisher.

Printed in the United States of America

Cover design by Gina Fox
Interior design by Cyrus Wraith Walker

Publisher certification awarded by Green Press Initiative
www.greenpressinitiative.org

For Eric and the amazing men of Bravo Company 2/162, Infantry

And for Mag—thank you for showing me that
each word is just as important as each idea

Contents

Preface

Ten years ago a good friend of mine was killed in an explosion that put me in the hospital for a couple months. Another friend of mine was critically injured that day. In all, four men in my company were killed during our tour in Iraq: Eric McKinley, Kenny Leisten, Ben Isenberg, and Dave Weisenburg. I hope to hell this book honors these men.

After coming back hell-broke and feeling ruined, I fell into a place I didn't think I could get out of. Not even the people closest to me knew how bad it was. I thought about taking my own life and many times wished I had died in combat. But this book isn't a complaint or a long list of the ways I think the war messed me up. I am proud of what my unit did over there. The men in my company were exceptional and I hope to show this, but I have two reasons for writing this book: I want to give the family members of combat veterans a glimpse of what their soldiers went through, and I want to let other soldiers in that dark place know they're not alone. They can get through it and lead successful lives.

Most things in this book are true. I changed the names because everyone remembers traumatic events differently, and not everyone can be at their best all the time, especially when they don't know someone is going to write about them. Hundreds of people in and out of uniform became huge parts of my life during the period of time contained in this story. I wish I could have listed them all, but it became clear early on in this project that I would need to merge some of them and not mention many others. A few events were changed, but the war stuff is true: we were shot at or mortared every day, many people died, and we helped who we could.

'Thinketh, such shows nor right nor wrong in Him,
Nor kind, nor cruel: He is strong and Lord.
'Am strong myself compared to yonder crabs
That march now from the mountain to the sea;
'Let twenty pass, and stone the twenty-first,
Loving not, hating not, just choosing so.

"Caliban upon Setebos," Robert Browning

Holes

The morning Simon Scott was killed he sat in the back of our Humvee with his elbows on his knees and told me his theory on life. He said he'd figured it all out. Everything we take in or put out goes through a hole. It didn't matter if a person fought in a war, drank himself to death, chased girls, or risked his life to be a hero; every action was made to fill one hole or another. We laughed and threw rocks at stray dogs while waiting in the Iraqi heat for our final combat mission, the mission that would take his life and send me home on a stretcher, bone-broke, bruised, and soul-wrecked. I skipped right over what he was trying to tell me that day and didn't think about it for a couple months after the ambush, but now I think about it all the time. When I remember each decision I made leading up to that one afternoon, I think about the hole I was trying to fill.

September 11, 2001: I was twenty-eight years old and had been a civilian for two and a half years since leaving the army after a six-year hitch. In all that time, I had never once thought about reenlisting, but the next day I jumped in my beat-up white Toyota and drove off to join the Oregon National Guard. The recruiter's office was a chaotic sea of college kids who had changed their minds about joining up now that the threat of war was on every channel, every station. I cut right through them, walked up to the desk, and told an old sergeant I wanted to do my part and reenlist. I remember him turning to another soldier and saying, "There's still hope for the republic after all."

Those words made me proud of my decision, gave me a sense of heroism. From then on, whenever people talked about that horrible moment in our history, I was able to say I reenlisted the next day.

Where I grew up, in the poor trailer parks of Western Oregon, the kids didn't see much of a future for themselves. The best we could hope for was a manager position at Les Schwab or Safeway, or maybe leaving for a season to be a fisherman in Alaska, but most ended up as loggers like their fathers. I wanted to create beautiful art and stories, to get people's attention and approval. Looking back at this I can see Simon was right; I was only trying to fill a hole.

Because of her pregnancy with me, my mother left high school during her sophomore year, never to finish. Dad stuck around long enough to have two more sons, and by the time my mom was twenty years old she had three children and no husband. She didn't make it two years before she gave up her sons to be raised in the green mountains of Oregon by our paternal grandparents. After a few years, our grandparents realized they were too old to raise boys and forced our father to come back, to marry, to raise his sons.

My brothers and I ended up in the Cascade Mountain Range, in a poor logging town made to stop logging because someone decided the spotted owl was an endangered species and needed miles of untouched forest to breed. Between jobs, Dad sold most of our food stamps for half their worth in cash so he could buy liquor. He worked hard when he was employed and drank hard at home. At school, children were cruel to my two brothers and me for being poor, and at home we were beaten for trivial things like not cleaning our plates, not bringing in the firewood, or forgetting to feed the dogs.

I used art as an escape and read books about uncompromising heroes. I was an odd child who wanted to be Cyrano de Bergerac, Jean Valjean, a Musketeer. Many times the books were too smart for me, but I read through the *Divine Comedy* and *Paradise Lost*, and I'd memorize a line I liked even if the bigger story was too difficult for me to understand. This didn't make me smart, just weird, an outcast. I only saw one way out of that small, mountain town life, and when I was old enough I raised my hand, said the oath, and left.

The US Army Infantry sent me around the world. I lived in Hawaii, New York, and Germany; I deployed to real-world situations with a rifle in my hand. During my first three years as a private, I learned that the human body can withstand ten times the amount of punishment the mind thinks it can. I ran marathons in Hawaii, went through cold-weather training in thirty degrees below zero in upstate New York. During the second three years I was sent on deployments in some very poor countries where I discovered much of the world doesn't have the same respect for human life that we do in the United States.

I read or scribbled pictures during my downtime, and eventually the other soldiers in whatever unit I was stationed with would figure out I was an artist. The commander would always task me with painting the company murals. Dozens of my eagles still fly on giant rocks in training areas around the world. My skulls loom in the halls of my old company CQ rooms and common areas. My bulldogs, too. But my biggest piece, the one I am most proud of, filled the walls of an entire room in upstate New York.

I painted an ocean of sharks in a weight room at Fort Drum, paying special attention to this mural because I saw the similarities between sharks and infantrymen. A shark is nature's perfect killing machine; if a shark stops swimming, it can't breathe, it dies. Infantrymen never stop training to be killers. I sat for hours in the small room breathing in the paint fumes, suffering the headaches, going days over my deadline in order to get it right. With plastic on the ground and the walls and ceiling painted like the ocean, I spent hours on each shark until I was almost covered with the same blue shade, just one more shark in the aquarium.

At the end of my second tour I left the army. My last duty station was at a small military intelligence base in the Bavarian countryside of Germany. I had been away from the United States for two years without watching US television, reading US news, or even visiting. When the end of my tour came I decided to get to know my country again. I flew into Pensacola, Florida, and rented a truck to drive across America all the way to Los Angeles with the hopes of becoming a famous artist like Chuck Close, Roy Lichtenstein, or Franz Kline.

Driving through the main arteries of the United States filled my chest and mind with colors and feeling: southern hospitality, New Orleans jazz, endless Texas sky, lightning storms over a New Mexican valley—every place had a unique type of person living there, so many types I felt maybe the world wouldn't mind one more. But it only took a couple of weeks in LA for me to realize that I needed to go home.

The Pacific Northwest was where I belonged. I settled in a place on Southeast Hawthorne Boulevard in Portland, Oregon, and used the GI Bill to enroll in art school. Finally I was an artist. I had the charcoals and canvases and paints and brushes to prove it. My experiences in developing countries gave me a perspective the other students didn't have. My worldliness gave me an advantage. The faculty knew me to be gifted, and soon I had made friends with a tight group of artists, including a small man of Spanish descent named Francisco Cabra. He was from New Mexico and had long, curly hair and earlobes stretched from plugs. We had a number of classes together and went to the same parties. I met Jaime through Francisco.

She spoke about going into graphic arts so she could get a job after graduation. My degree would be in fine arts, and when someone would ask what I would do with that degree, I always said, "Be an artist."

I was all in, and she admired that. She loved my work and my crazy lifestyle, but more than that she believed in me. She was my first beautiful thing, my first beautiful thing to feel deeply about. We laughed and drank wine, and she would pose nude for me by candlelight in my little apartment so I could draw her with charcoal. Her long, dark curls were natural, and even when she didn't smile the traces of her dimples made her look serene. She had a strong jawline with beautifully defined neck muscles that the light danced along. Yoga and biking gave her a compact, muscular-but-feminine frame. Her vision of my future was even greater than mine, and after months of being together I couldn't see a future without her.

At the end of winter term we went a week or so without seeing each other. It was finals so I didn't think too much of it, but when she grabbed my hands with her fingerless gloves and sat me down in the common room of the art college I knew something was about to go wrong. She told me she had met a drummer in an Elliott Smith cover band. In an even and honest voice she told me I would be great one day, and she very much enjoyed the time we had together, but it was over.

A year later, I was living in a shitty little town seventy-five miles south of Portland. I had left school and found a state job on the Internet. After reviewing the military experience on my résumé, the managers at the Oregon Department of Transportation hired me on for a new position called an incident responder.

I spent most shifts driving in three-hundred-mile circles on state highways and didn't see or talk to another person all day. I learned that a pitchfork, not a shovel, was the best tool for getting rid of raccoon, opossum, or nutria carcasses. The flat blade of a shovel caught the sticky intestines and I'd have to spray it off, while the sharp points of the pitchfork rolled the animal into a ditch or culvert nicely. The morning was the best time to scrape them, too, because the heat of the afternoon hadn't yet caused their stomachs to bloat.

But even with all the roadkill, this was a government job with sick days and good benefits—the type of job people I grew up with would kill for. My boss wasn't that bad; he was just an incredibly lazy and gluttonous man whoppered down in his youth. A fifteen-minute conversation would wind him, so we didn't talk much. I drove to work, jumped in the incident response truck, and drove in big circles on the state highways for ten hours a day. On my least busy days, I dealt with a dead raccoon or the carcass of a deer; on the busiest days, I helped the police reconstructionist control traffic and clean up fatal car accidents. At the end of these shifts, I strapped a five-gallon jug to my back and sprayed bleach over the asphalt to dilute the blood and wash the car fluids from the road. Then I returned to the garage, jumped in my shitty, beat-up car, and drove to my shitty, cluttered duplex. I never painted, never drew pictures, and never read anymore. Eleven months. For eleven months I gave up on art, beauty, and trying to become that person I'd imagined myself to be.

I slept in the day the towers fell. We all remember the moment we heard the news of the attacks, and I was in my underwear with my house phone cradled against the side of my face, my mom telling me to turn on the television.

On September 12th, 2001, I signed a six-year contract to serve Bravo Company 2/162, Infantry, in the Oregon National Guard.

The armory was twenty miles west in the college town of Corvallis. National Guard soldiers reported to their armory one weekend a month and two full weeks out of the year. I had to wait until October for my first drill, and by that time every yard and porch displayed flags showing their wind-whipped American pride under a sky that refused to be blue. Every radio and television outlet played the worst of 9/11 on heavy rotation, and in the couple of weeks since it happened many reporters had the time to focus on one horrible, tearjerking story of bravery or death, each one meant to break your heart.

On the day of my first drill I showed up early, parked in front of the one-story brick building, and sat in my car questioning my decision and staring at the armory for at least twenty minutes. I could hardly take my eyes off the red brick walls or the row of small, curtained windows. A couple of college kids rolled down the sidewalk on skateboards and I envied them so much. I wanted to be them. I wanted not to have a care in the world.

In one sudden and violent movement, I sat forward, turned my car off, flung the door open, popped out, and walked with purpose toward the armory. The building sat like an island in a field of freshly cut, bright green grass. A cement path framed with small, colorful flowers led from the sidewalk to a set of blue metal doors. Some landscaper had planted rosebushes on each side of the main entrance, probably in the hopes of making it more beautiful and inviting, but the tangles of bare, thorny branches appeared to be slowly dying, and they had the exact opposite effect. Halfway down the cement path stood a soldiers' memorial made of three black marble slabs about four feet high, arranged in a C shape. A metal pipe with a saucer on top like the Space Needle shot out of a block of concrete behind the marble slabs. I stopped to read some of the names. They were dead Oregon soldiers from past wars etched into the black marble. I forgot the names as fast as I read them.

The blue metal door scraped against the concrete landing, and the horrible sound made me jump; it was a sound I imagined the gates of the City of Dis would make in Dante's *Inferno*. I turned to see a man in forest green dress uniform walking toward me, lighting his cigarette with a Zippo lighter. He walked with such a determined look on his face I thought I had done something wrong, but when he got closer I found I wasn't the focus of his attention. He walked right up to the metal pipe, puffing on his cigarette, making the cherry nice and hot before climbing up on one of the black marble slabs and holding the end of his cigarette over a hole in the middle of the metal saucer. With a smile he said, "The goddamn eternal flame went out again."

The gas flowing from the hole ignited and he hopped down.

I looked at my steel-toe work boots and then back at him, knowing I should say something. He probably guessed that, too, and made it easy on me by introducing himself. Staff Sergeant Danny

Addison was the first person I met there, and he had an easy way about him. Danny always had raised eyebrows, but this didn't make him look confused, just friendly like he was open to whatever a person had to say. When he spoke, his hands never stopped moving, and his eyes were the color of a worn brass handle. He told me right off that he was one of two full-time National Guard soldiers who staffed the Corvallis Armory. I shook his hand and started to ramble nervously, telling him my whole story.

Danny smoked another cigarette and listened to me talk about my job, my prior service, the places I had lived. When that was done, I told him about my favorite artists, and I was going on without thinking about it this turned into a story about Jaime and how she was the one that got away. This, out of everything I said, made his face light up. He stuck his cigarette between his teeth, unbuttoned his uniform top, and pulled his right arm out of its sleeve to show me a tattoo of a pinup girl with the words "man's ruin" underneath. His eyes didn't leave the tat when he said, "Women: the only trouble worth getting into."

Small drops of rain sizzled as they hit the hot metal saucer near the flame. I smiled and asked him who I needed to report to, it being my first day in the company and all.

"Oh, shit. You're Sergeant Davis." He stuck out his right hand.

I shook it and gave him a nod.

"Fucking glad to meet you. Let's get you a uniform."

The first night back in the army was awkward and clumsy. The lower enlisted wouldn't talk to me, afraid I was an asshole. Soldiers my rank wanted to know how full of shit I was and quizzed me on my prior duty stations. They asked what restaurants were in the food court in Fort Drum's Post Exchange or what the biggest gulch was nicknamed in Schofield Barracks' training range. I didn't talk to the higher enlisted, afraid they might be assholes. I ended up passing most of the night reading.

I was issued uniforms, a gas mask, field equipment, and my rifle. The unit had different rifles than I was used to. During my first stint in the army we had the old M16s, but Bravo Company had the updated, lighter M4s: new and improved teeth for the shark.

Sean and the soldiers of Double Deuce
training at Fort Hood, Texas.

The Big Game

During weekend drills, I led armed men through the wet, forested hills of Oregon and trained them to kill people and blow things up. Between those times I scraped roadkill, took orders from a morbidly obese government employee, and drank enough to believe the characters in sitcoms were my friends. The routine was comforting, but a year and a half slipped by without change. I dated a divorcée or waitress every once in a while, but they all ended badly after a few weeks. These romantic failures made me think about how perfect it was with Jaime for that one year. I hated doing it, but in my darkest and drunkest times I dialed Jaime up just to listen to her voicemail. It made me love her and hate her at the same time.

In the summer of 2003, after dangling the opportunity for promotion in front of me, the Oregon Department of Transportation finally told me that they didn't feel I could supervise one guy driving in circles on the state highways and promoted a turkey-necked bald guy of Eastern European ancestry to replace my old boss, who took a promotion in Eastern Oregon. The new guy's swollen red eyes blinked constantly, and he spoke slower than I've ever heard a person put words together.

I tried not to be insulted, but the military had inflated my ego just enough to make it sting like hell. There was no telling what they saw in him, what he had that I didn't, other than a complete disregard for hygiene and modern dentistry. I threw around hints that I was going to quit, but they didn't register. He would just blink at the wall.

In the end I couldn't do it anymore. I told Turkey Neck I was off to pursue a more challenging line of work. I told him I wanted to give cryptozoology a try. He didn't move except to blink, so I explained that I felt tracking Bigfoot and collecting the beast's feces appealed to me more than working under him. They gave me a bit more than two thousand dollars when I cashed out my 401(k), which bought me a few weeks to come up with something else.

The next Saturday morning, I found myself sitting through a class on how to make a bowel movement in a combat zone during a chemical attack. The long and short of it involved a charcoal-lined suit, a poncho, an entrenching tool, and as many baby wipes as a person can get a hold of. I laughed with the guys after the class while all two dozen of us funneled through the one door. I was heading to the drill floor when I heard Sergeant First Class Schofield call my name. His voice was unmistakable. Schofield was the guy you didn't want to piss off, the guy you tried as hard as you could to make proud. Most soldiers just wanted to stay off his radar altogether. He was the other full-time National Guard soldier who ran the armory with fast-talking Danny Addison. Schofield had his ranger tab, which was intimidating enough, but the story behind how he got it was worse. Ranger school is hard as hell for eighteen- to twenty-year-olds, but he made it through without issues on the first try when he was in his late thirties. Everyone knew him to be the driving force behind Bravo Company.

I stopped and moved to the position of parade rest, the military's way for a subordinate to show respect to a higher-ranking NCO. He was a few inches shorter than me physically but much larger in prominence. He took a second before speaking to look me up and down, inspecting me, making sure I was setting a good example for my men. I had never seen eyes the color of his before. They were gold and bounced around his sockets, reminding me of a bird of prey. He said, "Sergeant Davis, you are now my Second Squad leader."

That was all he said and he walked away right afterward, leaving me in the hallway thinking. He had the best platoon in the battalion, and his other squad leaders had ranger tabs too, or were prior Special Forces, or national-award-winning sharpshooters. I had no idea why he would choose an art school dropout to lead a squad of eight infantrymen in his platoon. Nothing he had done had given me a clue he even knew my name until that moment. He would expect more, which meant longer hours and harder missions, especially during our yearly two-week training period, which was scheduled for the following month. He also told me that the paperwork to promote me to staff sergeant was in, which was a good thing because a solid two weeks' pay at that level would help me save up a down payment to get my shit together. I decided I would take that money and move back to Portland at the end of the summer. This little self-imposed exile was killing me; I needed culture, friends, and art.

The two-week training was held at Camp Rilea, a small coastal base the government had used during World War II in case of a Japanese attack. Very few improvements or renovations had been made in all the years since. The barracks were open bays with bunk bed-lined walls. Quonset huts lined the grounds like giant half-buried trashcans turned sideways. Small wooden one-story buildings painted bleached-bone white served as administrative offices.

On the first day we unloaded our gear in the sunshine and lined it up. We sat on our rucksacks waiting for instruction. Our company commander drove up in a Humvee and called everyone to gather up in a horseshoe formation. Since I had joined the unit I'd only heard him speak once or twice at the end of a weekend drill, and that was only to give safety briefings before the major holidays. We all thought he was going to instruct us on how to be safe while training the men to shoot each other. A hundred of us surrounded a five-ton truck and looked up at him as he stood on its folded-out tailgate.

I was in the back with the other squad leaders, expecting to hear that alcohol was strictly forbidden during annual training, or how we shouldn't blow our full two-week paycheck at Thong Thursday at Sancho's Bar when we got back. Standing next to me was Staff Sergeant Tom Cederman, the First Squad leader for the platoon, second in charge after Sergeant First Class Schofield. Tom worked some sort of industrial job in Washington state and volunteered as a county sheriff a couple times a month. The man could tie forty different types of knots and tell you the names for each. Hell, he gave out laminated cards with useful information like radio procedures, nine-line MEDEVACs, or the army phonetic alphabet, and not only did he give them to the guys in his squad but to the other squad leaders, too. The year before, he had made the President's Hundred, a shooting competition to find the hundred best marksmen in the United States. To Tom, every bit of training was something to be observed closely and disseminated, so it was a bit out of character when he tapped me on the shoulder and told me he needed to take a shit. He asked jokingly if I would fill him in on anything he missed.

He wasn't gone two minutes before the CO — the commanding officer — announced we had been called up by the Pentagon and would be deployed as part of Operation Iraqi Freedom. He announced this with the gravity it deserved and let the words sink in. I looked from him to the blue sky and listened to the summer wind blow through the branches and the gravel crunch under the boots of everyone around me as they shifted their weight. We would leave within two months' time.

The captain went on talking about the logistics, but I didn't hear him anymore. Instead I pictured tanks with red crescent moons painted in blood, shimmering in the desert sun. I saw the vast Persian army of Xerxes. I imagined gritted teeth and angry eyes piercing through loose headdresses and gnarled fingers firing rocket-propelled grenades. I had been to Haiti my first time around, but that wasn't anything more than police action. We were only shot at twice and the guns might as well have been homemade.

But this was Iraq.

Iraq. We would be going in right after the initial push into the country. Soon I would be on the other side of the world with a gun in my hand. There was a reason I reenlisted in the Oregon National Guard and not the regular army. I wanted to do my part, but thought my part would be patrolling the airport or guarding Umatilla Chemical Depot in Eastern Oregon.

Iraq. Looking at the faces around me, I could tell they were all as surprised as I was. Memories of CNN reporters live in Baghdad ran through my head. I would know that place soon. Two sentences repeated in my head: *This is real. This is really happening.*

Iraq. None of us spoke. Behind me I heard the returning footsteps of Cederman, and I turned to look at him with a cocked eyebrow; he was aware that he had arrived in the middle of a heavy moment, but he wasn't sure of the reason. "What happened? What did I miss?"

The missions started right away. This two-week period turned out to be more difficult than any of us would have thought. The colonel started us on road marches and continuous operations. We marched up and down the beach, along gulches, and through the small fake town they'd built out there for urban warfare simulation. The fake town was what the army called a military operations in urban terrain, or MOUT, site, and it was essentially a bunch of empty buildings made from cinderblock and wood. We crawled over small cement fences and through basement windows, second-story windows, and underground tunnels. We shot blanks at each other while sprinting across alleys, roads, and fields with our wet, heavy gear.

The colonel and a couple majors came to watch every once in a while with their chests all puffed out. Sometimes one of the majors would call us over to give a big speech about how wars weren't fought in jungles or deserts anymore. We were in a new era of modern warfare; every street was a linear danger zone, every window a sniper, every door a funnel of death. We were all an Army of One and needed to be hard, suck it up, do more than we thought we could. Then they would get in a Humvee and drive back to their nice rooms, leaving us to run around in the woods, soaked to our bones.

The real-world deployment meant a restructuring of the company. We had three platoons that were sixty percent full, but we needed to deploy at one hundred percent strength. This meant getting volunteers from other units, and if they weren't experienced infantrymen we would train them up. We called this reclassing. Our platoon was restructured and I was issued a new squad. Specialist Nicholas Melvin, a skinny kid with bad posture and sunken eye sockets, was my Alpha Team leader. While I had never worked with him before, he had a reputation as a man who could find things. This skill bordered on thievery at times.

My Bravo Team leader was Specialist Baldwin, a blond-haired, blue-eyed kid around twenty-five who could have doubled for Captain America, and what he lacked in perspicacity he made up in loyalty. He and Melvin were new to leadership roles, and it would take me a while to help them get their footing, but they weren't the biggest challenge I faced.

I had eight men total, including my two team leaders, but the two problem children were Simon Scott and Mechaiah O'Brian. I didn't know if he thought giving them to me demonstrated Sergeant Schofield's confidence in my leadership abilities or if he just plain didn't like me, but either way it was my task to turn these two around.

Tall and skinny, Mechaiah had been a truck driver before being reclassed. Of course, he did have two DUIs and his license had been revoked, but he could pull a trigger so someone volunteered him to be an infantryman. His trigger finger might have worked fine, but he couldn't hit shit and had no clue about any of the infantry tactics. On the day I met him I asked why the hell his parents had given him a fucked-up name like Mechaiah, and he told me with a straight face, in a quiet voice, that they were going to name him John but didn't want other people making fun of him. "You know, because John is another name for the bathroom, Sergeant."

"What is Mechaiah another name for?" I asked.

"They own a Christian bookstore, Sergeant."

I would give him long blocks of instruction on a weapons system or how to pack his ruck, and he would just stand there behind his god-awful army-issued glasses and hardly say a word. O'Brian really wanted to do well; in the beginning he just didn't have the ability, but that wasn't really his biggest issue. I would find that the main problem with O'Brian was that when he got a couple drinks in him, he was done. The lanky boy wanted to fight as soon as he felt the beginning of a buzz, and once he started drinking he didn't stop until he blacked out. The first time he was late for drill, I called the phone number he had down as his home of record only to find I had called the pay phone outside the Circle K on the Oregon State University campus. I had to take a Humvee around town and search the bushes in the backs of pubs for him.

Simon Scott was my other troubled youth. The army runs on a belief system that everyone must follow. Everyone must believe the rank system gives authority to the men holding the ranks. The higher-ranked men must have the character, knowledge, and experience to be good leaders, and their charges must adhere to protocol, etiquette, and procedure. Every once in a while a soldier comes along who doesn't buy into all of this. He doesn't want to play pretend. Simon was one of these. For some reason he didn't separate his civilian life from his military life, and instead of snapping to the position of parade rest and calling me Sergeant Davis he would look at me with that half smile of his, wave, and say, "What's up, Sean?" I would tell him to do push-ups when he screwed up and he'd laugh, and then get mad when I really made him do them. He didn't think of himself as Private First Class Scott when he put his uniform on; he was just Simon wearing the pickle suit.

Every day of the two-week training, the commander assigned us to be good guys or bad guys, to raid a house or to defend one, to walk into an ambush or to set one up. Most of the Bravo Company squads followed the infantry tactics to the letter, but I tended to use my imagination to solve problems. We baited other squads into ambushes, used the terrain to our advantage, and flanked the soldiers trying to flank us. What really worked was giving the squad a nickname. Once we started calling ourselves Double Deuce—we were Second Squad in Second Platoon—the boys really gelled, and we started getting the attention of the higher-ups. Even Simon started to soldier up, so much so that Sergeant First Class Schofield called him over and asked him what the hell had happened to turn this skater punk into a steely-eyed killer. Simon told Schofield that it was real now, we were going to war, so he might as well start paying attention and doing it right.

At the final formation of the two-week training, all four-hundred-plus soldiers of 2/162 Infantry Battalion stood tall in an open field at Camp Rilea. The battalion commander announced to us all how proud he was to go to war with men of our caliber. Then he completely surprised us by calling my squad to stand in front of everyone to be recognized as the best in the battalion. We just looked at each other before moving because we were all at the position of attention. I looked to Sergeant Schofield for permission to move and he jerked his head in the colonel's direction. We ran up and stood in a column. One of the majors started up with the attention-to-orders speech like they do when handing out awards, and the colonel walked straight up to me.

He fumbled with a medal before pinning it to my chest like he was installing a part on a machine. I saluted him; he returned it, leaned in, and whispered, "Good job, Sergeant. Your men are real killing machines."

Killing machines, I thought, and sharks swam through my head. They swam around my broad chest and down my strong arms and up my sturdy legs. I was a shark again.

I thanked him and watched him go down the line, pinning pieces of shiny gold to the chests of every man in the squad, even O'Brian. Even Simon.

Robots Love Car Bombs

Once we returned from training and were sent back into the real world, the first person I called was my little brother Vince, to tell him about being sent to war. The words seemed so strange coming out of my mouth. I was back at my shitty duplex, in my civilian life, and a silly thought crossed my mind: maybe it didn't happen, maybe it's not real. But it was, and Vince asked me a question I wasn't prepared for. He asked, "What are you going to do over there?"

This should have had an easy answer. War meant fighting the bad guys, but none of the briefings included information on exactly who the bad guys were. They didn't include much information at all, actually, and the lack of an enemy didn't seem to matter to anyone. Most people in the country felt a deep need to do something about the 2,977 innocent lives taken on 9/11. Shit, I did too. The soldiers in Bravo Company were no different, except we had the opportunity to do something about it. Seeing those flaming towers on repeat filled me full of anger and rage, but I didn't call it that; I called it patriotism and duty. Although these primal emotions were natural to feel, for some reason I thought I was above them. I wouldn't admit to myself that I had a need for revenge, but how would that play out in Iraq? Saddam was a tyrant that gassed his own people and according to Colin Powell he had WMDs and terrorists training camps, but I saw right away there was no connection to the attack on the Twin Towers, the Pentagon, or the White House. So when my brother asked me that question, I had no real response. I hadn't thought about it until right then.

The obvious answer was that we were being sent to a lawless Middle East to kill evil people and break things. Before, when someone had asked me what the infantry did, that's what I'd say. But now that I was actually going to war, I stopped to think about it. I knew from experience what a real-life deployment meant: real people facing desperation, violence, and death. Back in 1995, I had played my small part in an infantry line platoon in Haiti. Our larger mission was to provide the country with stability, and nothing says stability like a couple brigades of highly armed American soldiers patrolling every street corner.

Haiti was only classified as a police action, but I saw some fucked-up shit. The people there were so poor that some of the less ethical soldiers traded C batteries to young girls for hand jobs through the chain-link fences. My squad responded to a riot outside of President Aristide's palace only to find that a woman had squatted between two parked cars and birthed a baby in the gutter. When the United Nations decided to put in place a program where people could trade guns for food, some of them tried to turn in toy rifles carved from blocks of wood or thick tree branches. One time a man was killed fighting for something he found in our base's trash pile.

During one miserable patrol in the hills around Les Cayes, we followed the stench of burnt shit and garbage into a village and found a couple dozen Haitians kicking a man to death. We pulled the broken man out of the mob without knowing or understanding what the hell was going on. The captain ordered another private and me to load the dying man into the back of our Humvee. I spent the next hour sitting over him, listening to him die a slow and painful death as we drove around trying to find a hospital that still had electricity. Every time the Humvee hit a bump on the unimproved roads the broken man gasped ragged breaths through his crushed windpipe until he finally died at my feet. In the end we dumped the body at a makeshift police station, ignoring the protests of two cigar-smoking Haitian volunteers.

I remembered that the army mission briefings during that deployment had taught me only enough to fear the people I was there to help, and I decided this time would be different. My answer to my brother's question surprised me as much as it did him. I said we were going to help the Iraqi people get their lives back together. I went on to say I was going to learn their language and read up on their history and religion. The next day I bought *The Complete Idiot's Guide to Understanding Iraq* at a bookstore and started reading it.

I broke the lease on my shitty duplex and moved in with fast-talking Danny Addison. Danny worked full-time at the armory with Sergeant First Class Schofield, so I would get all the up-to-date information on the looming deployment. Being unemployed gave me time to read my Arabic language or Iraqi history books and do physical training. But even this and the drinking couldn't fill the empty time between finding out I was going and actually getting on the plane.

I called my other brother Keith and told him. I spoke to my mom in San Francisco and my dad and his wife in Los Angeles. Maybe it was selfish, but I liked telling people. When I explained it to someone else, I was also talking myself into it. The reactions of my family helped with the fear of it all. The problem was that after a week I had no one left to tell. I had even called my grandma. One night I finally decided to call Jaime.

Jesus Christ, I can't figure out why the hell I stayed fixated on that girl, but I couldn't help remember the winter nights we walked in the bad weather from my one-bedroom place on Hawthorne to the 7-Eleven to buy cheap red wine, laughing, rain dripping from our noses. Those were the nights I spent drawing her in charcoal by candlelight as we sloshed the wine in our cups. Now I was sleeping on a twin mattress on the floor of an unfurnished guest room, living out of a suitcase and studying for the big game, waiting and waiting. I wanted just a piece of that old life back, just a taste to convince myself that I could still be that artist. Maybe not today, but someday.

I'm not sure why I thought she would answer, but after the fifth ring her voicemail kicked in. I hung up without saying anything and felt as empty as the dark rooms of the apartment. I decided to hit the college pubs so I could watch all the pretty coeds make bad life decisions. The first place I landed was a college-town version of an English pub called the Fox and Firkin. I couldn't turn my head without seeing a tight sweater riding up to reveal a tattoo on the young pink flesh of a lower back. Meathead jocks in striped rugby shirts hovered around like dogs waiting to be petted.

The joint had a dartboard in one corner and served fish and chips. That was the extent of English culture except for a giant Union Jack thumbtacked over the polished wood bar. Under this flag I saw Simon and his girlfriend June smoking cigarettes and laughing. Seeing them there was like an answer to a prayer. I walked up and grabbed Simon's shoulder. He turned with his half smile and not a hint of surprise. "Hey, Sean, have a seat."

Simon had his nose ring back in and wore a ripped black T-shirt with the name of some obscure band on it. His right forearm had a tattoo sleeve of a honeycomb, or maybe some Celtic design, and his baggy jeans had a silver chain coming out of the back pocket, the other end of which was latched to a belt loop. Simon and his famous half smile. I called everyone else in the company by their last names, but not Simon. It just didn't fit him, the formality of referring to him by just his last name.

I didn't know too much about Simon before he was put into my squad, aside from the stray story or two. I knew he was a skater kid into tattoos and piercings. I'd heard about the Red Dragon. Whenever we got a new private in the company Simon would introduce them by showing them the Red Dragon. His pubic hair was red and he had the head of his penis pierced. If you asked me what Simon's genitalia had to do with initiating new soldiers I would be at a loss, but it seemed to be the way things worked.

Simon and June sat only inches apart and seemed to always be touching, with a hand on a knee, a shoulder, a leg. They communicated with each other through just a glance or an expression. June was a small and quiet young woman with long, straight hair the color of redwood. She had the alternative style I expected Simon's girlfriend to have with her long black skirt and odd jewelry, but I didn't expect her to be so intelligent and observant. Sometimes when she looked at me I thought she could see too much.

Simon was a baker in his real life, and when he talked about it his words came fast, like he didn't have enough room in his head for all the ideas he had to improve the craft. His hands zipped around and he smiled while he told me about the best type of butter to use, how to glaze the bread, or which grains were best. The way he spoke about rolling the dough reminded me of the time and care I used to take setting up my paints, straightening the easel, and preparing my brushes before starting a new piece.

He said they wanted to open a tattoo shop that served fresh-baked bread. June watched him tell the rehearsed story like it had already happened and he was accepting some sort of prize. Her proud eyes even followed him away after he excused himself to the bathroom. Then she looked at me. I didn't mean to lock eyes with her, but she made sure I did. "You're going to be in charge of him?"

"Yes, and that's scary because I have no fucking idea what I'm doing," I said, and laughed.

She kept looking at me with the same intensity. "Is it going to be dangerous?"

The mood was too heavy, awkward. I tried to smile but it came off skewed and dumb. "It's war."

She wouldn't let go of my eyes; even when I lit my cigarette, she wouldn't let go. "We're going to get married when he gets back. He hasn't asked or anything, but I just wanted you to know we talked about it."

"I know, and open the bread-and-ink shop." I picked at the coaster under my pint.

"You're not some robot, are you?" Her nervous fingers unwrapped the plastic from a new pack of cigarettes.

"Robot?" I broke away from her gaze and exhaled.

"Who'll just follow orders no matter what." Now she made a point not to meet my eyes again. "This war is only to make the rich richer. They don't care about people like Simon, or you." Her voice cracked, and the fear she felt made her one of the most beautiful women I had ever seen.

Simon returned with a dimpled smile and ordered two Irish Car Bombs. These drinks consist of a shot of Jameson, a shot of Bailey's, and a pint of Guinness. He gave me one and we toasted to the Union Jack before dropping the shots in the beer and throwing them back. After we closed the pub down, we staggered back to their basement apartment. They were happy to let me sleep on the futon in their living room between two very large and warm dogs.

Lying there that night, I thought about the beautiful fear June felt for Simon. I knew that if I could just feel a bit more like a soldier I could ignore the anxiety that goes with being sent to war and view it as a way to escape my problems, as an opportunity. Maybe June was right, and they didn't care about soldiers like Simon and me, but the war would be a way to meet a need I had but couldn't explain. I call it the Viking gene. My life was too ordinary and too dull, and being deployed was going to give me something exciting and important to do, something worth dying for, something that would make it beautiful to be alive.

Trained Stupid

I was activated on Monday, October 6, 2003, and put on permanent orders for Operation Iraqi Freedom a full week before the lower enlisted soldiers. In that week, Battalion told us that before heading to war we would be sent to train stateside for half a year. What they didn't tell us filtered down anyway: since we were one of the first National Guard units to be sent into combat, the brass at the Pentagon decided we needed to be trained up by the regular army. That way they could be confident we weren't beer-guzzling weekend warriors who would end up scalping someone or shooting each other. The orders sent the whole battalion to Fort Hood, Texas, for five months before we ended up in Louisiana for one last month-long training exercise.

Texas was hot and flat, two words a person would never use to describe the Pacific Northwest. The whole place put me off kilter. The artist in me wanted colors and balance; I couldn't find either. The day I got off the bus, the first sergeant pointed us toward some old barracks before my eyes could even adjust to the intense sunlight. We grabbed our gear and found our assigned rooms.

The barracks were vacant because Fort Hood Command had scheduled them for demolition in order to build modern living quarters for new troops. Fluorescent light fixtures hung open, their wires snaking out from gaps in the ceiling tiles. Holes of all sizes decorated the interior surfaces, and ancient drywall crumbled into dusty piles on the thin carpet. We were paired up, and my roommate was Second Platoon's Third Squad leader, the crazy former Navy SEAL Dave Zabat. Sergeant Zabat had the hunched back of a caveman from carrying too much weight for too many years. His father was an Irishman and his mother was Greek, which made him a short, angry man almost as wide as he was tall, with hair everywhere except on the top of his head. He had graduated from Navy SEAL training years before enlisting in the Oregon National Guard, and I was sure he felt that shooting someone from a distance was almost like cheating. He was the type of soldier who wished the world had no weapons, only because that would mean we could all beat the shit out of each other with our bare hands. He taught the platoon a mixed form of hand-to-hand combat during downtime. We had a corner room on the third floor that over-looked the Burger King, the on-post movie theater, and the Class VI, the military's version of a liquor store. It was the perfect place to put a unit if you're worried about them being fat, lazy drunks.

We jumped out of bed the next morning, excited to be in a new place with a new mission. At 0500 hours, we stood, rank and file, in the cold dark of morning and loaded up on Blue Bird school buses, then headed out to a close-quarter shooting range.

Government-employed civilians ran the ranges, so things moved slowly and were oversimplified. The army used return-ing Iraqi soldiers as primary trainers for our battalion. Some of them had just returned from tours less than a month before, and there was a reason they were removed from their old units. No unit wanted to lose a functioning and successful combat veteran of any rank, and no functioning and successful combat veteran would ever volunteer to become a trainer. Some of the soldiers getting us ready for combat were the broken-spirited and war-wounded; they hated the fact they hated war.

Some of them came back with limps, unable to carry even basic equipment. Most of them hardly spoke unless they were instructing. When they did, their instruction came in the form of anecdotes that involved the incident that messed them up. No matter the lesson, it always led back to the time they got shot, or the time a friend of theirs got blown up, or the time they shot someone at point-blank range.

Our platoon's main trainer had finished his second tour of Iraq only a couple months earlier. His skin had the sallow color you could only get from being wrapped in bandages or under a cast for a month or two, and he had absolutely no hair, not even eyebrows. But the most peculiar thing about him was the way he spoke in whispers, as if the words he used were constrained by the weight of their meaning. He looked through us when speaking like we were the ghosts that haunted him. We called him Captain Intenso.

Captain Intenso had no problem road marching or shooting with us, but when we moved into the MOUT site he would lose his shit completely. He would start whispering to himself, and the tics in his speech and his movements would amplify and become more frequent, until they were almost funny. We began to see him as a joke, a warrior who had lost his craft and become a caricature of himself. I wondered why he didn't just give it up and get on with his life. Why continue to torture himself by staying in?

The MOUT sites were real enough at Hood; each one was like a little town, complete with houses, stores, and schools, all full of beat-up furniture. The army used its deep pockets to make the training as realistic as possible. They spread garbage all over the streets of the training area, just like we would see in Iraq, and they even hired Arabic-speaking civilians and dressed them appropriately. Between these missions, when we drank water in the shade, I would look over and see Captain Intenso's hand shaking while replacing a canteen or going over his notes.

At the end of one MOUT missions, he called the entire platoon into a fake church. We sat in the pews with our rifle butts between our feet, barrels pointing to God, listening to him speak in his low, raspy voice. He told us about Private Rosewood. To us Private Rosewood was just a name, but the way Captain Intenso spoke I had no problem believing that he saw the private in the back of the room. Rosewood had gone over to pet a stray puppy and a second later had his guts blown out like party streamers.

The captain's whisper trailed off into a barely audible mumble about the downright unsportsmanlike conduct of the aggressive combatants on today's modern battlefield.

"The ragheads don't have the common courtesy to give the American soldier a fair fight. They shoot from shadows and run away. Some of the ragheads aren't ragheads at all. Some of them are blond-haired and blue-eyed Serbian mercs looking for the bounty on the head of every US soldier."

Captain Intenso paced between the rows of pews, and the sound of his combat boots hitting the wooden planks of the fake church's floor gave rhythm to his words. "You think it's just a Pepsi, but then, *fucking boom!* Now you're waiting for the MEDEVAC chopper to fly you to the CASH, thinking about how your wife will have to wipe your ass for the rest of your life because you got no fucking hands."

I didn't know what the CASH was, but I sure as hell wasn't going to ask. I don't think he expected us to know because he stepped back up on the fake stage behind the pulpit and said slowly, "Combat. Army. Surgical. Hospital."

The boys laughed about it when he left, but later that night I heard many of them on their cell phones repeating the same lines to family members back home: Combat. Army. Surgical. Hospital.

The rest of the training at Fort Hood went on like this: we were attacked by Russian helicopters; we protected convoys from a

platoon-sized ambush; we breached two- and three-story buildings; we did many other things that had nothing to do with our
mission in Iraq. We started to call it CTB training, or Check-the-Box.
We figured the colonel had a big list of tasks regular army men
did and wanted to show the Pentagon that we were just as qual-
ified. The problem was that while we ran ourselves ragged with
these missions, we didn't do much physical training, and we did
absolutely no language or cultural training. It seemed to me we
needed to prepare for our upcoming role in a war, not try to jus-
tify being sent. Of course, my view on things from the bottom was
completely different than the big picture of the brass, but I remembered being a private in Haiti. The people terrified me because I
didn't understand their language, history, or culture, and it doesn't
take a genius to know that we fear what we don't understand.

On one of our few days off, about two months in, Zabat and I
played a drinking game while watching damn near all of *Band of
Brothers* on his laptop. We pounded a beer or threw back a shot of
Jameson every time something blew up. I couldn't imagine doing
the shit they asked soldiers in World War II to do, like performing
an amphibious assault on fortified beachheads, or walking miles
in the snow with shit gear, or crouching at the bottom of a foxhole
hoping an enemy artillery round didn't find them.

Our generation had better weapons and better equipment, and
we severely outnumbered our enemy, but Dave and I talked about
how that era of soldiers had something more important: a reason
to fight. Everyone in the armed forces back then knew what the
hell they were fighting for. They knew what the enemy looked
like too. Sure, Captain Intenso told us daily about all the dangers
of "today's modern battlefield," but no one explained why they
were even sending us to Iraq. Saddam was a real son of a bitch,
but he wasn't trying to take over the world and force fascism on
everyone. I was caught up in the excitement of doing something
in response to 9/11, but was doing something I couldn't understand better than not doing something at all? Colin Powell stood
in front of the United Nations and told the world Iraq had WMDs.
"WMD" was thrown around by everyone on the news. It was the
new buzzword, but what made something a weapon of mass destruction, and how did you know if they were bad? Hell, I was a
weapon of mass destruction, or at least I soon would be. Pakistan,

North Korea, Syria all had wmds too. Shit, India and China had nukes. Damn if I knew what any of it meant.

Angry thoughts and whiskey were a bad combination. I needed to breathe deep and calm down. I stepped out on the windy balcony and looked down at the long lines of lampposts, car headlights, and house lights spiderwebbing away from our barracks. Most of the other buildings on base were one story, probably due to hurricanes or twisters or whatever other messed-up weather conditions belonged to that part of the country. I was in the middle of a blurry and sparkling world that went on to the horizon. Reality looked upside down because all the stars stretched and blinked on the ground and the sky was one big black tarp. The ground over my head and the stars under my feet made me feel better, like all the crazy wasn't just happening in my head. I'd joined the military so my life might make sense again; I didn't know it at the time I reenlisted, but that was the reason just as much as anything else. And it almost worked.

Until I thought about it. I was being shipped to the other side of the world to fight in a war I didn't understand, but at that moment on the balcony, whiskey-drunk and lonely, looking at the upside-down universe, it all almost started to make sense. All I had to do was spend the night drinking the better part of a twelve-pack, shooting Irish whiskey, and getting teary-eyed watching my mortality unfold on a seventeen-inch laptop screen in a series of three-act dramas. The reason didn't matter. I wasn't sure what did matter; maybe it was the act of going, maybe it had something to do with that Viking gene.

I was so close to finding the big truth; in that particular moment, the thought of calling Jaime seemed like a good idea. I pulled my flip phone from the pocket of my cargo shorts, the wind whipped at my open Hawaiian shirt. I punched in her number, held the phone tight to my ear, and sighed.

After five rings her voicemail clicked on and my heart almost broke. I read the signs wrong. Must have. I snapped the phone shut and leaned over the rail so far I scared myself a little. Doubled over like that, I had to look up at the ground. My jaw burned with stomach acid and I spit. The poison was coming back up ail at once and there was no stopping it.

I jerked myself upright with violent haste, and the jarring motion churned my stomach. The room was pitch black when I flung the door open. Dave had turned the lights off to try and sleep.

I tripped over his bed and a chair, slammed into a wall locker, tripped on some clothes, and crashed into the bathroom like an avalanche, a score of beer bottles clanking behind me. I was still four feet away from the toilet on my first heave, but my aim was true. When the vomit hit the water it splashed everywhere—on the tiled floor, the side of the tub, the wooden cabinets under the sink, and all over my face and torso.

I didn't hear the phone ring until I finished the third heave. I fumbled with my cell, saw it was Jaime, swallowed hard—drug mule hard—and answered.

"Hello?"

"Hello, my name is Jaime Hansen. I'm returning a call from this number."

"Yeah, Jaime, it's me." I panted hard and pulled some toilet paper from the roll to wipe my mouth. I could hear faint club music in the background on her end. She hated club music.

"It's me. Sean. Sean Davis."

"Sean?"

I heard Dave's bare feet slap on the tile floor. He flipped on the light in the front room, walked to the bathroom door, and looked in. "Jesus fucking Christ, Davis."

"Jaime, Jaime—so, how are you?" I felt the cold porcelain against my chest and the vomit soaking through my Hawaiian shirt.

Dave stood hunched in the doorway with his thick forehead scrunched. "What the fuck did you eat? Is that spaghetti?"

"Sean, where are you?" Jaime asked.

I looked back at him. "Calamari, from TGIF. Give me a minute."

Dave shook his head and walked away.

"Where?" Jaime asked.

"Texas, sorry. I got a little sick and my roommate's here, but… anyway, where are you? I hear club music. You hate clubs." I laughed a type of laugh I didn't remember ever using before.

"Are you drunk?"

I laughed that laugh again. "No, I just wanted to talk to you. I got a new cell phone and thought you might want the number. They said we're heading to Baghdad, Jay."

More muffled music filled the gap before she answered, "I know. Francisco told me." I was trying to think of the next thing to say but she beat me to it. "Why did you join up again? What was going through your head?"

"They needed good people, Jay. You know, 9/11."

"Yeah. Well, you take care of yourself, Sean. I'm out with my parents and need to get back. I applied for Pratt, and I thought you were them calling me back."

She paused like she wanted a reaction, but I had no idea why.

She continued, "It's a very prestigious art school in Brooklyn." She paused again. "New York."

"I know where Brooklyn is, Jay."

"I didn't recognize the number, thought you might be them."

"That's what you said. Art school, Brooklyn, great." I spit in the toilet and saw that my gums must've been bleeding. I had the taste of copper in my mouth and the smell of vomit around me. I took my shirt off and started wiping off the side of the tub and the wood cabinets. "When are you going there?"

"That depends if I get accepted. Pratt's hard to get into."

"'Cause I have some leave coming up when we're done out here. I was hoping that we could spend some time together. I was going to drive to San Fran to see my mom and then to LA to see Dad. We can go on a road trip."

"I have to go, Sean."

"Yeah, me too. I'm sorry I called so late, but are you going to be around in early March?"

"I don't mind you calling me. I just don't want you to think we're going to get back together. That's not fair to either of us."

I closed my eyes and felt the cold curve of the toilet against my forehead while the muted beat bounced around over the static on the line.

"I'm sorry, Sean."

"Ah, don't worry about it. I'll probably be busy anyway. I have to go, Jaime. You know the army, always a bathroom floor to clean, people to yell at. I have to get up early for some fast-rope training. We're sliding down ropes out of hovering helicopters, just like *Black Hawk Down*, no shit."

"You take care of yourself. Be safe," she said.

"Of course. They can't kill me." She had already hung up.

The Part Where I Have Drunken Sex with a Cowgirl and Later Eat Lunch with the President of the United States of America

Danny saw me moping around and decided the next night we had off he would take me to the Market District in downtown Austin. Soldiers were discouraged from going to Austin because we didn't do well with crowds after being deprived of normal social settings for a couple months, but we were in our last week of Texas training so it was our last chance to see the big city. Plus, I thought it would be a great way to get Jaime off my mind, hopefully for good.

A couple of privates, Private First Class Trace Ford and Private Craig Walken, heard us planning the trip and asked to come along. Ford was a chicken rancher from a small town named Damascus in Oregon. He had soft blond hair, softer blue eyes, and a beak of a nose. I had never met a chicken rancher before I met Ford, but I couldn't imagine anyone looking more like a chicken rancher after meeting him. Everything about him gave it away, from his quick movements to his feathery hair, and when he was excited I swear the kid clucked.

Craig Walken was another one of the guys in Double Deuce, my squad. Walken happened to be the youngest soldier in the battalion. His parents had signed a waiver to get him in the army at seventeen. He claimed New York City as home, and even tried to have the accent at times, but the truth of it was his family left the city when he was five to start a Christmas tree farm in a small mountain town called Alsea, thirty miles west of Corvallis.

Danny rented a giant SUV with tinted windows and a powerful sound system. I sat up front. I had been away from civilization so long, I kept the window down so I could smell and hear everything: the food from the corner hot dog stand, bus exhaust, horns honking, people yelling.

The blue and yellow neon signs of the Market District spanned a dozen city blocks along Sixth Street. Most of the pubs or clubs were made of brick, with storefront-big windows that showed the world how much fun the pretty, young people inside were having. I watched them talking and laughing while Danny paid a lot attendant to park the car. The only pretty women I'd seen for months were the two-dimensional types in the pages of a dirty magazine. I thought I could smell the perfumes and shampoos of the women from where I stood.

The closest pub jumped with people, music, and drink. No one seemed to know there was a war going on, and somehow that was comforting. Maybe I would forget too.

The colors, my god. I had gone so long seeing only green and tan that the platinum-yellow hair, sapphire-blue eyes, pink- or mocha-brown skin, and magenta-red lips drove me crazy. The vitality of the night made me feel like a real person again. Training for war had taken all my focus. Being a good leader of men in combat left no room for anything artistic in my life. I hadn't even had the time or inclination to scribble or read during the downtime, but being in that bar full of colors and laughter made me suddenly want to paint. The artist in the back of my head wanted to capture the moment. The music flowed around the smiling people so loudly that I pictured using thick paint strokes like Van Gogh. I'd use his yellows and blues as well, give every person their own outline. The whole scene reminded me of his café terrace paintings.

Danny leaned over the bar and ordered four pints. We started with a toast and vowed to get laid that night. We had a couple rounds before Walken and Ford were riled up enough to talk to the opposite sex. I put them over the top by pulling two crisp hundred-dollar bills from my pocket and betting each of them they wouldn't get any. They pushed themselves away from our table like men on a mission.

I racked some pool balls on a red felt table. The fear and excitement I'd felt on the way into town had settled into a smooth and mellow confidence. I wasn't there yet, but playing pool in that Austin pub, listening to good jazz, and smiling at a couple of hot girls across the room was part of the journey. I was proud of myself, and I don't think I would have changed my path—no matter how many times Captain Intenso told us about the CASH. Combat. Army. Surgical. Hospital. It was the goddamn Viking gene again. Silly human men court death to feel alive. My ancestors built rickety ships and sailed into the unknown, joined crusades, fought world wars. I joined the most powerful and technologically advanced army in human history to go and fight illiterate thugs living in mud huts. But still it was something.

Three rounds of pool and five pints later, Danny and I found ourselves playing doubles with two blond veterinarians in tight jeans from Rockdale, Texas, a town they said was an hour from everywhere. They had come to Austin for an equine health convention. The girl I partnered with had a cheerleader type of beauty. The color of her hair came from a box and her fingernails were as manufactured as her tan, but she had the body of a runner and small perky breasts that I hoped were as fake as the rest of her. She told me a story of being elbow-deep in a horse's vagina, helping the miracle of life along. I gave all the nods and exclamations of someone who was interested, all the while eyeing her curves and cleavage. Everything about her was Texan, from the lazy drawl coming out of her highly glossed lips right down to the yellow stitching of her little boots.

When the bar closed down the girls agreed, between giggles, to let us give them a ride to their hotel. They flirted in the back of the suv with Walken and Ford on the drive, but when we finally parked Danny found a radio station playing old-time big band songs, and with the door open we swing danced with them under the streetlights in the parking lot of their hotel. Walken and Ford fell asleep in the car.

We twirled, spun, and groped for a half-dozen songs while the old fat guy behind the counter of the motel office watched with nervous glances. Every twirl smelled like exotic flowers, and I could feel my heartbeat in her laughter. I pulled her tight and we touched foreheads for a second. I could do anything at that moment in time, and what I chose to do was hold that small girl close to me, make out for ten minutes or so, and then suggest we take it to her room. She agreed.

The lights in her motel room flickered on and she immediately went to packing up the outfits she had left spread out on the bed, all the clothes she didn't wear that night. She stuffed them into a pink suitcase with a grandma floral pattern and motioned to the mini fridge with her head. There was a half-full bottle of Vanilla Stoli and some Big Red soda. I made a couple drinks in red plastic cups, handed one to her, and moved close enough to feel her breath on my face. We kissed a little more, and it was awkward until we found each other's rhythm. We made our way onto the bed and then she pulled away and asked if I had ever been to a rodeo. I told her no, but I hoped to. We went at it until six in the morning. I had her leave on those boots with the little yellow stitching.

Two things about infantry colonels: they're all fast runners, and they all have a sadistic sense of humor. The day before we were to pack up and move on to Louisiana, the colonel decided to celebrate our time in Texas by taking the battalion out on an eleven-mile run. These runs were usually pretty slow because each company lined up and had to stay in step. They were monotonous but tolerable on most days, but the colonel didn't know we didn't need any more celebrating. We had all celebrated proper the night before. Every single man there swayed with a hangover that morning. I hoped and prayed it was just an accountability formation before being told to pack all our shit up, but then I heard the command for right face, then double time.

The colonel darted through the parade grounds and ran us through alleys and fields. The fucker wouldn't stop and the Texas temperature was rising faster than whatever I had drank the night before. I could smell beer and whiskey squeezing its way out of the pores of every man around me. A couple of the privates broke ranks to throw their guts up, but they all managed to sprint back into place. The only person to fall out and not catch up was our thick-necked, red-haired company commander. This was a big fucking deal.

When we finished, the colonel had us all do push-ups as some sort of twisted morale booster. About fifteen minutes into this, our CO came jogging in, looking like a refrigerator being pushed on a dolly. The colonel stopped everything until our commander fell back into formation.

Before the end of the day our company had another formation. The colonel had our captain apologize to us for his failure and introduce his replacement.

To me, this was the first in a long line of decisions that made little sense. Imagine a coach leading his team to the Super Bowl, and then the owner replacing him right before the game. It takes a company commander months to win the respect and trust of the soldiers in an infantry company, and that respect and trust is necessary for the unit to perform. The fact that the colonel gave us a brand new captain that late in the game made no sense to any of us, but maybe they had a big plan that we grunts at the bottom were not privy to. I didn't know. The closer we got to war, it seemed, the weirder shit got.

I couldn't bear to watch our old commander stand in front of our formation and humiliate himself by apologizing to us. Instead,

I examined the fidgety, dark-eyed replacement in captain's bars. His spit-shined tanker boots went higher than they should, almost three-quarters to his knees. His new company stood in front of him at parade rest and he was more interested in whatever was under his fingernails. When our old commander was done speaking, his replacement stepped up and introduced himself as Captain Charbonneau. I couldn't see the pupils of his eyes, just big, black balls on white orbs darting from one face to the other before resting on a small leather-bound journal he pulled from his starched cargo pocket.

One hand was tucked into the small of his back and the other held his journal as he read aloud. The pages held the highlights of his experiences and he read them like a grocery list without emotion. It was the same even when he came across something that probably should have had emotion, like when he said he very much appreciated the opportunity to lead us into combat, or the part about our company having a special role to play in history. The pitch and volume of his voice remained consistent while he told us all about the dangers of today's modern battlefield: every window a sniper's nest, every alley a linear danger zone, every door a funnel of death. Our old commander backed up slowly, a half step at a time, until he turned and continued on to the parking lot. Then he was gone.

I smoked four cigarettes and listened to the lower enlisted spew tales of debauchery while waiting for the buses to take us to the brush and swamps of Louisiana. A couple of them said they double-teamed some townie girl they'd picked up at Applebee's, and they did this while her father and five-year-old daughter watched *CSI* in the living room. They said the father turned up the TV to drown out the noise.

Others spoke about their families and what their children were doing back home. Home felt as far away as Iraq. I wondered what Jaime was doing, and then wondered why I still thought of her. I had pined over old girlfriends before; the same thing had happened to me when I went through basic. But Jaime felt like something more than that, more than just the one that got away. I still pictured myself being an artist after the deployment, and I still pictured her in that future.

I pulled my waterproof leader book from my left cargo pocket and flipped through pages of serial numbers that belonged to the equipment my soldiers carried. Some pages had birthdays, social security numbers, names of wives, parents, siblings, and children. Other pages had sector sketches and notes on other military tactics. Somewhere in the middle I found an empty page, and pulled my government-issued ballpoint pen from my left breast pocket. Right there, I started sketching the men in my squad, the way they sat on their rucksacks in the sun.

I sketched Private Craig Walken texting furiously on his new phone. I drew my Alpha Team leader, Melvin, hunched over and looking out at everyone from his deep eye sockets, holding his cigarette with just his index finger and thumb. I outlined Mechaiah O'Brian's long legs stretched straight out while he lay with his hat over his eyes. I captured the motion of Specialist Baldwin as he threw pebbles at a squirrel in a tree.

Simon's shadow darkened my page.

"Damn, Sean, that's pretty good," he said.

I thanked him without looking up.

"You draw tattoos? I have this idea…"

"I have before, but I don't like to. I don't like the idea of something I doodled being a permanent part of another person."

"I guess, but don't you think you're going to remember all this shit for the rest of your life? The things you do are going to be permanent memories for me, man. Just like what I do you're going to remember. I mean, we're going to war, Sean."

I looked up at him, but only saw his silhouette against the sun. The buses pulled up, and I flipped the book closed and slipped it back into my left cargo pocket, the pen into my left breast pocket. Everything has a specific place in a highly trained infantry platoon.

We loaded up our equipment in the cargo compartments. These were coach buses, the type with cushioned seats that take tourists to see pretty sights. Each one of us was counted, checked off a list, and then counted again after we sat down. I used the ride to Louisiana to catch up on sleep. I tried hard to dream of rodeos.

JRTC stands for Joint Readiness Training Center. This was not as fun as it sounds. The only weed there was of the noxious variety. The army carved out a big, ugly chunk of land in the middle of Louisiana. We called it the Box. US Army units from all over would send a unit of unfortunate soldiers there to suffer all the heat, humidity, and bugs the South had to offer. I had been there three times during my prior service years. If I were asked to design Hell, my own Inferno, the Box at JRTC would be my starting point, the top rings.

We were counted again once the bus stopped, just in case one of us had decided to jump out the window during the trip, and then we trudged through the gaggle-fuck of finding our equipment and putting it on. We walked like a giant turtle exodus to a set of World War II barracks.

The air was different in Louisiana, as if the smaller trees somehow made it taste different. Bugs chirped as loud as power line transformers from every direction. The first sergeant stood in a Moses pose with his arm pointed at a row of weather- and rodent-ravaged two-story buildings. I looked right past them, thinking that our barracks couldn't be those old buildings with the paint peeling from the wood siding and windowpanes so old the glass appeared to have melted.

The first sergeant told the assembled platoons that two of the six buildings were condemned, and we weren't to sleep in them. Then he hurried off to a meeting, leaving us to figure out which two of these hovels he meant. Each platoon took a building, and Second Platoon lugged our shit into the nearest one. I told Sergeant First Class Schofield that my squad would sleep on the top floor because I hoped it would be easier to survive a fall than to have the top floor land on us.

We had no training that night, and we weren't slotted to head into the Box for three days. I emptied my bags and refolded all my T-shirts, underwear, and socks, placing each carefully in the wall locker. I hung my two changes of civilian clothes and my Hawaiian shirt up. I had learned a trick from an old master sergeant I used to talk with back in Haiti. He told me that when I became a squad leader I should always tell my guys to have a Hawaiian shirt and a flask on their packing list. A Hawaiian shirt could trick your mind into thinking you were on vacation in some exotic land. Of course, you never really consciously forget that you're in a shithole eating bad food from plastic pouches and actively exploring new diseases you can't pronounce, but if even one tiny little part of your brain buys it, then maybe you can hold on to some sanity in a fucked-up situation. The flask, well, that was to carry alcohol. These two things have been on every packing list I've given out since.

We stayed in a very remote part of Fort Polk, miles away from the normal folk who lived and worked on the base. A swamp surrounded the Box, and the old barracks sat right on its edge. While out smoking on the metal fire escape I could see a motor pool full of tanks, a circular road cutting through the weeds that was no doubt a running path, and, almost a mile away, a small PX, or Post Exchange—the army's convenience store. I called for Simon to follow me and slid down the fire escape ladder, because I knew that as soon as the rest of the battalion discovered the PX they would descend upon it and buy the place out of cigarettes and beer within an hour.

An hour later we returned victorious, with three twelve-packs apiece and a carton of Marlboro Reds. It was a good night. Even Lieutenant Chris Caius, our platoon leader, said we did a hell of a job securing supplies for the men. Caius had to have been a Viking in a previous life. He was tall, bulky without being fat, and had a bit of a clumsy streak, but he could take apart a weapon in a minute, fix it, and shoot the hell out of it. The more he smiled, the more his eyes squinted, and with me he spoke mostly with squinted eyes.

A platoon leader is the lone officer in a platoon and, while he is usually younger and less experienced, he outranks even the platoon sergeant. Think of them as mother and father: the platoon leader is the nice mom and the platoon sergeant is the mean, cranky dad. Caius was a prior enlisted soldier who got his college education and became an officer, so he knew to listen to Sergeant First Class Schofield when his sentences started with, "Sir, I strongly suggest that…"

Another thing about Caius was he always surprised the hell out of me. One day he saw me reading *Animal Farm*, and we proceeded to have an hour-long conversation about Stalin, Lenin, and Trotsky. I would hear him speaking Russian one minute, Korean the next, and the day after that I'd see him pick up a musical instrument and play it like a pro. On that cool February night in Louisiana he found a guitar, and the entire platoon sat around outside the beat-down barracks and sang every Jimmy Buffett song we could remember. The air smelled sweet as tree sap, and we drank and took pictures of each other to send home. When the sun went down we all went in the barracks and kept singing, smoking, bullshitting, and messing around. I never saw a group of people so incredibly content, completely peaceful, and genuinely happy. We had the shoulder-grabbing-and-smiling-without-having-to-say-a-word type of understanding. This was it, the family I was looking for. Though I hardly had anything, I lacked nothing.

If you were to ask our colonel, the training at JRTC was a huge success. Bravo Company in particular showed such an improvement that *his* higher-ups fought over the opportunity to put us in special roles for the upcoming deployment. The two-star general came down to see how the training was going and saw an assault planned by Captain Charbonneau and executed by the company. This visit was purely routine, but the general left so impressed he told one of his aides to use "those Oregon boys" as his personal QRF, or quick reaction force. When this got out all the battalion commanders wanted us, too. We were a great infantry platoon—really, one of the best—but that wasn't the reason we got the general's attention. The reason we were so wanted rested squarely on the shoulders of fast-talking Danny Addison and one of our machine gunners in weapons squad we all called Dirty Burt.

After a week of living in the World War II barracks, the entire battalion moved into the Box to live within a warlike scenario for the rest of the month on a fake FOB, or forward operating base. A series of tents of all sizes made up the FOB. Some were filled with hundreds of cots, while others housed logistic needs, things like industrial-sized washing machines or mailrooms or chow halls. Every tent was wired with electricity and every wire led to a diesel generator. These generators became so commonplace in training and in combat that I can't pull up a single memory of being at war without their smell of diesel or their low hum. A few tents within the FOB were called TOCs, tactical operations centers. The TOC was where most of the bad decisions were made. Every few days we were sent to the field, where all of the good decisions were made. It worked like this: A real colonel would call us for a fake mission, and we would throw on our really heavy gear and trudge to a fake city to play laser tag. When we got "hit" and started beeping, we'd find some shade to be dead in and smoke cigarettes until everyone else was dead. Then we would lug all our shit back to our tent to hose the mud off, and start again next time we were called. All the little missions built toward the big mission at the end, when Danny and Dirty Burt turned us all into heroes.

The soldiers we played laser tag with were called the OPFOR, or opposing force. They took their jobs very seriously, as they should. They were training men and women for combat, but not in the way you'd expect. Most of their training taught people how to not get themselves killed rather than how to kill others, which of course was a big bonus for all concerned.

OPFOR consisted of soldiers stationed at Fort Polk, Louisiana. The people hired to be Iraqis actually spoke Arabic and wore the dishdashas and head wraps, but they were civilian federal employees and, being such, they took weekends, holidays, and sick days off. It took a while, but even us infantrymen started to see a pattern. Most of the fake missions came Monday through Friday, so on the weekends we went to firing ranges, grenade launcher ranges, or Humvee driving courses.

We lazed around on our off time, but the rest of the FOB buzzed with busy little bees. The administrative, bureaucratic, and logistical jobs always went on, but the killing jobs only came when all the other jobs lined up right and the enemy had enough people to fight. After we read all the books, got tired of playing cards and jerking off, and wrote everyone there was to write, we were left with an amazing amount of time to think of very stupid things to do.

Our path to glory started the night before the two-star general came to watch the big battle. Danny Addison bet Dirty Burt he couldn't daisy-chain twenty nine-volt batteries together, lick his thumbs, and hold them for ten seconds. This turned into a competition where a young private could make a name for himself by showing how much pain he could take. By the end of the night, we had learned that the maximum amount of batteries that could be snapped together and held for ten seconds was exactly forty-two. We knew this because Dirty Burt wouldn't volunteer to do forty-three. Still, forty-two was more than the twenty they had bet in the first place, so Danny had to hand over his prized possession, the Anna Nicole Smith Special Edition *Playboy*. Dirty Burt took his prize and headed directly to the Porta-John.

The nine-volt batteries they drained that night were supposed to be used in the harnesses for what the military called MILES gear. MILES stands for multiple integrated laser engagement system, which is just a high tech game of laser tag. Without the batteries, they didn't beep when we were shot by the enemy, and without the beep, we didn't die. We became ninja. Vikings who could not be killed. That's what we were, those Vikings pulled from battle by the Valkyries to sit in Valhalla to drink all day, fight all night, die, and drink again the next morning. The Norse legends call these warriors the Einherjar.

We fought like maniacs and fired our blanks at the OPFOR, and no matter how much they fired back we kept advancing. Our battalion commander would tell us later that he had never been so proud of his boys. He had personally heard the general lean over to one of the majors and say, "Those are the types of boys I want on my QRF."

While the big battle raged, the engineers improved the chow hall on our FOB. A raised plywood path from the hand-washing stations to the entrance helped us to keep from tracking mud in. They hung cargo nets on the inside for aesthetics and served better food from heated buffet-style trays instead of chili mac or powdered eggs from Cold War-era metal cans.

It made no sense. We were only going to be there for another week. Why the hell didn't they fix the place up sooner? I found Schofield to ask what the hell was going on.

"Bush is coming tomorrow." He was on his cot reading a book called *The Moon Is a Harsh Mistress* and didn't look up. "He's going to speak at the football field on post. We'll be bused there at 0700 and bused back at 0900. If any of your boys are interested in having lunch with him, have them write down their social security number, DOB, hometown, and three questions they would ask."

I laughed.

"I'm serious. That's what they're asking for, and I don't want any fucking cuss words in their questions or any stupid shit. They might actually be called to ask one."

I don't know why, but I immediately wanted to do this. "Are you going to eat lunch with him, Sergeant?"

"Hell no. What would be the point?"

The next morning, our battalion and just about every other soldier in Fort Polk packed into the parade ground, under the biggest American flag I ever saw. I stood in the middle of thousands of the nation's finest servicemen and women and stared at the giant flag. I had never seen the Stars and Stripes so magnificently presented, but what really blew my mind were the two sniper teams above the flag on the roof, one stationed at each corner. They were so high up there I could barely see them, but there was no mistaking what they were.

The president walked through the crowd, up to the podium, smiling and waving the whole way. The speech he delivered could have been pieced together from sound bites on any news station. It was vague and unmemorable, but delivered with conviction. Then he smiled and waved his way through the crowd again.

It took a lot of convincing, but later that afternoon I found myself eating one table away from the leader of the free world. About forty of us from different companies in the battalion sat at tables with honest-to-God tablecloths and meals in sturdy trays instead of on flimsy paper plates. I stood up with everyone else when the president entered and watched him walk to the center of a big table.

President George W. Bush wanted to be one of the boys, he said. He didn't want any special treatment. That was why he'd decided we would all enjoy a Meal Ready to Eat, our field rations, instead of having a big lunch cooked for us. But we didn't eat them out of the bag like we usually did; that day they were heated, prepared, and served to us by the president's staff. The thing was, in a standard-issue MRE there is a chemical heater pouch into which a soldier is supposed to slide his main meal and add water. The chemical reaction heats the food up. I later found out from a cook that the Secret Service had decided that the MRE heaters had the potential for use as a weapon against W.

The president thanked us all for coming and asked our chaplain to say a nondenominational prayer over our field rations. Everyone bowed their heads except the Secret Service agents and the press. The cameras clicked so much it sounded like an ocean wave. After we were instructed to sit, I nervously sipped at my orange powder beverage the whole time the president spoke. Then I was thirsty through my meal because we were instructed not to get up while the president was in the tent.

Staring at him sporking spaghetti in meat sauce into his mouth didn't do anything for me. I really thought I would see something in his eyes, something to prove he deserved to be in that position, but all I could think was how nice his hair looked. I wondered if his barber traveled with him.

If his eyes told me anything, they said he was unconcerned. His attention would shift with complete indifference, and this made me believe he was filled with either general apathy or childlike amusement. This wasn't the guy who had addressed us at the football stadium that morning; something was missing, I was sure of it. Something I couldn't really place. I considered it for a while as we ate in relative silence, my thoughts only occasionally interrupted by hushed whispers. I came up with what I thought was the answer: there were no television cameras, no viewers. I thought how exhausting it would be to be watched by millions of people all the time. Now that the video cameras were off, it was just him and a couple dozen run-of-the-mill soldiers. There he was, only fifteen feet away, sitting at the same type of fold-up table I was, sitting in the same fold-up chair. Just a man. Maybe meeting any president under these circumstances would fill a person with disappointment. They can't be great men every second.

Half an hour went by and I hoped to hell they wouldn't call on me, because I couldn't remember the question I was authorized to ask. It was a fluff question I had only used to get in the tent, anyway. All I really wanted to know was who's driving this war machine and why. Imagine if someone actually asked that. When the questions did start, the first kid asked how it had felt to own a professional baseball team. Everyone laughed, and I poked at my brick of salty meatloaf, one of the worst MREs in my opinion. Each one came with a different entrée and different pouches of side meals.

A few other forgettable questions were asked. I waited, hoping something remarkable would happen. Here I sat, only a few feet away from the ruler of the free world—the man who played such a huge part in this massive, impending deployment, the man who had every leader of the United Nations on speed dial, the man who threatened through the television screen to kill, capture, or destroy all the evil in the world—but no one asked about anything important. It was all so anticlimactic, cliché, jejune.

He answered the questions by speaking about faith, a just God, and an America filled to bursting with freedom. I'm sure as a man he sincerely felt for us who were weeks from combat, but I didn't hear the man: I only heard the political rhetoric of a president. What he said made for good sound bites but lousy motivation. Other people liked his answers, though, and they clapped their callused hands with enthusiasm. At the end of a loud round of applause, someone decided to end on a strong note. Lunch was cut short. A staff major I had never seen before called the room to attention, everyone jumped up, and the president was ushered out, leaving everything on his plate except a few bites of spaghetti. The rest of us sat back down without ceremony and ate our meals at a low murmur. I stood, walked over to the chow line, and refilled my orange beverage drink.

Twenty-Five-Dollar Whores, Victorian Literature, and Humane Killing Machines

At the end of our six-month training, the colonel gave us two weeks' leave before we headed to the Middle East for combat operations. We signed the paperwork in Louisiana, so all we had to do was fly back to Oregon and take the buses to the armory to store our equipment. We landed at an air force base in Eugene, loaded Blue Bird school buses, and headed back to Corvallis.

The bus seat squeaked every time I moved around, and I moved around plenty. Usually the hum of the engine would put me to sleep, but I had slept the whole flight back. Every time I closed my eyes, I imagined Iraq in the springtime. There was nothing to do other than lean over the aisle and join the ongoing conversation—Danny Addison, Baldwin, and a few others were talking about killing. Hell, it was on everyone's mind. How could it not be? I believed myself to be a rough man who stood ready to do violence on behalf of the American people so that they could sleep peacefully at night, but there was a difference between theory and function.

Dirty Burt said he would have no problem with it. He hunted every year and gutted deer in his garage. Using the knife to cut from neck to asshole was his favorite part. "I use my army-issued bayonet, too, and find it's the best thing for it. You just can't stick it in all the way or you'll burst the shit sack and ruin the meat."

"The way you want to fight is through a scope," Danny said, smiling. "You don't want to get too close, either. The Hajis might not know how to shoot worth a shit, but they have AK-47s and plenty of ammo. Those rounds tumble."

"What do you mean?" I asked. I was eight years in and had never heard about tumbling rounds.

"Yeah, when they come out of the barrel they fly end over end. You didn't know that?" Danny asked.

I shrugged because I didn't know that.

Dirty Burt slapped his knee and spit some chew into an empty Coke bottle. "Damn, Sergeant. I thought everyone knew about that."

"Well, I live the way of a peaceful warrior. I have an artistic soul," I said, and smiled over at Simon.

Danny said, "I don't know about the Russian AKs, but the Chinese AKs shoot tumbling rounds so when they hit they tear flesh, cartilage, and bone. Then it bounces around inside you, really fucking you up." Danny talked like he was telling a dirty joke. It was.

Staff Sergeant Cederman leaned into the conversation. No one even knew he was listening. "What we carry, the M4 rifle, is the most humane weapon on the battlefield. There is a tight spiral cut into the barrel that sends the round flying at the enemy just how it's shot, limiting the damage as it penetrates."

Simon leaned out of the conversation and put his patrol cap over his eyes. "Well, I'll sleep easier knowing we don't want to hurt them any more than we need to while we're trying to kill them."

I had to find something else to do besides talk shop. It didn't matter if the rounds tumbled, twirled, or somersaulted, as long as they moved away from me when I pulled the trigger. I went through my pockets and was surprised to find the little booklet they had handed us during training. The cover said it came from the Defense Language Institute Foreign Language Center. Inside, it had Arabic phrases spelled out phonetically. The pamphlet seemed more like an afterthought than anything else, but at least it was more than I had received when I was in Haiti. These were phrases the DLIFLC thought we might find helpful during our time in combat. The first page had two lists of cultural notes.

If you are in Iraq it is OK to do the following:
   Shake hands with men
   Kiss men on the cheek
   Dress properly: dark or white colored shirts are preferred for men

It is NOT OK to do the following:
   Look directly at or talk to women
   Hold hands with or kiss your wife or girlfriend in public
   Talk about politics
   Get drunk in public
   Whenever you're in doubt about the impact of a conduct, try to avoid it

This changed my notions of war completely. Combat sounded like a cultural gathering. All the officers talked to us many times about the dangers of today's modern battlefield, and explained that this was not our grandfather's war. I had no doubt that there would be some shooting involved, but maybe there *could* be some hand-shaking and cheek-kissing. I probably wouldn't get the chance to wear black or white, but maybe after enough cheek-kissing they'd be okay with the tan of the desert uniform. As for the *dont's*, I didn't plan on looking at or talking with women. I had no girlfriend or wife to kiss, and alcohol would be prohibited while at war, so all I really had to deal with was trying not to talk politics. I hated politics. Politics were for the stark raving mad and made no sense to the rational mind. My current position was a great example: a bunch of Saudi Arabian men with ties to illiterate thugs in Afghanistan planned 9/11 in the Philippines and killed almost three thousand innocent US civilians, so I was being sent to Iraq to oust a dictator the US government had helped put in power. If anyone besides a lunatic tried to explain to me with a straight face how we got from point A to point Z, I'd punch him in the teeth.

I tried hard to convince myself that the Iraq war wouldn't be full of explosions, gunplay, and final prayers screamed to God. Hell, this was the land that created law and the written word. Iraq was where the Tigris and the Euphrates rivers met; it was the goddamn Holy Land, the cradle of civilization. The people who wrote my language pamphlet must have been there at some point, and the booklet made the place sound civilized still. Maybe it wouldn't be that bad, I thought, but then I turned the page:

Stop or I will shoot	*awgaf te-ta ar-mee*
Don't shoot	*le-termee*
Put your weapon down	*dheb sla-Hak*
You are a prisoner	*inta a-seer*
Surrender	*is-tes-lim*

As the pages went on, nicer phrases like *Can you help me fill out these forms? (mum-ken it-sa-aad-nee am-lee haee el-is-ti-ma-rat?)* or *Are there rental cars available? (aku sa-yar-at lil-ta-jeer?)* peppered the pages, but none of it was something I would say before I kissed a guy on the cheek.

The bus rolled on for several hours, and eventually even the conversations stopped. Some of the men slept, but most stared out the windows deep in thought. When the bus turned off I-5 and onto Route 34, eyes lit up and a few of the guys stood to get a better look at the familiar landscape—we were only ten miles from home. This would be the last homecoming for a lot of us. No one made a big deal about the four Blue Bird school buses returning from training in Texas and Louisiana, but I wondered about the next time Bravo Company would drive into town. I imagined people on every corner waving flags or holding homemade signs of support, but then a thought occurred to me: the odds said that not all of us would be there for that homecoming.

We filed out of the bus with very little talking. Blue sky began to poke through the familiar gray above us. I grabbed my gear and stuck most of it in my locker in the back of the armory, then stood in front of the open locker door thinking about how the next time I saw my gear I would be hours from landing in Iraq. The last thing to do was hand in our rifles to the armorer, so the entire company lined up and bullshitted about how much we were going to drink or who we were going to screw that night, much like I imagined convicts talked on their last day in prison. Only after I turned in my rifle did I realize my situation. I had nothing to my name but a beat-up Corolla full of books and art supplies.

I walked out the front door and lit a cigarette under the blue awning. The thorny bramble of rose bushes on each side showed small signs of spring, an ugly blossom here and there. Simon pushed open the heavy door behind me, stood for a while, and said, "Hey, Sean. What're your plans?"

"I don't know, man. See my parents I guess. Isn't that what we're supposed to do?"

"Not if you don't want to."

"It'll be good to get out of town. I'm looking forward to the drive."

Simon packed his smokes against his left wrist, opened the pack, pulled one out, and turned it around before putting it back in. Then he took a different one and lit it.

"What do you do that for?" I asked.

"Luck. Want to grab dinner?"

"All my clothes are at Danny's house and he's with his girl, Clara. I'm not even going to try to put on the civvies in my A bag—they'd probably get up and crawl away. And I'm sure as hell not going out in my desert uniform."

"We're about the same size," he said.

"June is going to want to spend some time alone with you."

He took a drag from his cigarette and shrugged. He grinned, let a second go by, and said, "She thinks I'm coming home tomorrow. I wanted to surprise her. She's at work until ten."

"What were you going to do for the next four hours?"

"I don't know. Fuck it, let's grab a pint."

I played with his two big dogs in his basement apartment while I waited for him to find some clothes for me. The thought of having an Irish Car Bomb or two at the Fox and Firkin took precedence over a shower. He came out of the bedroom and threw me a Dead Guy Ale T-shirt, a ripped pair of cargo shorts, and some flip-flops. He dressed much the same, but with a black beanie. I asked him why he was wearing a beanie, since it was almost summer weather, but he just gave that same half smile. He never answered a direct question with anything but that half smile.

I breathed in the fresh spring air as we walked, and I could taste that it came from the big evergreens of the Pacific Northwest. The ten blocks between Simon and June's basement apartment and the pub were filled with a ridiculous amount of absolute beauty; the slanted light of the setting sun shone low on the blossoms that dotted the trees, and birds sang like tin whistles. Spring hit me from every direction, and it was so staggering that I almost had myself one of those Joycean epiphanies.

Being an artist, I hate to admit to people that I'm slightly color-blind. The second after I tell someone, they start pointing at things and asking, "What color is this? What color is that?" It is difficult to explain how color blindness works. I still see all the colors everyone else sees, but something in my brain has a hard time distinguishing between hues of a color, or spotting the variations among subtly different shades. Red, brown, and green are difficult to tell apart. So are blue and purple. Sometimes I can talk my brain into thinking green is red or the other way around. So, not only do I see things differently, I can also influence how I see them. Maybe this isn't a bad thing; it's difficult when you want to be an artist, but not bad. I navigated around the problem by memorizing the color wheel. I learned that color is just light in different wavelengths. The colors in a rainbow are always in the same order, and they go from the shortest wavelength to the longest. I was aware of all colors and understood how to use them, but I could really only enjoy the most vibrant colors. This was not a bad thing, to my way of thinking. But that morning, walking to the pub, I saw every color: deep blue, lush green, rich brown. The colors were so vibrant because I had spent so much time in the colorless training areas of tan Texas and mud-brown Louisiana.

The Fox and Firkin had added another dartboard in the corner, but otherwise the place looked the same. We walked through tables of college kids eating patty melts and sat down at the bar. I looked at the long line of taps and knew I belonged there at that moment. The hot bartender wore a torn black Johnny Cash T-shirt that revealed enough cleavage to fill her tip jar. She had bright red dreadlocks and a tattoo on her right forearm that spelled out "namaste" in a lovely font.

"The guy said it was called Fairy Dust," she said.

"What?" I brushed my fingers against hers when she slid me a pint of Boddingtons.

"The font, it's called Fairy Dust," she said.

I initiated eye contact. "What's it mean?"

"Peace."

"Piece of what?"

"You know what I mean."

"Yeah, I guess I do." I sipped my pint.

She chuckled, and her business took her through the rubber doors that separated the bar area from the kitchen.

Simon elbowed me. "That's Viv. June knows her. She's got a boyfriend. A power rower."

"I know who she is. I hang out here more than you. Wait, her boyfriend's a what?"

"A power rower. He rows those boats on the river."

I thought about how privileged a person must be to even think of becoming something like a power rower. What a quaint hobby. In my head I immediately compared it to humping sixty pounds of equipment through triple-digit heat while hunting men. But I compared everything to that in those days. I found that when I was busy building a sense of superiority I was able to ignore the fear. Knowing that I was going to be sent over in an infantry-line company picked by a two-star general to be his personal quick reaction force hung over every other thought like the Sword of Damocles. It scared the hell out of me, even if I didn't admit it to myself.

Simon turned in his chair and looked the room over, then pointed at the empty stage in the far corner. "I hope there's some music tonight. I think I'll miss that the most, over there."

"Hell, man, I'll sing for you when we get there, but until then let's promise not to talk about *over there* for at least a week."

"Yeah, you're right," he said, and we clinked our glasses on it.

Two hours later, Simon and I were doing our best to impress Viv by telling her about all the high-speed training we did in Texas while preparing to go *over there*. I was four pints full of happy and tipping big. We found out an Irish band was going to play later that night, and Viv's shift ended at nine. As the place filled up she had to spend more of her time with the patrons at the tables. The Johnny Cash shirt rode up her hips, revealing smooth white skin that inspired all kinds of sinful thoughts. Every once in a while, she would look over and catch me thinking them.

"I'm unstoppable tonight," I told Simon after catching a sly smile from Viv.

"It's the cash you're dropping," Simon said, and checked his watch. "Her boyfriend comes here most nights too. He's big."

"I'm big, too," I said. "You've been checking the time a lot. You have a hot date?"

"Yeah, I'm going to head out a little early to surprise June at work. That okay?"

Danny and Clara couldn't go all night, and I knew they'd probably be at the Fox and Firkin soon, so I said, "Go get your girl. Now I feel like an asshole keeping you here."

Simon left me there to spin on my barstool and follow Viv with my eyes while she worked the room. She swung those hips back to me when I finished my pint. I decided to make the move and ask her to stay the night with me. I was a handsome enough guy, I could tell she dug me, and in an hour's time I would have at least five guys from Bravo Company in the joint to back me up in case the power rower showed up. So the next time she leaned over the bar, exposing a little bit more of God's beauty, I asked her what she was doing after she got off. She giggled a cute little giggle and asked me why.

"I was thinking maybe we could start an epic romance," I said. I felt those slithers inside my chest and the jitters in my fingers. She paused for a second, and I tried to look indifferent while breathing short breaths. Then she let me off the hook. "You know, my relief is here already. Maybe I can join you now."

The rubber kitchen door swung open, and there stood Jaime. I coughed, a deep stomach choke, almost a gag. For a second I didn't understand what was going on.

"Jaime, do you mind if I clock out a bit early and have my after-shifter?" Viv asked. I heard it like she spoke through a tunnel.

"Sure, hon, not at all," Jaime said, tying a black apron around her thin waist. She didn't react to me. She had to have seen me but it must not have registered, or she didn't recognize me. Her curly brown hair had been straightened and pulled up in a ponytail that flowed like rapids down the right side of her long neck, showing off her razor-sharp jawline and dimpled cheeks. Her skin was darker than I remembered, making me picture her out on a road trip or on some adventure I wasn't a part of. I wanted to know where she'd been, what she was doing now, and why she was in Corvallis.

I wanted her instantly, but more than that I needed her to want me. I immediately made it my number one priority to show her how big a mistake she had made by ending our relationship. She had hurt my pride back when I was just an art school dropout, and now that the infantry had inflated my ego to massive proportions, I couldn't just let it go.

Viv had clocked out and now stood next to me, but I couldn't take my eyes off Jaime. My mouth opened before any words came to mind, and hung there like I was the village idiot trapping flies. I could feel a layer of sweat between my fingers and the bar.

"Do you know each other?" Viv asked.

That's when Jaime looked up. "Sean?" She walked over and I couldn't focus on anything else. "How did you know I worked here? I only started a few days ago. I haven't told anyone."

"I live here. We just got back from training today. I had no idea you worked here, but it's good to see you, Jay." I turned to Viv with a big smile. "You ready to have that drink, doll?" I used *doll* on purpose; that's what I used to call Jaime.

Viv smiled back. "Give me a second to get my things." Then she disappeared behind the rubber door to the kitchen.

Jaime stood in front of me like she always used to, with her spine arched, and I couldn't help but remember when she would walk completely naked around my little one-bedroom apartment on Hawthorne. I loved the way her flat stomach curved into her hips like the legs of a capital K. Her complete confidence made her supernatural.

Damn her. She could get whatever she wanted from me and she knew it, but I didn't go for it that time. "Hey, so what happened to that place in Brooklyn?"

Her cheeks deflated. "Pratt? I decided to go to Oregon State instead."

"How's that going for you?"

"Great!" Her expression made me think she was about to recall a whole story about her trials and tribulations, her hero's journey, the herculean obstacles she had to overcome, but I cut her off.

I put a twenty on the table and asked for another pint and whatever Viv wanted, then turned in a very disinterested fashion to watch the band set up. I said, "Keep the change."

She did.

Danny and Clara showed up with Corporal Liam Quinn. Quinn was a Ranger from Third Squad in my platoon and a small, third-generation Irishman who had joined with his brother. His brother Brennan Quinn was a team leader, a part of sharpshooting Tom Cederman's squad. Liam had the hyperbole of an Irishman, which is to say every joke was the funniest thing he'd ever heard, every girl the most beautiful, and anyone he'd fought was the biggest man in the city. He was strong as an ox but also so short that, when sitting down, his legs lifted off the ground every time he laughed. And his laugh was the type you couldn't help but share.

Viv and I sat with them, listened, clapped, and even danced to a song or two. There were two bartenders on, and I noticed Jaime covered the all the tables except ours. I felt confident that she didn't like it when I snaked my arm between Viv's red dreads and bare shoulders. I waited until she was in my peripheral vision to lean in for a kiss.

The band stopped playing around eleven and the place slowed down a half hour later. Danny and Clara talked about heading to a pub a little farther down the road called the Top of the Cock, a second-floor bar above a pub called the Peacock. Viv said she had half a bottle of vanilla Stoli at her dorm and was ready to leave. I went to close out my tab and found Jaime waiting to help me. She lifted my credit card from the box behind the bar and slid it through the machine. "I didn't recognize you at first."

I picked at a coaster. "Yeah, well, it's been a while."

"No, I mean your hair—it's all chopped off. And you lost some weight."

"Hey, I wasn't fat, Jay."

"No, I didn't mean that. You just look shrink-wrapped or something, more compact." She handed me the slip of paper and a pen. I signed and left a big tip, and when I looked up she grabbed my neck and pulled me across the bar. Her tongue felt warm, with a cinnamon taste. I felt each turn and curl in my gut. When she let go the stars in the corners of my vision surrounded her.

"Jesus, Jaime."

"Call me in a couple hours."

"My cell isn't charged."

"I get off at midnight."

"I'll be here."

The next morning she stood completely naked in the kitchen of her studio dorm and made us coffee from a French press. The morning sun cut through the dozens of plants on her windowsill and made her and the white counters glow. I stood in my boxers on the opposite side of the half wall that separated her kitchen from the rest of the place and sipped my coffee from a small white cup. It was the best I ever tasted, even without cream or sugar.

Jaime told me she had left the art institute a couple of months after I dropped out. She transferred to Portland State University to pursue a graphic design degree. She went there for a semester or two before deciding she didn't like it there, either, so when she never heard back from Pratt, she transferred to osu to major in graphic design. But her dream was to go to school in Eastern Europe or some obscure country. She would learn some absurd discipline from some ancient culture and bring it back to Portland to start a movement.

"Like where?" I asked.

"Greece." She took an exaggeratedly small sip from her cappuccino cup.

"I'm going to Iraq."

She sipped again. "I know, Sean."

"I only have two weeks left, Jay." I walked around behind her and with one hand scooped up all her hair and moved it over her left shoulder. I pressed my cheek to her ear, lightly placing my hands on her bare stomach, pulling her tight against me.

She asked, "What are you going to do until then?"

"Road trip to see my mom and dad."

"Your father still live in LA?" She laughed when I kissed her neck.

"Yeah. You want to come with me?" The words spilled out of my mouth.

She pulled away, turned, and stepped back. "No, I have my classes, but I'll be here when you get back." She stepped closer, her warm cheek touching the center of my chest.

The drive to San Francisco ate up twelve hours of my remaining time in the real world. I passed mountains that refused to give up their snow, and rolling hills, and all the Americana stuff I knew I'd miss in the cradle of civilization. When I arrived at my mom's apartment, she had a twelve-pack of amber ale and fresh-baked bread she'd made from scratch.

My mother was still young, only sixteen years older than me. She lived in Union City, outside of San Francisco, but she was a horticulturist that took care of the plants in the skyscrapers of the city. The war really pissed her off, the Bush administration too, and the general unraveling of humanity. I told her that we were doing our part to fix the world. I explained that our M4s were the most humane killing machines on the battlefield, but somehow she didn't get it. There was no way I could make her understand why I wanted to go, but in her watering eyes I was an American hero. It surprised me, her thinking me a hero, but society in general was doing the same thing. Television news, radio, and newspapers all called every serviceman and woman a hero no matter what job they had. Yellow-ribbon magnets appeared on most cars. The US supported the troops but not the war. A broken line of a Blake poem crossed my mind: "a lamb misused breeds public strife, and yet forgives the butcher's knife."

Who did they think pulled the triggers? If given the choice of being the lamb or the knife I'd be the knife without doubt. I didn't get into a deep conversation with my mom, but no one in my generation had been drafted. She was remembering the Sixties and maybe overcompensating for how the troops were treated back then. I didn't know, but an infantryman in the US Army trains for war from the very first day of boot camp. I knew what I was getting into. Sure, the thought of going over sometimes scared the shit out of me, but it also excited me and made me feel more alive than I had ever felt.

To change the subject, I told her the good news: Jaime and I were seeing each other again. It was wishful thinking at best, but maybe if my mom knew I was in a relationship she wouldn't worry about me as much. I'm not sure now how that was supposed to work, but for some reason it made sense at the time. It annoyed me that the news didn't excite her.

My mom had always been difficult to figure out. I understood that she had had to start fending for herself at an early age, but, for reasons I could never understand, she picked boyfriends over being with her kids. Still, when I visited her, she did everything she could for me. She cooked great meals, took me to her favorite places in the city, and, even though she couldn't really afford it, took four days off work. She may have never been the perfect mother, but I have no doubt her worries about me going off to war were sincere. It was important to her to fill those days with good memories. We took trips to Chinatown, Mission Park, and Half Moon Bay. We drank good beer in the city, in the wooded hills, and at the ocean.

My little brother Keith lived in the Bay Area, so he was over to visit every day. Keith owned a struggling art gallery and frame shop and was an amazing painter, better than me. We drank beer and spoke about what I'd learned in my year of art school. I listened to him talk about how hard it is to make any sort of living with art today. Taxes were killing him, the frames and equipment were outrageously priced, and when he was actually commissioned to do a portrait the people hated it because it looked too real, which means he didn't ignore double chins, get rid of wrinkles, or make people taller than they really were. After a six-pack, we made a pact to paint together as the Brothers Davis when I got back from the war.

I spent five days there, in all, sleeping on the futon in the living room of my mom's one-bedroom apartment. When she hugged me goodbye, it felt awkward—somehow not as real as I wanted.

My dad lived another couple of hours south, in a Los Angeles suburb called Whittier. After he was hurt in a logging accident he left Oregon, took a settlement, and drifted down to Bakersfield, California, where his big brother gave him a job in the oil fields. After being injured in the oil fields, he was awarded a few more large settlements, and moved to Whittier. While most people would believe he was taking advantage of worker's compensation or filing frivolous lawsuits, this isn't the truth. My dad had strange luck. It started when he was sixteen. He and his big brother got drunk off their asses and crashed a car into a brick wall. The accident should have killed them, and after he'd had a couple beers he loved to tell anyone who would listen that the doctor in the emergency room said that if he hadn't been so intoxicated during the wreck it would have killed him. He said that being drunk saved his life, so why stop?

My dad had an irresistibly deviant charm, and his luck was in not only surviving the near-death experiences but actually benefiting from them. In Oregon, he was run over by a tree that snapped off the choke while logging, and it crushed his leg. A piece of machinery dropped from a great height, severing the end of his left thumb right there in the oil fields. My dad was given a string of settlements and set up with a new profession. He decided he wanted to be a nurse, but during his vocational rehabilitation program he got drunk and had sex with another student on an operating table in a hospital and somehow contracted hepatitis, rendering him unable to work in a hospital. So he moved to Whittier with his wife and became the handyman at a high-rise retirement complex in the middle of LA's Koreatown.

He named me after him. Philip Sean Davis: my full name. It bothered him that I had stopped going by Philip after grade school, and he mentioned it sometimes. He and my brothers still called me Philip. My mom didn't have a problem calling me Sean.

The morning I got to Dad's place, he woke me up and we drove to a market to buy the best steaks they had and a fifth of Johnny Walker Black Label. He told me that since there was a good chance I wasn't coming back we were going to spare no expense. I laughed and said that they couldn't kill me; I had the strange luck just like he did.

Dad loved baseball, so I watched Giants games with him on his big television. He took me down to Hollywood Boulevard, Sunset Boulevard, and a bunch of other places you saw on TV. In those couple of days, it was like we weren't at war at all. I heard no one talk about it, and there was little mention of it on the news. In LA, nobody gives a shit about anything but LA. A ridiculous thought crossed my mind: maybe the war didn't exist. Maybe I could just stay there or drive down to Mexico and forget about all the training, the weapons, the equipment, the men. It wasn't that I didn't want to go to war, but the fear was there. I was never the kind of soldier that couldn't wait to fight in combat, but I had a talent for it, a knack for the military. I knew I would be a good leader of men, but it still scared me.

Only a maladjusted person would want to fly thousands of miles from home to kill other human beings he doesn't know or understand, right? Maybe the US government was banking on the fact that I was mad. Maybe I was, because the patriotic fog I had been in when I joined up had dissipated, and I still wanted to go. I needed a purpose. Without a purpose, I would end up driving in circles, cleaning up roadkill with twenty-seven years left until retirement. This scared me more than the thought of combat.

Keith drove down on the last night before I was to head back, and we all smoked cigarettes and drank whiskey in Dad's living room while his wife barbecued steaks on the patio. Every few minutes, Dad broke from our conversation to yell at the television.

Dad's wife called through the sliding screen door that dinner was ready, and we filed out to fill our paper plates with meat and grilled potatoes. The steaks were so good that no one spoke. The sports announcer filled the gaps between the clashing of knives and forks. The food settled in my stomach and leveled out my whiskey buzz. Dad lit another cigarette, crossed his legs, and looked across the shag rug with heavy-lidded eyes. He surprised me by saying we should go for a walk. I said it was dark and I didn't trust the dirty streets, but he told me that the people knew him there and he was well liked. He got up, staggered a step back to catch himself, and said, "Come on, son. I have a surprise for you."

"Seeing you is all I want, Dad," I said.

He didn't say anything else, and walked out the door into the lobby of the tower. I looked at Keith for some help, but he only smiled and shook his head. We both knew whatever he was up to wasn't any good. This is how it's always been. I followed him mostly out of obligation, although I did have a flicker of curiosity.

We strolled through the garbage and graffiti of Koreatown at dusk. All the driveways were fenced in, all the store windows barred. Everything smelled like car exhaust, burnt fish, and sour cabbage. The indecipherable scribbles and words painted on the buildings started getting denser and more closely intertwined as we walked.

"Come on, you're going to war—don't let the gooks spook you."
Dad laughed and said, "Spooked by the gooks."

After ten minutes of winding through the dilapidated blocks of old houses and convenience stores, he stopped outside the unmarked door to a stuccoed warehouse and knocked heavily on the steel plating. He looked at me and smiled for a few seconds. The door opened and a big Mexican in a black tank top leaned out. He had more tattoos than I'd ever seen on one person, and each one looked like a saint off a church candle.

Dad smiled. "Eddy, Eduardo, this is my hijo. The one going to Iraq."

Eddy or Eduardo stepped toward me but kept one foot against the metal door to keep it from closing. He nodded quickly and stuck out a big, callused hand with the word "VERITAS" tattooed across the arch between his thumb and pointer finger. I shook it. He turned back to Dad and said, "Fifteen minutes?"

"Maybe thirty, let's see how he does," Dad said with pride.

The warehouse smelled as though someone had tried to drown the smell of five-day-old body odor with a floral spray. "What's going on, Dad?"

"I rented you a whore." He patted me on the back, trying to move me toward the door.

Eddy scanned the street and moved to the side to make room for me to go in first.

Dad motioned for me to head down the hall. "Come on, son. Don't embarrass me."

The hallway turned to shadows ten feet in. I looked back to Dad.

Eddy jutted his chin toward Dad. "Are we going to do this?"

"Thanks, Dad, Eddy, but I just got back together with Jaime. You remember Jaime, Dad. I meant to tell you before—"

"Phil, I'm closing this door in thirty seconds." Eddy's neck muscles bulged, and I swear Saint Anthony winked at me.

"The girls are clean, son. I come here almost every Tuesday. Come on. Live a little. Besides, I already paid for her."

"You already paid?"

"Well, I'm going to owe either way."

"Okay, that's it," Eddy said, and started to go back inside.

"Hold on," Dad said. "Son, I'm telling you, these girls are worth the money. There's one in there that knows just what she's doing. She has this move…" He put both his elbows together, fists up, and gave a couple of drunk pelvic thrusts into the night.

"Why don't you go, Dad? I mean, you'll owe either way."

Somewhere in the distance a dog barked.

"You're sure, son?"

"One hundred percent."

"I don't give a shit which goes, but they go now."

Dad went in and the heavy metal door slammed shut. I walked a few steps in the direction we had come from and sighed at the dark streets. The sun had set and the flickering streetlamp lit up a dancing piece of newspaper scuttling along the broken pavement. That's when I realized I didn't know how to get back.

I walked half a block and sat on the curb under a billboard advertising Coca-Cola in a language I didn't understand. The sky had turned a bright orange and I breathed deep, but the air tasted stale and metallic. Every person who drove or walked by gave me a look like they wanted to do me harm, even the children. I would leave for Oregon the next day, and if this was the last time I saw my parents I figured I had spent the appropriate amount of time with each.

The drive to Oregon robbed me of fifteen hours of the three days I had left. It was three in the morning before I got back to the green beauty of the Pacific Northwest. I pulled into Danny's apartment, and he was good enough to let me sleep on the futon of his guest room for a solid ten hours. I woke up at five in the afternoon and called Jaime from his house phone. She wasn't at her apartment, so I left a message for her to call me. I took a shower, shaved, and dressed in an outfit I thought she would like. I still didn't hear from her by seven, so I walked into the living room where Danny and Clara were watching TV and asked if they wanted to go out for a pint and some dinner. Danny knew what I was up to, so he talked Clara into going to the Fox and Firkin with me.

When Jaime saw me she ran from behind the bar and jumped on me, wrapping her legs around my waist, and if any man in that joint wasn't jealous it could only mean he was dead. Her hands ran along either side of my jaw and she pulled me in for several deep kisses.

"I'm so happy to see you," she said.

"Me too," was all I could say.

Danny and Clara sat down at a table behind me.

"I'm so sorry I have to work. Viv called off." She looked so crushed.

I was crushed too. "I leave the day after tomorrow."

She told me she'd comp me a pint or two to make me feel better and headed toward the bar. "I've had the worst week. I'm so sorry, but tonight is so hectic. I *have* to study for this exam in Victorian literature, but I'll get it done tonight and we'll have that big dinner tomorrow night to celebrate." The way she smiled when she said "celebrate" made me okay with things.

I sat down at Danny and Clara's table with the biggest smile on my face. "God, she's beautiful."

"She's a looker," Danny said. Clara gave him a fake glare and laughed.

"Hey, what's the best restaurant in town?"

"Big River," Clara said.

"I mean the type that takes reservations." I watched Jaime's hips slide back and forth and imagined them naked as she brought me my beer.

"Big River," Clara repeated.

Jaime set the IPA in front of me. I snaked my arm around her hips, above her low-cut jeans. "Hey, sit down for a second."

Jaime plopped down next to me. "Of course. My feet are killing me. I've been on the go, nonstop."

"My mom says hi. She's really excited we're seeing each other again. You'll never guess what my dad pulled."

"Oh my God, how rude. I didn't get you guys your drinks. I'm so sorry, honey. I'm the only one here. I want to hear all about it. Tomorrow night." She popped back up. I watched her beautiful breasts bounce.

"Yeah, I'll get reservations to Big River; what do you say, around seven?"

"Perfect," she said, and took Danny and Clara's order.

We stuck around and had a couple beers, but Clara didn't want to eat a patty melt or fish and chips so we headed out and had some Italian at the Old World Deli around the corner. Then we hit up the Top of the Cock and a few other places. While we were out, I saw Viv with a big guy who could easily have been a power rower. It pissed me off that she had lied about being sick, but Danny told me to drop it. We didn't need to get in a bar fight two days before we shipped out.

At seven thirty the next night, while sitting alone at a table for two, I received a text message from Jaime. She had typed a very nicely punctuated letter, with flawless grammar, so I figured her schooling was paying off. I could tell she took a lot of time picking the perfect words for apologizing to a ruined soul heading to war. The gist of it was she didn't want to get into a serious relationship with me again at this time. She had a lot of schooling left and didn't need to be distracted by having a boyfriend who could get killed any day. She said it prettier, but I was sure there was more to it, so I went looking for her so she could explain. But I couldn't find her. She wasn't at work or in her dorm room.

I couldn't find any of the guys from Bravo Company at the bars, either. They were all probably saying their last goodbyes to their families. So I spent my last night in the US alone and made it my mission to get tore-down, shitty drunk. My first shot I toasted to the lost opportunity of bedding a twenty-five-dollar Korean prostitute. My second toast was to my hatred of Victorian literature. My third toast was to humane killing machines, and so on. When I was sufficiently drunk and had been thrown out of the last bar that would have me, I slept in the back of my Corolla. I left for war the next afternoon with what was the worst hangover of my life.

Starving in the Belly of a Whale

A single-file line of soldiers stretched from the mouth of the civilian airline 747 down the stair car, across the tarmac of Portland International Airport, and almost all the way back to the real world. The ground crew loaded our A and B bags into the belly of the plane, and we all lugged our rucks and rifles as carry-ons. I shifted my shoulders against the weight and looked at the overcast sky, fully aware that I would miss the clouds, even the threatening, papier-mâché-looking ones overhead. The officers walked around outside of the line with an elevated sense of privilege, but sooner or later they were getting on, too. They made sure no one smoked while waiting to get on the plane that would take us to the other side of the world to kill people we had never met, because smoking is illegal at an airport.

The line moved slowly because one of the majors on the battalion staff stood in the door of the plane, checking to make sure the firing pins had been removed from each weapon. They wanted to make sure that none of us knuckleheads shot a hole in the side of Omni Air's pretty plane.

I saw Captain Charbonneau taking small but quick steps toward Lieutenant Caius. While I watched them trade salutes and talk, an unsettling feeling came over me, one that I couldn't really put a finger on. The line moved another few feet, but I couldn't keep my eyes off of them. They weren't upset, and whatever they talked about didn't seem to be an emergency. In fact, the topic appeared to be totally trivial. That was the problem: everything was too trivial. Suddenly, my uneasiness made sense. I was upset because this wasn't how going to war was supposed to be.

I wanted Patton. I wanted Teddy Roosevelt. Hell, I would have taken Schwarzkopf. I wanted my chance to be picked by the Valkyries and taken to Valhalla to be one of the Einherjar waiting to fight at Ragnarok. I wanted to rush in at high tide and storm a fortified beachhead. I wanted to come in hot, flying low in a Huey, a door gunner with a handlebar mustache, lighting up the countryside. Instead, I shuffled in line, waiting my turn to ride coach into a combat zone, hoping the in-flight movie wasn't a romantic comedy.

Sean training in Kuwait.

The captain walked smartly away, and Lieutenant Caius called for the squad leaders and platoon sergeant. I didn't mind the leadership meeting because it meant that I could step out of line with a sense of elevated privilege, too. The lieutenant told us that a couple of the Arkansas boys were hit and one kid was killed. They had left two weeks before we did and an IED, an improvised explosive device, hit one of their convoys on the way up to their base. The engines of the 747 roared to life and I couldn't hear the rest of his speech, so I stood there nodding appropriately and pining over the girl who had stood me up like I was some sort of asshole. I thought of a particular memory, one in which I sat at the desk in my one-bedroom apartment on Hawthorne with a full cup of coffee, sketching a sad clown in pastel colors on an orange piece of construction paper while Jaime slept on the couch under an old afghan blanket. The white of the clown's face makeup and the Elizabethan frills around the neck and wrists really made it pop from the page. The emotion in the face was so subtle that it somehow magnified the sadness. I saw myself, so intent on drawing each fold of the polka-dotted, one-piece outfit. I thought that if maybe I could just go deep enough into that memory, I could start again from that point.

Instead, I stood on the tarmac under papier-mâché clouds, waiting for my turn to get on the plane, trying to look soldier-like while doing my best to hide my subtle sadness.

Fourteen hours later, the pilot announced our descent into Kuwait City, Kuwait, local time 1:00 a.m., ten hours into the future for those in the US. The temperature was an uncharacteristically cool seventy-four degrees Fahrenheit.

We landed, and the muffled voice of the colonel came over the cabin intercom. The first order I received in a combat zone was to remain seated until the plane came to a full stop. I leaned over to look out the window, trying to catch a glimpse of something exotic, like an oasis or a camel, but only saw the yellow-striped cement of any airport runway. The normalcy of it all was driving me fucking nuts. The plane took fifteen very dull minutes to come to a stop, and when it did the seatbelt sign went off with a ding. I got my rucksack from the overhead bin, slung my rifle over my shoulder, and stood in the aisle thinking that maybe when I got off the plane the war stuff would start happening.

The line poured out the door and I stepped into air without the taste of any trees in it. I had to smack my tongue a few times to realize that the freshness I was accustomed to had been replaced by a tinge of mutton and salty dirt. A battalion staff major armed with only a clipboard directed each company to a designated waiting area under generator-fueled lights. I wanted to finally experience this part of the world, but I was disappointed to find that everything—except the air—was the same: the waiting, the sitting on our gear, the fatigue, the bullshitting, the smoking, the complaining, the complete lack of knowledge regarding what the hell any of us were doing.

But when Sergeant First Class Schofield called for the squad leaders, the intensity in his eyes burned into us the seriousness of our situation; however familiar things seemed, we were indeed in a combat zone, and there was work to be done. The cherry of his Marlboro Red lit up. He breathed in and started his speech with the smoke still floating in his mouth. "The two-star general and the 2-7 Cav are fighting over us to be their QRF. Either way it goes, this means Bravo Company is being separated from the rest of the battalion. We're going to be asked to do some serious shit. Make sure none of your boys left any of their shit on the plane and that you have all the information you need on each soldier, in case the worst happens."

We all said, "Yes, Sergeant."

We started to disperse, and he called after us, "And make sure the firing pins are back in their fucking weapons."

We waited until 0300 hours, Kuwait time, before three buses rolled in to pick us up. When the doors swung open the sound of Middle Eastern music poured out, a cacophony of violins, woodblock percussion, and nasally singing that bounced all around the vocal register. All similarities to any other deployment ended at that moment.

Tassels above the rows of windows shook from the weight of each soldier walking to a seat. The cranked air conditioner pushed a thick smell of stale incense and livestock around the bus until I was saturated with it. Even the squeak of the seat sounded different when I sat down and tried to get comfortable. I tried to see out of the black window, but it only showed my reflection.

After every seat was filled with soldiers and their gear, the driver swung the door shut and lit a cigarette. We were packed in uncomfortably tight, and none of us knew how long the drive was going to last. I couldn't do anything but lean back with my eyes closed and listen to the twang of some exotic string instrument accompanied by bouncing vocals. Twenty minutes into the drive the adrenaline surge from being in a new land faded, and no one spoke. I was about to doze off when the music stopped.

Lieutenant Caius's bulky silhouette stood at the front of the bus and yelled back that our time at Camp Wolverine would be brief. He kept talking about how we would use the time there to train and acclimate, but I only half listened because I was trying to figure out why the hell anyone would name a military base in the middle of a desert after a subarctic-dwelling mammal. I was just beginning to wonder if there was a Camp Batman when he got to the part where he said we were heading to a place called Taji in about a month. So far, every unit that had convoyed up there had been hit.

Camp Wolverine was a gypsy city made of tents and air-conditioned trailers in the middle of the desert. Not the flowing-dunes type of desert, but a packed-as-hard-as-concrete desert. A giant communications antenna stood like an erect penis in the middle of the camp in defiance of nature, God, or whatever force decided that nothing living could exist in this complete desolation. Sand blew constantly to gum up the eyes, nostrils, ears, and any other wet orifice that belonged to a human being.

The camp looked like a shantytown built in the impact crater of an atomic test site. The US government and the contractors spared no expense to bring all the comforts of home to one of the worst wastelands on the planet; we were surrounded by Burger King, Subway sandwiches, a gym complete with treadmills and brand-new weights, a post office, a PX where we could buy all the latest popular CDs, DVDs, and even laptops and digital cameras. The soldiers stationed there lived in air-conditioned trailers that were built for two, but many didn't have to share. The chow hall was as big as a sultan's tent and came complete with indentured servants flown in from the Philippines, contracted by Halliburton to slop chow on the soldiers' plates. This was real combat, where the army cooks didn't serve the soldiers food—they supervised contracted labor to do it. American contractors offered the cook jobs, janitorial jobs, laundry jobs, and other menial labor to the desperate people of poor nations around the world.

I couldn't fathom the amount of taxpayer money it must have taken to get running water to that false oasis, let alone diesel fuel to power all the generators twenty-four hours a day. It had to be comparable to colonizing Mars.

We were just passing through on our way to the front, so the command stuffed our platoon into a small tent that looked to be handmade. A local family must have taken months to embroider the outside of it with beautiful, intricate curls and webbing that made me think of an Arabian circus. Most of the guys just filed into the front or back flap to throw their bags on the cots, but Lieutenant Caius came up beside me. He reached out and touched the intricate pattern of the embroidery. "You think it says something?"

"I don't know, sir, but it took a long time to make. I'm sure they didn't count on us using it."

"Probably sprigs or something."

"Sprigs, sir?"

The tent was cool, too, much cooler than anything in the middle of the desert could expect to be. We hit the rack for a few hours on the most comfortable cots I'd ever slept on. Then I brushed my teeth and shaved with hot water in the shower trailer before loading up in the back of a five-ton truck bound for the shooting range.

After seeing homogenized America in the middle of the desert, the going-to-war enthusiasm faded. I had watched war movies since childhood, and I knew it was supposed to be a harrowing experience filled with danger and heroism. So far it felt as if I were Neil Armstrong stepping out of the *Eagle* to find myself in the middle of a warehouse in Queens filled with lights and cameras.

We drove an hour into nowhere before stopping and piling out. The firing range looked like one of a dozen we had trained at in Texas. Eight targets stretched away from the firing line, mounted on wooden posts at twenty-five-meter intervals, just like back in Texas. The only difference was a house made completely of brand-new Firestone tires that we would later use to practice clearing rooms. To the right of that was an air-conditioned trailer for the two retired military men hired by the military contractor Kellogg, Brown, and Root to run the range.

We had driven there in order to make sure the weapons we carried were as accurate as possible. We called this zeroing our rifles. To zero a rifle, one needed to fire three shots at the same target, tweaking the sights between sets until the three shots fit into the circumference of a quarter, right in the middle of the silhouette's chest. This was hard for some units, but we did it just fine when we were left alone. We could have done it ourselves with a couple hundred rounds (thirty-eight cents apiece) and a few MRE boxes (free) with targets drawn on them.

The two contractors were both former Navy SEALS who made sure to tell us all their war stories from the first Gulf War. They said that back then it was their job to make the Iraqis think there was going to be a huge amphibious assault on a certain part of the Kuwaiti coastline. They did this by riding Zodiacs, small boats perfect for either whale watching or naval beach assaults, to about five hundred meters off the coast and swimming to the shore, each man strapped with at least five charges of heavy-as-shit explosives. They said once they got to land the whole platoon set up all the explosives to go off at once, in the middle of the night, so the Iraqis would think a shit ton of Marines were storming them.

Sergeant Schofield did his best to guide the conversation back to the present and get the training started, but the stories kept coming. The SEALS laughed and hit each other on the back and told us how they shot up the beach with machine guns and grenade launchers when they got back to the Zodiacs. They thought it was funny as hell that they were shooting at a bunch of nothing, and then the Iraqis started shooting at a bunch of nothing, too. Saddam sent two divisions over, but when they got there they didn't see anything but a bunch of blown-up driftwood and a nice ocean view. Meanwhile, they left the back door open to the real invasion. We all laughed like they wanted us to, but I didn't give too big a shit about all that. I was finally here and, good or bad, I wanted to get my war started, not hear about theirs. I wanted to have my own war stories to laugh about, stories of courage and camaraderie. I wanted the ability to win the respect of people I'd never met with tales of heroism, and all I had up to that point were stories about tassels on a bus and diesel fumes.

Thirty minutes of fake laughter and sweating my balls off went by before they even started the range safety briefing. But then they interrupted themselves to tell us that we should all look into becoming contractors ourselves. The food was better, they could cycle back home when they wanted, and they made four times as much money. This made them so proud of themselves that they started to joke around again, as if they were on vacation. These fuckers were ruining my war.

When they finally got on with it, they handed out special bolts to replace the ones we had in the upper receivers of our weapons. Each bolt probably cost a couple hundred dollars to fabricate and was extremely challenging to get into the weapons, but we changed them out. My spirits lifted a bit with the thought of shooting something. The bolts made it so our rifles shot special blue wax bullets, which also had to be expensive to make. Each squad leader was given responsibility for two shooting lanes, where his squad would fire the wax bullets at targets.

It only took ten minutes of sitting in 110-degree heat with an ammo can of wax bullets to figure out this was a bad idea. Every third or fourth round would misfire, or not fire at all. The ones that did fire made a little thud without a kick and landed all over the place. We wasted our time tweaking the sights the best we could, but it didn't help. After two of the guys fired at the targets, I realized we were making the weapons less accurate. I called a ceasefire for my lane and walked over to Lieutenant Caius, who was in the prone position doing his best to fire off his rounds before they melted.

He raised his Kevlar helmet and looked up at me.

I kneeled down beside him. "Sir, why aren't we shooting real bullets?"

The lieutenant clicked the safety on his rifle and sat up. Smudges of sand stuck to his cheek, and he gave it a swipe or two with the back of his hand, met my eyes, and said, "Because the army logistical command is full of cockwaffles, Sergeant Davis."

He went on to say that after the first Gulf War the Pentagon wanted to cut down on deaths in training, so they decided giving us real ammunition would be too dangerous. Caius was also fairly certain that the shit-bird who thought it up was given a medal and a promotion.

"Will we have any real rounds to shoot, sir?"

The lieutenant lay back down in the prone position, clicked the safety off, and fired with a light thud. "Hell, imagine what we would do with them. Someone might try to sneak one into combat." He pulled the trigger again, but nothing happened.

A few days later, Schofield told the squad leaders to go sign for our Humvees, two per squad. I grabbed young Private Walken and headed out. The motor pool was three trailers and a fence that surrounded an area the size of five football fields. A short, fat man in a grease-stained jumpsuit with a lieutenant's bar drawn in Sharpie on the front met us at the gate. He shuffled through a bunch of crinkled papers on a clipboard and pointed to a couple of flatbed Humvees without doors. They were skeletons. Worse than skeletons, they were used skeletons with chips and nicks on their hoods and chassis. One of the tires on the front Humvee was flat.

The jumpsuit lieutenant must have seen the horror on my face, because he tried to reassure me. "Relax, Sergeant, they haven't been hardened yet."

"Holy fuck," Walken said.

"Hardened, sir?" I asked.

The officer squinted at Walken and said, "All the vehicles going up north are reinforced to protect the crew driving them. I need you to sign for the two vehicles, and we'll drop them by your tent when we're finished."

"Holy fuck. We're driving that?" Walken said.

"You expecting armored Cadillacs with oil slicks and rocket launchers? I got news for you, kid; the army ain't made of money."

I signed for the trucks and thanked him.

The hardening process for the Humvees consisted of nailing four-inch by four-inch wooden posts into the frame so they stuck up vertically around the perimeter of the flatbed. Two layers of plywood were nailed to these posts, making a big square. There was an interior and an exterior layer with four inches of space in between. This space was filled with sandbags. Then three-inch steel-plated doors with four-inch Plexiglas windows were installed. The windshield was not modified, nor was the fiberglass hood. In fact, nothing else was modified. The whole process was a bad joke and everyone knew it. The fucking thing was flimsy and extremely flammable, and we would later learn that the suspension needed to be replaced monthly due to the incredible weight of the sandbags and steel doors. Also, the fact that the back was built like a coffin didn't inspire any confidence. We were at war, and unless the enemy was shooting slingshots that plywood wasn't going to stop anything.

The Kid

When the sun came up over some nameless dunes, the shadows raced back across the sand in the direction of a hundred military vehicles, all lined up nicely, waiting for the word to convoy up into Iraq. Somewhere in the middle of all those Humvees, five-tons, and semis painted with desert camo, my truck idled on the verge of dying. The day had come, and all the battalion's vehicles had been staged on the northern border of Camp Udairi, Kuwait, waiting for the movement to start.

According to the army, we had been in country long enough to acclimate, which made us ready to move to Taji, a small city about a half hour's drive north of Baghdad. I tried hard to believe I was acclimated, but the Kevlar helmets and flak vests added at least ten degrees to my body temperature. I tried to prepare mentally for all the different scenarios we might encounter, but the vibrations of the engine, the godless heat, and the inhalation of pure diesel fumes made my head just a lump to hold my helmet.

Simon sat in the driver's seat of my Humvee clicking the heater vent open and closed. I sat in the passenger seat and pulled the Velcro of my flak vest open just a bit with a hand-mic clipped under my chin strap. Baldwin and Walken sat in the back of the Humvee, in the middle of the coffin-like plywood box, using the equipment as a cushion and trying desperately to make themselves small enough to fit in a small patch of shade in one corner.

My squad's other Humvee was driven by Mechaiah O'Brian, with Alpha Team Leader Melvin in the passenger seat and Specialist Tully Patterson in the back on the machine gun. Double Deuce, originally a squad of eight, was now shrunk to six men most of the time because of the needs of the company. Our lieutenant needed someone to carry his radio, and Third Platoon needed a team leader for one of their squads. They picked my guys because they were the killer sharks in this ocean.

Patterson was a good man, squat and strong, so much so that the rest of the guys nicknamed him Beast. The squad automatic weapon, a light machine gun, fit in his hands like it was home, and he had no problem carrying the belts of ammo for it. He never complained about the weight or the heat, and even if I asked him to do something that I knew was difficult he would only squint his eyes, smile, and say, "Okay, Sergeant, let's see how this'll go over." We stuck, tied, and jammed the entire squad's duffel bags into any available space. All of our equipment probably would have fit, but the platoon equipment had to be divvied up between the squads as well: communication wire, extra parts for night vision devices, radio equipment, different-sized batteries for all the equipment, extra weapons, and ammo. Each of us carried seven magazines with thirty rounds for our M4s, night vision devices, three days' worth of food, a couple porn magazines, two canteens, a CamelBac filled with three quarts of water, as many packs of cigarettes as we could get our hands on, a compass, two smoke grenades, a flak vest (which was heavy as fuck), and a Kevlar helmet. My Humvee alone carried enough armament to level the fake village back in Camp Rilea: eight hundred fifty rounds for the .50 cal machine gun, 1,500 rounds for our squad automatic weapon, ninety shotgun shells, 190 M14 rounds, two anti-tank weapons, and two boxes of claymore mines. Carrying all of that ammunition gives a man an erection the size of God.

Of course, all of these things would only come in handy if they weren't buried under the gear. We laced a cargo strap through the metal frames of our rucksacks and ratcheted it tight around the plywood box in the back so that our rucks hung outside the vehicle, giving us the appearance of some sort of post-apocalyptic junk collector.

We weren't the only ones going to the ball in a homemade dress. The long line of Bravo Company Humvees looked like the caravan of a heavily armed carnival. The engine of our hand-me-down Humvee had been constantly running for so long that I became intimately aware of each whine and shimmy. Every hour or two, some major would tell us to rearrange the rows of trucks, and our Humvee would usually stall or die a few times before getting into position.

Sergeant First Class Schofield and Lieutenant Caius were both given up-armored Humvees, as were most officers and senior noncommissioned officers. To Lieutenant Caius's credit, he did try to give his up-armored Humvee to one of the squad leaders, but Captain Charbonneau told him it wasn't allowed. I figured the reasoning was that the experience and leadership skills of an officer or senior NCO would be harder to replace than a private, team leader, or squad leader. Of course, this reasoning came from officers and senior NCOs.

I saw Lieutenant Caius walking toward us between some big rigs twenty meters back, so I got out of the cab to meet him. The droop and puff of his eyes showed he hadn't slept for at least twenty-four hours, but when he saw me he smiled that big smile. We were heading to Taji, he said, and the rest of the companies from the battalion would go to the Green Zone in Baghdad. The two-star general had relinquished his claim on us sometime in the last twenty-four hours, and Bravo Company was now officially attached to 2-7 Cavalry. He explained this to me like it was very important, but I didn't feel any different after hearing it. I didn't care about who we would work for when we got there, because I had my doubts about our ability to get there. Even if the shitheads that hated us didn't hit us with explosives or fire weapons from an overpass, my piece-of-shit Humvee would probably break down.

Lieutenant Caius said our new battalion had been broken into seven chalks, or lines, of about a dozen vehicles, and most of Second Platoon would be a part of the fifth chalk. One chalk would head out every three hours, with the first one scheduled to leave immediately. He also told me that a truck from Alpha Company was hit on their way into the Green Zone the day before, on the same highway we were going to be using. One of the boys lost a leg and another one was killed.

Every three hours or so the trucks in the very front headed out, and all the other trucks had to move up to fill the gap. These short drives were filled with nerves and anxiety, and it didn't help that our piece-of-shit Humvee died almost every time. The last time the engineers came to jump it, they attached a tow bar to the front in case we broke down en route. The tow bar was a five-foot metal V that attached to two points on the front bumper and folded back across our hood, partially obscuring Walken's field of vision while driving. The hope was that if we broke down, some helpful five-ton truck would pull over and I would fold the V down onto the trailer hitch so we could be tugged into combat.

When we finally got to the front of the line, where we would be the next chalk sent up, a skinny Puerto Rican first sergeant called all the NCOs and officers to his Humvee. He gave a pep talk in an accent so thick that I am positive that no one understood. It took ten minutes to figure out that one of the words he kept using was "soldiers." The speech seemed to me like that of a holy man speaking in tongues to the converted. It would have had the same effect if he were screaming at us in Klingon.

He paused for a moment and pulled out a camouflaged clipboard that he either bought from a catalog or made himself. I tried to decide which was worse while he called off names and assignments. It took a couple minutes before he said, "Soryent da viss, hoo soryent da viss? Soryent da viss? Gadammit, sumone fine soryent da viss."

I looked around at a sea of confused faces. The first sergeant said it again, "Soryent da viss." Unsure, I slowly raised my hand.

"Soryent da viss, watta u deef?"

"Sorry, First Sergeant."

"You two trks, QRF." He looked back down at the clipboard and called someone else's name and assignment. I understood QRF. This is meant that if some shitheads attacked Chalk Five, the first sergeant would expect us to handle them while the rest of the convoy blew on through. After we resolved the problem, we would catch up.

I raised my face to the heavens hoping some god or angel would give me the ability to communicate with the very animated, foreign-tongued man, to tell him that my truck probably wouldn't make it fifty miles before breaking down, but nothing came. Instead I stood there and forced myself to think of home. I thought about the beautiful aroma of painting, the smell of turpentine and linseed oil, and how it smelled nothing like diesel fumes or sun-bleached dirt. I thought about sipping Rogue Brewery's Hazelnut Brown Nectar while listening to a spring shower on the windowpane. I thought about Jaime.

Lieutenant Caius walked over after the first sergeant was done and broke me out of my trance. He clapped a hand on my shoulder and said, "Soryent Davis."

"Does he know QRF means quick reaction force, sir? The only way I could get that truck over fifty miles an hour is if I had Simon drive it off a cliff. We're too weighed down, not to mention the thing's stalled on us a dozen times since we got it."

"Do the best you can, Sean. I'll be pulling up the rear."

The call came out over the radio: Chalk Five was heading out. The Puerto Rican first sergeant drove in the dead center of the chalk, flying a yellow flag adorned with the cavalry shield from his Humvee.

I'm sure in his head he was defying the terrorist war machine. I hoped that the terrorists would oblige and shoot at him first.

A staff major from our new battalion stood at the position of attention in the front of our chalk and whipped his straightened hand from his side to his forehead at the passing of every truck. He held each salute for a few seconds, then whipped it down again with dramatic flair.

"What a fucking knob," Walken yelled up.

I had a long list of things that just weren't right—going to war in a secondhand jalopy, being led by a man that I could not communicate with, test-firing our weapons with bits of wax, having the guys in the back of my truck use two crates of highly explosive claymore mines as seats while driving through a combat zone—but this guy left me more unsettled than anything else. I didn't know if he was told to stand there and salute everyone or if he chose to do it. Whatever the reason, he changed something for me. Until then, I couldn't tell if anyone at all knew we were going to war. They all acted clueless or macho, like going to war wasn't that big of a deal, yet this one guy was taking it seriously. Maybe a bit too seriously, but he gave me the war experience I had wanted since landing in Kuwait. When our turn came, I returned his salute from the passenger seat, right before our truck sprayed him with fine sand and exhaust.

The flat land ran so far into the horizon that I thought it might be possible the world wasn't round at all. Kuwait was an absolute wasteland of blinding light and unbearable heat. It took hours before we saw patches of brown grass squeezing their way up through the sand. The only signs that any type of civilization had ever been there at all were the melting plastic bottles, curled cardboard, crushed aluminum cans, and pieces of Styrofoam dropped by the other military convoys on the way up.

The dead bodies started with the sun-bleached bones of what might have been a mule or a horse. Every hour or so after that we would see a dead goat, or something indistinct and bloated to the point of exploding, or an occasional camel laying sprawled and searing in the heat, decaying under a coat of flies.

Sweat ran down from under my helmet, my flak vest, and my armpits and pooled in my crotch. I sat in a puddle of my own perspiration, steaming in a heat I had believed possible only as an oven setting back home. I opened the small Plexiglas window in the middle of the reinforced metal door to let some air in, and that worked for a very short while until, in just a matter of seconds, fine sand covered every inch of my exposed body. Every movement spread the grit and sand onto my unexposed skin, making my entire body itch constantly. The sand wedged itself under my collar, along my belt line, between my boots and shins, and rubbed at my nipples. Scratching only caused more itching somewhere else.

Our long line of overburdened trucks drove on the MSR, the main supply route. This was the most important road in Iraq. According to the US government, we couldn't easily move men or equipment into Iraq without it, but for some reason no one stopped some asshole from naming all the checkpoints after brands of semi trucks: International, Sterling, Peterbilt, and so on.

We parked at Checkpoint Freightliner for the night, right before the sun went down. The temperature probably didn't get below sixty degrees, but as soon as it got dark it dropped fast, and the fifty-degree swing was a shock. Suddenly, we were freezing our balls off in the middle of the desert. We dug into our A bags to find our snivel gear, anything that would keep us warm through the night, but, as any soldier knows, everything you need in your A bag is always at the bottom.

We started driving again at 0330 hours and traveled endlessly through a black void, like we were flying through space. The headlights lit up the asphalt to our front but died on the shoulders of the road. I imagined us on a narrow bridge, sailing through an abyss. My eyes got tired searching the nothingness on either side, but then I saw lights on the horizon. A half-dozen flaming oil wells spewed fire twenty feet into the air. I had never seen fire shoot so high. They were how I imagined the torches that lit the way to Valhalla. The light from the fire spouts turned that small part of the horizon a dull orange.

"Christ," Simon said. "How do you fix that shit? That is fire shooting from the ground at least three stories tall."

At 0900 hours I noticed the salt stains dried into my uniform start to darken with sweat again, and the first sergeant's RTO, or radio telephone operator, announced to the convoy that we had crossed into Iraq. There was no line in the sand, no fence, no boundary marker—only more of the same nothing.

An hour or so later, the convoy slowed down, and we hit a fueling checkpoint called Kenworth, a three-mile-wide spot in the highway where the US Army had placed cement barriers two feet high and four feet long. Two barriers blocked the entire right lane, and then an eighth of a mile later two more blocked the entire left lane. We had to swerve around them over the whole stretch. This was so a vehicle borne IED couldn't speed up and bust into a sensitive area. With the concrete barriers making the car slalom they'd have to stay at a very slow speed and could be shot before getting too close.

Messages with misspelled words from past units were spray-painted over each barrier: *367 Maintenance Company wuz here* or *2123rd Transportation kix ass.* Some had the names of hometowns or loved ones: Kansas City, Charlottesville, Baton Rouge, Chicago, Penny, Katie, Shannon, and others. The smart-ass messages were my favorites, like *I found Nemo.* I imagined the first soldiers to come to Iraq posing in front of them with their rifles in both hands, smiling for pictures to email back home.

After another hour of driving we passed a couple palm trees, and a few minutes later we saw our first blown-up armored personnel carrier or APCs. We couldn't tell if it was one of Saddam's or one of ours. Soon there was another, then some burnt-out cars, then the skeleton of a bus. With the top blown off and the glass shattered, it looked like the giant ribcage of a charred body.

There were posts running along the highway, but the guardrails had been removed. I didn't know why until I saw them used as siding on the houses in the next settlement. The adobe huts looked like they were made back in the days of Muhammad.

"Jesus Christ, people actually live out here," Simon said. "Why don't they move?"

I looked over at him to see if he was serious. "This is where they were born. It's all they know."

"I would fucking move," he said, looking out at the horizon. "This place is a shithole."

I started to argue with him, quoting some of the facts from my *Complete Idiot's Guide*, but I was interrupted by the first sergeant's RTO over the radio. He said that one of the maintenance trucks blew a tire and both of the Humvees in my squad needed to stay with it.

My Humvee parked in front of the five-ton maintenance truck and Sergeant Melvin's Humvee parked behind. Other than our three vehicles I couldn't see anything but flat land for hundreds of miles. There wasn't a terrain feature or any discernible hill within sight. The wrecker with the blown tire hadn't been desert-painted yet, so it was still green, the only green for miles. I jumped out of my vehicle and walked over to talk to the driver of the big rig, fully aware as I stepped out that it was the first time I was setting foot on Iraqi soil.

The tire was definitely blown out. I had seen it a couple times when I worked for the state. The temperature affects the tire pressure, and if it goes too long without being adjusted—*boom*.

No one from the truck got out of the cab, so I climbed up on the running board and looked in. I saw two white male soldiers and one black female soldier; all three had decided they weren't getting out of the cab. The most I could convince them to do was roll down the window. When they did, all three wide-eyed faces were framed in the passenger side window. I asked if they could change the tire, being maintenance and all. That was pretty much their job. The female buck sergeant told me they didn't have a spare.

"How the fuck are you driving into combat without a spare?" I jumped down and looked under the frame of the truck, hoping they were wrong. She told me her supply sergeant couldn't get her a spare. One of the specialists told me that it didn't matter anyway, because they didn't have a hydraulic jack. She then said her supply sergeant couldn't get her one of those either. I walked back to my truck, leaving them calling out a list of all the equipment they should have had but didn't.

I swung the door open on my side of the Humvee, plopped down on the seat, and shut my eyes tight, letting the sweat bead up and run down my cheeks. The sun shone so intensely that when I breathed in I could feel it warm the inside of my lungs.

"Are they pogues?" Simon asked. Pogue was sort of a dirty word in the infantry. It was slang for non-infantry, or someone who didn't have to go through the same stress we did.

"Yeah, mechanics without a jack or a spare. Imagine if we went to war and forgot our guns." I opened my eyes and sat up. "We're going to need help getting these guys moving. Call it in to the next chalk, see if they can help."

Baldwin yelled from the back of the truck, "Holy shit, Sergeant, there are kids out here."

I turned and saw four boys dressed in rags and dirty dish-dashas—ankle-length, shirt-like garments that most Iraqis wore—but with all the caked-on dirt and stains, they could have been wearing colored burlap sacks. The oldest had on green and couldn't have been more than fifteen. A kid in blue with a block-shaped head almost as wide as his shoulders pushed a kid wearing an old gray private's shirt with the word "ARMY" on the front. He must have gotten it from a soldier somehow. The youngest had to be around four years old, in brown rags that folded up around his feet and dragged in the sand.

The oldest recognized that I was in charge and walked toward me with a thumbs-up and a smile. I told him to go home in his language, but he kept moving with that smile like he had no doubt I would help him. He pinched the fingers of his right hand together and bounced them off his pursed lips.

"He wants food," Baldwin said, standing in the back of my Humvee.

I looked back at him. "I know."

My first instinct was to give them food and water, but one of the staff majors told us before heading out not to give them any. I didn't want to start out my tour by disobeying orders. They were dirty, disheveled, and thin, but didn't look starved. I hesitated for a second before shaking my head no, and the kid knew that hesitation meant I still had enough sentimentality in me to exploit.

The kid turned without missing a step and walked toward Melvin's truck, giving the same motion and pointing to the four-year-old. The youngest child gave us all starving eyes. These kids were practiced actors and talented at playing the GIs' heartstrings. They had to be; surviving in the desert demanded focus and determination. Every desert creature needed to be quick, and when the kid in green saw that he wasn't going to get any scraps from my guys he produced a stack of Saddam bills from under his clothes.

We all eyed those bills. He held in his hands our first opportunity for a war trophy. The kid pointed to O'Brian. The kid was pointing at his cigarette, but it took a second before O'Brian realized this. When he did, O'Brian unclipped his extra ammo pouch, grabbed his smokes, and pulled one from his pack.

The kid peeled off a bill and held it out.

I should have stopped the transaction. O'Brian had just given a cigarette to a kid. Instead I yelled, "That money isn't worth anything."

"I know, Sergeant, but it has Saddam's face on it."

Now everyone in the squad wanted to trade something for

Saddam money, and instead of putting a stop to it I decided to re-
move myself from the situation by stepping around the Humvee
to piss by the driver's side wheel well. I finished and zipped up,
and when I came back there were five more kids. "Where the fuck
did they come from?"

"I have no idea, Sergeant. It's like they just appeared from nowhere," Baldwin said.

I looked into the distance and saw the mirror effect the heat
waves created across the desert floor. It must have been cutting off
our field of view. They either walked from a settlement somewhere
out there in the complete desolation, which seemed impossible, or
they had a tunnel system, which seemed more impossible. Either
way, there they were. They called for food and water in their language and in ours. They pointed pleadingly at watches, pens, sunglasses, and anything else they saw. Then I heard Simon call my
name. I turned to find another small crowd around my Humvee.

"Hey, hey, get the hell away from there," I yelled. None of them
reacted to my voice, so I paused to remember my Arabic. "Lyl byet,
lyl byet!" I yelled, which I was pretty sure meant "go home," but
either they didn't understand or they just ignored me. I was helpless to stop them, and looking out at the endless sand I saw more
were coming. They started out as little black dots that broke the
mirror effect, grew into silhouettes, and then, almost like magic,
turned into little boys dressed in ragged clothes. It was the stray
dog effect: feed one and more come.

Stories were circulating, handed down from the brass—stories of these orphan panhandler children throwing grenades into
Humvees, onto the laps of unsuspecting soldiers. I pictured my
truck exploding. I yelled at them to leave and waved my arms at
the swarm of beggar children. This time I got a few looks, but they
soon went back to yelling and jumping at the guys in the trucks.
How was it that these children didn't recognize our chain of command? Our rank structure? They washed against the trucks like a
wave. Some children started climbing up the big rig and this terrified the maintenance pogues. They quickly rolled up the windows
on the cab of their truck.

Those kids crammed flush against our vehicles and pulled
against the padlocked shovel-and-pick set mounted on the outside
of the big rig. Little dirty hands grabbed at the rucksacks hanging
off the outsides of the Humvees. If they hadn't stolen anything
yet, they would shortly. My arms shook and my chest jittered. I

walked through the swarm of desert children to the older boy in green and hoped he spoke enough English that I could use him to get the mob back. He saw me approaching and looked me right in the eyes.

"We want food, water," he said with a smile that let me know he had me right where he wanted me. I wondered how often he was able to play this little game of his.

"We don't have enough. Make them leave and I'll give some to you and your brothers."

He set to work instantly, yelling in Arabic to the kid in blue and the one in the army shirt. The three of them screamed, pushed, and kicked the others until mob dispersed. They acted with such enthusiasm that I almost changed my mind. Their hands waved wildly in the air and the stubborn kids who tried to stay received kicks in the stomach or bloodied noses. I had just put a small despot in power. The scene looked like a riot at an orphanage. Finally, they chased them all away into the desert, and soon only the original four stood there. The violence of the whole thing started the four-year-old crying, with snot running down his nose, over his lips, and down his chin.

"Jesus Christ," Simon said, standing outside the driver's side door with the radio hand-mic clipped to his chin strap. The whole event had taken maybe thirteen seconds.

"B, give me four bottles of water and four MRES," I said.

"Yes, Sergeant."

I handed a thirty-two-ounce bottle of drinking water and an MRE to the kid in green, then the kid in blue, and down the line, but when I gave one to the four-year-old, the kid in blue grabbed it from him. The four-year-old started to cry louder.

"Hey, give that back to him," I said. ."

The blockhead held both the water bottles and the MRES tight to his chest and stared at me.

"Give it back." I took a step toward the oldest to have him tell his brother in Arabic. As soon as I broke eye contact, the block-head took off running. The one in the ARMY shirt chased after and tackled him, and they went tumbling into the sand wrestling and gouging at each other. I thought for a moment that the second kid was getting the little one's stuff for him, but when he grabbed the MRES that fell to the ground, he tried to take off with all of them himself. The one in blue caught the ARMY-shirt kid's leg, and they rolled around wrestling and biting each other. The oldest ran over and gathered up all the food and water that tumbled out, and took off sprinting. When the other two realized there was nothing left to fight about, they ran off chasing the oldest.

The four-year-old screamed like he was surrounded by devils. I looked at him and took a couple steps into the desert, but the others were gone.

I searched the horizon, but still couldn't see anything but the blurry, mirrored sand. "What the fuck?"

"Now what?" Simon asked.

"What the fuck?" I didn't know what else to say. I walked back to the truck and told Baldwin to give me another water and MRE. I opened the bottle, kneeled next to the kid, and held it out. He grabbed it and sipped between sobs. I unfolded a knife with my thumb and cut through the plastic MRE bag. Inside I found a chocolate-covered oatmeal bar and gave it to him. He went at it with both hands, shoving half into his mouth and letting his water fall to the sand, where it gushed out. I picked up his water bottle and sat beside him in the shade of my Humvee. While he started in on the meal, I took my helmet off and ran my hand through my sweat-soaked hair.

Fifteen minutes or so later the ground started to rumble, letting us know Chalk Six was coming.

Simon called from inside the truck. "Sean, I made radio contact. The second wrecker will be here in five mikes."

It took ten minutes to fix the tire. I told the female buck sergeant to fall into Chalk Six's convoy. She nodded but didn't say thanks. Both the wrecker and the big rig pulled off, leaving me, my squad, and the kid.

The kid was in the middle of finishing the main meal of the MRE.

"We can take him with us," Simon said, and jumped out of the truck to piss. His chin strap was always unbuttoned, his sleeves were rolled up almost to the elbow, and he left his flak vest pulled open so only half of the front was Velcroed together.

"What the hell, Simon? All your shit is fucked up," I said. "You can't even take care of yourself and you want to adopt?"

"I'm serious. We should take him with us. He can't be more than four years old."

"He's got to have a family around here somewhere." I looked down at the kid spooning the last bit of chili mac from the plastic pouch into his chocolate-covered mouth. A small feeling that I just might take him with me started itching in my gut.

Melvin came out of his truck to see what was going on. "This is something out of *Star Wars*. I can't believe people live in this fucking wasteland."

Simon climbed into the driver's seat, put his head down, and spoke into the hand-mic. Then he called out, "They want us to catch up."

The kid scratched some sand out of his hair, completely oblivious to anything else. I made a fist. "Shit."

"They want to know what's taking us so long," Simon said.

I lifted my helmet and ran my hand through my hair. "What's taking us so long? The big rig only left a minute ago." I knew we'd lose radio contact in ten minutes or so, and it would be at least another couple hours before Chalk Seven came through. I couldn't wait. We needed to get back to our chalk.

"Sean, come on, we have to take him with us," Simon said.

I looked at Simon and wanted to agree. Taking the kid with us was the right thing to do.

"Are you kidding? He'll find his way back to whatever mud hut he lives in," Melvin said. "If we take him, his parents will put a fucking jihad out on the next convoy."

"Fuck," I said. I knew that this was the first desperate kid in a country full of desperate kids. I couldn't go around saving them all and probably would be court-martialed for abducting the child, even if I did so with the best of intentions, but could I leave a four-year-old in the middle of a wasteland? "Fuck."

I squatted down next to him. This got his attention, and he smiled at me and rubbed his nose.

"I gotta go, kid."

His smile widened and I noticed he was missing a couple of his bottom teeth.

I looked up at Baldwin. "Give me two bottles of water."

Melvin jumped in the cab of his truck. "The minute we leave those other kids are just going to push him down and take them—you know that."

Sure, but at least they would come back. Then he wouldn't be alone in the desert. Baldwin handed down the two bottles of water and a bag of Skittles. I set the water beside him, ripped the bag, and poured some in his hands. He thanked me in Arabic.

"Let's get out of this shithole," Melvin shouted.

I stood up and looked over at him. "Shut the fuck up. No one is going anywhere until this kid finishes his fucking Skittles."

No one moved until every piece of candy was gone. I told the kid in his language to go home and got in the truck. He hugged both bottles of water to his chest and started walking. I tried to watch him in the side mirror of the truck, but we kicked up so much dust that he disappeared.

When we finally caught back up with the chalk, the first sergeant screamed at us in Spanish for being gone so long. He told us to go in front of the convoy to scout the freeway overpasses for snipers. We scouted forty-three more overpasses before reaching Baghdad.

The Cradle of Civilization

I had one thought going through my head when we first drove under the southernmost arch into Baghdad: I hoped to God that if we were hit I didn't shit my pants. Brave, courageous, masculine thoughts would have been better, but instead I remembered every story I ever heard about a person evacuating their bowels after death. I saw a movie once that said everyone shit themselves in near-death scenarios; the muscles of the sphincter relax, and whatever is in the lower intestines just comes out.

My hands were another worry. I planned on using them throughout my life to create beautiful pieces of art. I wanted to avoid owning a stump even more than I didn't want to shit myself. In fact, those were the first two rules I made for myself: 1. Don't shit your pants if you're blown up. 2. Don't let anything happen to your hands. These didn't seem like difficult rules to keep, but I would break one in three months' time.

I've noticed, in all my experiences in the developing world, that each encounter has its own distinct and memorable odor. Haiti was a thick stench that filled your nasal cavity with stagnant decay mixed with green growth because of the constant rain. I think the wet places always smelled worse. Water helped with rot, mold, and disease. Iraq wasn't bad. It had a constant, dry stench in the background that would hit you hard every once in a while when you weren't prepared—burnt plastic from the crooked old man burning trash in the gutter, the musk from a herd of goats running along the side of the road, feces drying in the holes in the ground because there are no flush toilets, unwashed clothes roasting in the heavy sun—but for the most part it wasn't bad.

Most of the battalion turned off the main road to find their place in the Green Zone, but Bravo Company was to continue north to Camp Cooke. It took another twenty minutes to drive through the city. Every flat surface of the box-like houses and office buildings radiated and reflected the sun's heat. It stifled me, suffocated me, but the people walked around in thick, full-body robes. Not one of them paid any special attention to the giant convoy of armed US soldiers thundering through their streets. The US military had become just another piece of the background, like the burnt palm trees and crumbled buildings and wild dogs.

Our chalk slowed down as we drove through a market in the center of town. There was hardly a building untouched by bombing or looting, but the people bustled around like they didn't notice, and this was very disquieting to me. I hadn't realized at that point people could adjust to living in the apocalypse. Just about every street had an arch at one end or another, and almost every corner had a statue, but the houses and buildings between were in different stages of devastation, making it look like ancient ruins abandoned and left to refugees. And, to a point, that was true. We drove by ten-story buildings bombed in half. They looked like dollhouses opened up, revealing metal desks, broken office equipment, and computers straight from the early '80s.

Tall fences of metal sheeting and rebar surrounded the nicer houses, the kinds of houses that Hollywood movie stars might have lived in during the '50s, but then the next house over would be a bombed-out ruin. That was the thing about Baghdad; the place juxtaposed decadence with destruction and decay. A woman in black-stained and blood-crusted robes rode a donkey pulling a cart past the ornamental gate of a three-story mansion; the metal bars on the gate were bent and welded into Arabic letters, maybe the family's name. The wooden-wheeled cart held a half-dozen cinderblocks—probably the only intact blocks she could find in the whole ruined city—a bunched-up plastic tarp, and a spooled length of telephone wire wrapped around a broken lamp without a lampshade.

Many of the houses we passed had been rebuilt using the rubble and ruins of others. Every ten blocks, we passed US checkpoints made of cement barriers and barbed wire, and parked Humvees with machine guns mounted on top. These soldiers had tired eyes, and if they acknowledged us at all it was with a solemn nod.

We drove under the northernmost arch of Baghdad, leaving the city around the time the sun went down. I heard Captain Intenso's whisper in my ear and suspiciously eyed every door, window, and alleyway. His hoarse voice didn't stop when we left the city, and the small degree of relief I'd been looking for never came. I imagined poor Private Rosewood, with his party streamer guts flying out of him, every time I saw a rock, a piece of garbage, or a dead animal. I quietly prayed that nothing would happen to my hands and that I wouldn't shit my pants.

I couldn't see much beyond the dirt-and-rock shoulders except for the silhouetted road signs and billboards. We passed villages but had no idea how big they were. I saw a few houses lit only by the unsteady, unmistakable light of a fire; none had power. We didn't see the first sign of electricity until we were almost a half hour outside of Baghdad—these were the floodlights on the high cement perimeter fence of Camp Cooke. Light poles twenty feet high ran along the razor-wire-topped walls of the forward operating base at intervals close enough to leave no shadows. The guard towers loomed a little farther back than the average person could throw a grenade but stood high enough for a good field of fire.

We rolled under an overpass with a guard tower in the middle of it. Then we turned onto a side road that led to Camp Cooke's South Gate. Our truck idled in line for an hour, waiting for our turn to enter the camp. When my Humvee pulled up, a barrel-chested Arkansas sergeant told me all the guys in my truck had to get out, take the ammunition out of our weapons, and dry fire into a barrel filled with sand. No loaded weapons were allowed in the camp.

I had absolutely no idea how to respond to that. This confused me greatly. "What if the camp is overrun or something happens where I need to shoot someone?"

This gave him pause. He stared at me for a couple seconds with tired eyes and said in a southern drawl, "Well, I guess that's why we're here, ain't it, Sergeant?"

"I guess so," I said.

"Safety first." He walked off, sat down on a foldout camping seat, and shoved a handful of sunflower seeds into his mouth.

We even had to take the heavy-ass .50 cal off the mount and dry fire her, though we all knew it was bad for her. Then we jumped back into our Humvee and fell back in line. The lieutenant came over the radio and said we would be led to our trailers by some MPs. Camp Cooke had been an Iraqi military base until we bombed the shit out of it and took it over. It looked like a military base, with the standard vehicle-maintenance bays, motor-pool yards, and even small administrative buildings, but many of these structures had the roofs or walls blown off. Of course there was no grass, maybe not in the entire country, but there were a scattering of palm trees amid the fields of fine dirt that gave it a foreign feel. Most of the buildings were decorated with stars—stars with eight points, like two squares on top of each other but with one turned so that the corners were all the same distance from each other. I figured that was the symbol for the Iraqi Army or something. We drove around strips of tarmac lined with rows of helicopters, then past the giant white mess hall tent. Finally we came down a road flanked by blown-to-shit warehouses and into a small field, where we parked like pioneers circling their wagons to fend off an Indian attack. My Humvee happened to be parked by a fuel truck's lighting unit.

I was in the perfect position to see Captain Charbonneau jump out of his Humvee and hurry to the MP's truck. The military police sergeant in the passenger seat saw the captain coming and straightened up, spit out the window, and wiped his chin. I could tell by the look he gave his driver he wasn't ready to answer any questions. I got out of my Humvee, faking a conversation with Baldwin so I could hear them.

The MP got out of his vehicle and saluted the good captain. Charbonneau returned it. They spoke in low voices for a moment before the captain yelled, "So you're telling me that we have *no trailers?*"

The MP said, "Sir, I was just told to bring you here. I'm sure they'll sort this out in the morning."

"What the hell am I supposed to do with my company, Sergeant?"

"I can call the battle captain and request to wake up the colonel if you want me to, sir."

Captain Charbonneau turned away from the MP and looked at the ring of Humvees.

"There's a warehouse over there that's not being used, sir." The MP pointed into the darkness.

Without looking at the MP again, the captain turned and walked back the way he came. The MP stared after him for a full minute before their break lights turned my world red and they drove off. I lit a cigarette, took a piss by the driver's side wheel well, and got back in my passenger seat. Ten minutes later Lieutenant Caius came over the radio, telling us we could either sleep in our trucks or in a blown-to-hell warehouse somewhere in the vicinity.

I called Melvin and Baldwin over for a team leader meeting and they asked me questions I couldn't answer, questions like, "Didn't they know we were coming?" "Are we sure this is our base?" "Who's running the place?" I told them to shut up and sent them off to their trucks. I headed over to Schofield for a squad leader meeting, and Cederman, Zabat, and I asked the same questions until Schofield told us to shut up and sent us off to our trucks—I'm sure Schofield and the other platoon sergeants asked

Captain Charbonneau the questions, too. In an hour's time we were all trying to get comfortable in the cramped trucks, wedged between our pointy and hard gear, in the hopes of getting at least an hour or two of sleep before the sun came up.

About an hour after first light, Captain Charbonneau and the officers scuttled off to some command meeting, and that gave the rest of the platoon time to smoke, joke, and do some hygiene. Most of the buildings in our area were abandoned and riddled with holes of all sizes, from bullet holes from small arms fire to gaping bomb holes. Even the dirt roads running between the ruins had potholes and craters in them. Right outside of our circle of trucks, Melvin found the mouth to an underground bomb shelter. He said he started to go down there but decided against it because the place smelled like a cesspool.

Privates Walken, Baldwin, Patterson, and O'Brian used an A bag as a table to play cards on. The dented speakers of a battery-powered CD player belted out Frank Sinatra's greatest hits. Ol' Blue Eyes was the compromise between the rock and country crowds. I hummed along to "Fly Me to the Moon" while digging to the bottom of my ruck for my hygiene bag.

I walked, naked to the waist, about thirty meters away from our circled trucks to piss in a three-foot ditch and wash up. Without my gear I felt weightless and cool, like maybe gravity had released me a little bit. I stood with my eyes closed and arms outstretched, feeling the morning sun on my chest, stomach, and shoulders, thinking maybe I could just float above all this mess.

I opened my eyes and there was Simon walking up with a blue toothbrush sticking out of his mouth. His chest glowed white except for a ring of dirt at his neckline. Every movement he made showed a muscle or bone under tight skin. The goggles he had worn the whole way up had left loops around his eyes, giving him an inverted raccoon look under hair that was packed down tight with a light coat of grit. I might as well have been looking in a mirror. He bent down to spit, took a swig from his canteen cup, and spit again. "Morning."

"Yep." I poured water that was still chilled from the lower temperatures the night before down my neck and over my chest—glorious. I used an old T-shirt to scrub a week's worth of grime from under my arms and around my neck.

"I heard this is supposed to be a new crusade," Simon said. He bent forward and poured water over his head.

"Who said that?"

"B did. He said Corporal Marr told him Third Platoon has to say the *Pulp Fiction* prayer before every mission. They said it on the way up here."

I laughed and used my dirty shirt to dry my hair. "Fuck, Simon, maybe it is. I smell like someone out of the eleventh century. I love the Crusades. They showed the world the importance of art."

"What? How?" Simon pulled out some baby wipes to scrub his armpits with.

"Half the world was dying of the plague while the rest fought over religion, and even with all that death some of the best painters and sculptors created movement after movement. Gothic, Baroque, Rococo, and everything else."

"What the fuck are you saying?"

"Serious, man. I know this shit. I went to art school." I poured some water into my palm and splashed it on my chest and into my armpit.

"Shut up."

"Yeah, well, there's a ton of shit you don't know about me."

"No one's going to force me to say a prayer."

"I don't see Schofield doing that, unless he starts Schofieldism." I squeezed some shaving cream out and rubbed it across half my face, but before I could finish the ground jumped and then fell away underneath my feet like I was standing on a wave. I widened my stance to keep from falling, but dropped my hygiene kit when the shock wave hit me hard. The sound of the explosion came a second later, then came again after bouncing off the wall behind us. A small patch of earth shattered like glass and shot rocks, shrapnel, and debris in all directions. Black smoke twisted in on itself and floated up from the impact of a mortar only about 200 meters away. I stood there half-lathered, squinting at the crater, trying to make sense of it, trying to make it fit into my logical world. At first I thought someone was doing construction work. I couldn't process the fact that intelligent beings were attempting to kill me.

Then Schofield yelled, "Incoming!"

The whistling of the second mortar round started faint but quickly grew stronger. It wasn't a constant sound like in the movies. I could hear the round spin as it screamed down at us. It hit a hundred meters closer than the last one, and when it did everyone threw down whatever they were holding and ran. I stumbled but caught a good stride and sprinted to my truck for cover.

Simon crashed into the hood of the truck next to me. His wet torso made a small outline on the side of the Humvee that quickly evaporated when he jumped up on the rear driver's side wheel to snatch his M203 from inside the plywood box. I reached into the cab, grabbed my rifle, and slammed a twenty-round magazine into place. I strained my ears trying to listen for another mortar whistle, but only heard Sinatra singing "I've Got the World on a String."

Adrenaline burned at my muscles and shot into my brain, slowing everything down to half-speed. Most of the soldiers in the company ran, flowing like an angry river toward the nearest cover. Lieutenant Caius saw they were running toward the fuel trucks and screamed that tanks of fuel make bad cover in a mortar attack. The herd turned instantly and surged toward the old bomb shelters, and then the third round hit. The ground bounced again and the concussion rattled my teeth. A few seconds later rocks, dirt, and jagged metal rained down on our trucks with thuds and tings.

Lieutenant Caius stood in the mouth of the old bomb shelter waving all the soldiers in. He stood there touching every soldier as they ran by, counting each one.

"We got to get over there." I grabbed Simon's arm and pulled at him to follow. We stayed low and used the trucks for cover. A fourth mortar whistled overhead, so close I thought I could look up and see where it was going to land. I peeked over the hood when the ground jumped but it had hit farther away, out of view.

I tapped Simon on the elbow and took off for the mouth of that bunker. I sprinted faster than I've ever moved. Halfway there I heard a fifth round coming, and could feel the vibration of the whistle in my spine the closer it got. My legs couldn't keep up with how fast I wanted them to go and I tripped.

In my memories of this moment, I see myself from the outside like a snapshot: frozen in mid-air, splayed out, arms flailing like a windmill in slow motion, half my face covered in shaving cream, screaming like death had a hold on my leg, maybe a glob or two of the shaving cream suspended in the air next to my face, eyes filled with fear of dying and the resolute determination not to shit myself. I twisted my body so I wouldn't land on my weapon. My shoulder hit the ground a second before the last mortar round did. I rolled and popped back up. Simon made it to the bunker a few steps before me. The last mortar hole smoldered two hundred meters away.

We huddled in the mouth of the bunker, poking our heads out to see where the round had landed but only seeing the smoke coming up from beyond the abandoned admin buildings around us. None of us had ever been in a mortar attack before. We didn't know how long we should stay in the bunker. The consensus was "a little longer." We stood in the mouth of the bunker listening to Sinatra in the distance. All of us searched the sky. None of us knew whether to breathe or not. We may have stayed like that for hours if Lieutenant Caius hadn't turned to me and said, "Good job, Sergeant Davis. It takes a great leader to show the men how to properly conduct a combat roll while under indirect fire."

Everyone laughed, laughed harder than the joke was funny. I laughed too. I laughed in order to get that tense ball of whatever it was out of my chest. "Thank you, sir." Slowly, we stepped out from the cave and into the sun again. We found later that one of the boys in First Platoon had caught a piece of shrapnel in the bicep. He said it felt like when you're sitting around a campfire and the fire spits a spark at you, hitting naked skin. He dug it out himself but the medic put a single stitch in it, and that was officially Bravo Company's first Purple Heart of the tour, received only a few hours after getting there.

Be Polite, Be Professional, and Be Prepared to Kill Everyone You Meet

Join the army, see the world, travel to exotic lands, get away from your small-town, white-trash roots, and travel seven thousand miles from home to be issued keys to a single-wide trailer. I stood in the shade of a cypress tree, waiting in a long line to pick up a folded cot, two sheets, a wool blanket, and an army-issued pillow from the quartermaster. All the buck sergeants and below had to share a room with two others. Staff sergeants were assigned only one roommate, and mine was sharp-shooting Tom Cederman. The Third Squad leader roomed a few trailers down with the weapons squad leader. This way, Sergeant First Class Schofield or Lieutenant Caius only had to go two places to gather the squad leaders.

I fumbled at the lock with my arms full of bedding until the door opened. The room had no windows, and the fluorescent lights made the white walls and floor glow like we had just stepped into a void. We had a half an hour to get all our bags and gear settled. I was unfolding my cot when Schofield opened the door and leaned in. Cederman yelled, "At ease!" and we both jumped to the position of parade rest.

"Don't do that shit in country." Schofield took a step inside and ran his eyes over my cot, my gear, and my face. "Make sure your guys clean their weapons tonight. They look like they've been rolling in a sandbox."

"Yes, Sergeant."

His attention bounced from me to Cederman. "We have a 0400 wake-up. We'll be out the North Gate at 0500 for our first patrol. Make sure your guys and all their equipment are ready. It starts tomorrow."

Schofield moved back to the door and stopped for a second. "Movement to contact. We're the only infantry unit in this camp. This mortaring bullshit isn't new. It's been happening for months. None of these pogues got off their asses to stop it."

Movement to contact means what it sounds like: we'd move around our patrol area until we contacted some shitheads and then we were to kill or capture them. Our mission was to stop the mortars from falling, stop people from getting hurt or killed. We were jumping right in, starting our tour off right.

When I finished setting up the cot I stared at it a while with the intense need to rack out, but instead I headed out into the evening heat to tell my team leaders about the mission. I found Baldwin, naked except for his tighty-whities and unlaced boots, throwing a six-inch knife at a sheet of plywood leaning against the outside of his trailer.

I watched the knife hit the board and bounce off, get picked up, and get thrown again. "What the fuck are you doing?"

"Practicing, Sergeant." He snapped to parade rest. "You never know."

"You never know what? When you'll have to fling knives at the insurgents in your underwear?"

He shrugged.

"At ease. Don't do that shit in country," I said.

He loosened up, then picked his buck knife out of the dirt and folded it up.

"Have your guys cleaned the .50 cal?"

His silence answered my question.

"Make sure that happens. The fucking thing looked like you rolled it in a sandbox, and don't have Simon do it all. You guys tear it down as a team and get that thing clean. Make sure everyone cleans their rifles, too. Then get some rack time because first call is at four; we have a movement to contact in the morning."

"Movement to contact already, Sergeant?"

"Someone's got to catch the shitheads lobbing mortars in here. Tell Melvin to have his guys do the same."

I walked back to my room hoping I did a good enough Schofield impersonation to impress upon them the importance of the mission. I sighed, and for some reason the stars caught my attention. I guess because they weren't the same ones I was used to looking at. The base hummed with generators near and far. I noticed a surreal peace coming over me, some type of feeling I didn't understand, maybe one that I'd never understand. Pride was a big part of it. Simplicity too. And satisfaction. Whatever need in me that Viking gene had created was being met. I was doing something that less than one percent of Americans did, and in the morning I would use loaded weapons to hunt man. The shark would swim.

I opened the door to my trailer and was hit with a wave of cold. Cederman had cranked the AC and it felt amazing. I dug out a uniform to wear on our first mission. When I pulled it from my A bag, my leader book popped out and fell to the floor. It landed on its spine and fell open to the pages of the sketches I had done of the men in training. Looking at them affected me in a way I wasn't prepared for. My first thought was that I hated those pictures. The urge to create like that was a weakness, a childish impulse. This was the moment I realized I had split myself in two, the artist and the soldier, and the soldier didn't like the artist. The soldier didn't like to think of home, of family, of a future. War was real. War was now. Nothing else mattered.

I reached down, picked up my leader book, and tore the silly pages right out. I ripped them up and threw them away. Then I grabbed my rifle and started to clean it in my sterile white room that looked like a ward for mental patients, void of any color, balance, or style.

The walls were so white that when I finally lay down to sleep I could project all of my swirling thoughts onto them. I reclined on my cot in my new uniform with my eyes half closed, watching the men who shot the mortars laughing big, evil laughs, dropping the high-explosive round down the tube before quickly plugging their ears at its thudding report. My private movie went on with them running through dank underground tunnels. They sat in their holes and planned the destruction of America because their lives were devoid of love, family, and peace. They were soulless men with snake eyes and cloven feet, hissing hate at one another with forked tongues. Somewhere in there I drifted off.

Throughout our first thirty days in country we were sent on more than thirty combat missions. Taji was right in the middle of what people called the Sunni Triangle. This meant that we operated in an area where people had been big supporters of Saddam. In fact, he had been captured just months before about ninety miles north of Taji. Before we borrowed it, Camp Cooke was called Al-Taji Airfield; it was an Iraqi Republican Guard base suspected to manufacture chemical weapons. It was also Saddam's biggest tank-maintenance facility. The entire northwest corner of the camp was filled with a tank graveyard. Rows and rows of tanks bought from all over the world rusted right there in the corner of our base, hundreds of them, more than you'd see probably anywhere else in the world. Every time we left for patrol through the North Gate,

I read the new graffiti. Some US soldier would write his sweet-heart's name or the name of his hometown in spray paint and pose next to the tank for a picture. I thought about doing it myself but never had the time.

Our new commander ran us ragged because we were the only infantry unit on base. We ran on continuous ops for the majority of that first month and patrolled around the clock. Not only were we patrolling the roads and fields around the base, we also had to guard a bridge ten miles south of Taji to keep it from getting blown up. On top of all this, we had our QRF missions coming in from the general. When he needed us, we jumped on helicopters and flew down to the Green Zone or wherever else.

The daily patrols were conducted in triple-digit heat while wearing at least sixty pounds of gear, on no more than two hours of sleep at one time, and on no more than six hours of sleep over a single twenty-four-hour period. This seems impossible, but we did it for almost two months straight. How?

Fear. Without fear there wouldn't have been any adrenaline, and we lived on adrenaline—it was the perfect drug. With it, I felt unstoppable. I could carry more weight, move faster, jump higher. My senses were in overdrive. I saw farther and clearer, heard more than I thought possible, and had greater control over my motor functions. I was able to process information and make decisions faster.

I was superhuman.

It wasn't uncommon to leave for a patrol and drive by an area hit by mortar barrage. The base had a fire engine and an ambu-lance like you'd see at traffic accidents back home, but the writing on the side was filled with Arabic squiggles and dots. When we'd drive by these scenes of devastation, I couldn't help but look over at the flashing lights. Sometimes I could hear the injured soldiers screaming in agony. Our job was to hunt the assholes killing our troops, and each day that went by without us finding them, more people died. Heading out on the job meant filling your chest with as much fear and anger as you could, because that's what kept you going, that's what motivated you, that's what kept the adren-aline pumping.

But being at war meant something else, too. It meant finding humor in as many places as possible. Laughter was a release—a way to clear out all that fear and hate when you didn't need it any-more, like an exhaust system. Gallows humor, sure, but the ironies of life became a bit more obvious, too. For example, after a month or so the general sent the Military Police out to patrol the base and pull over speeders. Their job was to pull over vehicles traveling over fifteen miles an hour on base because those drivers were being unsafe and kicking up too much dust. In a combat zone. They tried to pull us over once but we found that if we just ignored them and kept driving they wouldn't follow us out the gate.

There was another irony that was not lost on me; it was almost three years after 9/11 and I was over seven thousand miles from where I started, and I was still driving in circles on a highway, looking at roadkill and responding to incidents. Though there were a few big differences, of course: in Iraq, people sometimes shot at me while I drove, and the roadkill was potentially packed with high explosives. Hey, at least I was making a few dollars more an hour.

We made up names for all the towns and villages, names like River Villa, Red Bone Road, Hajji Highway, Compton, Hamtown. In order to cover more ground, it was common to have two platoons of four vehicles each patrolling different areas around the base. On April 12, 2004, my platoon patrolled the road to the east of the base that ran north and south, parallel to the Tigris River. We were out all night, and at ten in the morning we finally turned onto a small dirt road and headed west, back to base. A patrol from First Platoon was heading east on the same road. I had just barely made them out right before they disappeared in a giant cloud of dirt violently coughed up from the earth. A second later, I heard the explosion.

Lieutenant Caius happened to be patrolling with us, and he screamed at me over the radio to get there. I told Simon to floor it. He did. It looked like a lightning storm on the ground, the way the muzzle flashes lit up that dark cloud of dirt and cordite. The First Platoon lieutenant was screaming over the radio like a child, his voice cracking, his words making little sense as he tried to call out the roster numbers of the wounded. I jumped out of my Humvee with my weapon at the ready before we had even skidded to a stop. My squad ran after me with only the two drivers staying to pull security on our vehicles.

I ran into the swirl of blackness toward the screaming. Every breath tasted like ash. Most of the men were firing to the north of the road, and each time a trigger was pulled there would be a flash revealing the soldier, his gear, and his rifle. We rallied around the disabled vehicle and gained the superiority of fire like we had trained to do, but no one was firing back at us. The triggermen must have fled.

The dust cleared, and there was the medic and First Platoon's sergeant examining two soldiers from the Humvee that took the worst of it. They blocked my view of who was hurt and how bad, but between them I saw sticky blood trails running down from someone's hairline and heard another person screaming inside the vehicle. Everyone from the ambushed patrol tended to their own men or equipment. I ran by them, jumped into the irrigation ditch that separated the road we were on from a field of small date trees, and ran north after the triggermen. The men lifted fire so they didn't hit us as we ran into the date trees after the shitheads.

I didn't even get the length of a football field before having to stop and double over to catch my breath. The men in my squad crashed through the grove behind me. My equipment weighed heavy, and my heart strained. My muscles burned. We stood at the edge of the grove. If we continued north, we would be walking through an open field. This was always a bad thing to do while chasing shitheads.

I had no idea in which direction the triggerman (or triggermen) may have run, but I had too much hate in my chest to turn back. I decided we would head west, so we formed a wedge and walked through an adjoining orange grove. We moved quietly, more quietly than you would imagine men who were carrying so much equipment could move, through a thick bramble of twisted orange tree branches. At the end of that grove we came to another open field. In the middle of it, an old man in a white dishdasha was talking to a boy in dirty hand-me-down clothes. The boy couldn't have been more than twelve years old.

As soon as I saw them, I halted the squad and took a knee. Melvin crouched low, hustled over to me, and whispered excitedly, "Let's get these motherfuckers."

I studied his face, trying to determine what he meant by "get." I knew from my experiences in Haiti that blame was easily shifted to anyone of the same race in the general vicinity. It was easy for Melvin to see these two strangers as the reason we humped through triple-digit heat with all this weight. Maybe these two were the reason we were mortared every morning and every night. Maybe if we "got" them, it would stop.

I thought about killing those two farmers. I was sure nothing would come of it if we did. Despite what anyone thinks, today's modern army is not filled with robots or warmongers. We have strict rules, Rules of Engagement (ROE), that every soldier must adhere to, the biggest one being we can only shoot after being shot at or if we think someone else's life is in danger. But from where I stood, the old man could have had either an AK-47 or a stick he used to walk. I didn't know. The explosion had happened less than ten minutes before, and here they were less than a half mile away. Didn't they have to know something? And one more thing, one more thing that I hate to admit: I wanted to kill them. I did. I wanted to open them up and hear their screams just like I had heard my friends screaming ten minutes before.

That was how ground combat worked early on in the Iraq War: an IED exploded, an RPG was shot, a couple machine guns opened up, and the triggermen ran. Most of the time they ran into a populated area. The good guys shot back, sometimes killing a triggerman or two, every once in a while killing innocent people by mistake. The families of the real triggermen would swear to avenge their loss, but so would the families of the innocent dead, and the loop would repeat itself, ad infinitum, while the serpent ate its tail. The crowd supplied the actors in the comedy.

So there it was. Would I kill those farmers? The men in my squad would back any decision I made, but could I do it? Maybe I could have rationalized killing them by convincing myself they were the triggermen, but I didn't. The ROE isn't what stopped me that day. The real reason I didn't open up on those two poor farmers was because of the way the sun cut through those orange trees and fell on the old man's white robes. The scene was beautiful. The way he was leading that boy reminded me of a Gustave Doré illustration of *The Divine Comedy*. The old man looked like Virgil leading a young Dante through this hell. I didn't want to destroy something so perfect.

I don't know if they were the triggermen. I should have zip-tied and brought them in. But, after talking to them, I didn't see them as enemies—just a grandfather taking his grandson for a walk. I had them searched, and I released them when I didn't find anything.

Later I found out that one of our guys had a blown eardrum from the explosion. A couple more were pretty shook up from the explosion being so close, but for the most part the IEDs were buried too deep and the earth took the brunt of the explosions. No one was critically injured and no one died that day, but I started to see that real courage didn't come from running headlong into a combat zone ready to kill. I began to believe it took real courage to decide whether or not killing is necessary.

Sean with local children in a town outside Taji, Iraq.

Painting Daisies in Valhalla

One of the problems of having a new commander: when the dangerous missions come up, the new captain doesn't turn them down. He didn't know our names and faces, but he knew the names and faces of the men handing out the missions. At the bottom it seemed like he over-volunteered us for the toughest missions. We missed our old company commander very much. The new captain and Lieutenant Caius had a less-than-cordial working relationship, but our platoon was the best the captain had, and when the more difficult missions came along we were the boys he sent.

We heard about our newest assignment from the RTOS. RTO means radio and telephone operator, and it was usually one of the more intelligent of the lower enlisted. These soldiers carried the radios, batteries, and additional gear for the officers. A smart squad leader always went to the RTO for the latest information.

We were to patrol River Villa on foot and make friends. River Villa sat along the Tigris River, and the houses there were relatively nice. Some of the community had been well off, but now most of them were farmers using the river as irrigation for their crops of dates, oranges, or, in a few cases, wheat. They had electricity most of the time, and spigots spurted semi-drinkable water depending on the day and the number of iodine tablets used.

We needed to be friends with the people of River Villa for a few reasons. First off, the whole town was only a mile from our East Gate, and if they didn't like us they might let the shithead mortar teams hide there. The second reason was that, like I said before, Taji was in the middle of the Sunni Triangle. These people had been Ba'athists loyal to Saddam at one time. That was why they had been living in luxury compared to the rest of the country. They had riverside mansions while many people lived in mud huts. They had been Saddam's favorites, but now that Saddam was gone we had a unique opportunity to get them on our side. This meant winning hearts and minds. With a smile on my face, candy in my cargo pockets, and a rifle in my hand, I walked down the street we called Rodeo Drive.

I had found that the best way to win over a town was through the kids. Even the meanest stink-eye changed to a smile after I pulled a quarter out of some kid's ear. Handing out a couple of pencils and a bag of M&Ms was the best way to find myself a little buddy. After being friends for a couple minutes, the kid always wanted me to meet the fam. Sooner or later little hands would pull me toward a house or a business run by Daddy.

There were a couple problems with the plan. First, we carried the exact same weapons and equipment on our missions to make friends that we did on missions to kill. Second, we needed to be prepared for casualties even during these missions, so, though most of us walked, Sergeant Schofield drove his up-armored Humvee twenty meters behind us with Private First Class Ford, the chicken rancher, manning the .50 cal machine gun. This didn't always promote goodwill. And the final problem was that if the Iraqis answered any of the lieutenant's questions with anything other than yes or no, it was up to me to interpret what the hell they were saying. I had become the platoon's unofficial interpreter, a job I loved but one I was sorely underqualified for.

This town was tough. They didn't hide the fact that they were Ba'athists, or the fact that they didn't like us very much. I tried everything: I did bad magic tricks, gave out candy, kicked soccer balls around with a few kids. We stopped into a small store and asked to spend US and new Iraqi money on cold sodas and cheap US-knockoff cigarettes. At most places, we'd give a five-dollar bill for a soda or some gum and tell them to keep the change. Usually this was welcomed and we'd hit it off with the store's owner, but at this particular store they wouldn't sell to us. The man behind the counter shook his head no with his eyes closed until we left.

We were almost through the town and I was out of tricks. The children always asked for pens for school, so I kept a pocketful. I was down to my last pen when a child of around ten, holding a couple schoolbooks and a pad of paper to his chest, poked at my ammo pouches. When I turned to look down at him he asked for my last pen, but instead of giving it to him I pulled it out and motioned to see his notepad. He handed his books to a friend and opened his notebook. I slung my weapon across my back and drew flowers. Of all the things I might have drawn, I have no idea why I picked flowers, but I started there and then added a horrible, shakily drawn puppy.

It was an ugly little thing, but it made the boy smile. There it was. With one ugly little puppy surrounded by daisies, the artist did something the soldier couldn't. The boy told me his name was Farook. He smiled and asked me to draw Homer Simpson. I tried while asking him if his father lived nearby. As it turned out, his dad was named Hasheem and owned a small carpentry shop in town.

The father was a carpenter who had dark, curly, shoulder-length hair and a beard. He wore a white robe, and greeted me with a giant smile. It turned out he spoke pretty good English. Whenever I found an English-speaking adult, I made sure to politely introduce him to Lieutenant Caius. While we waited for the lieutenant, I posed for a couple pictures with Hasheem. The photos were more than just war tourism; I used them to document contacts in each town.

When he got there, Caius asked him about Saddam, and at the mention of his name all the kids pinched their noses, gave a thumbs-down, or booed. Then they yelled, in chorus, "George Boosh, number one!"

The lieutenant went on to ask the usual questions about weapons and bad guys, but all Hasheem said was, "No problem here." Then he told us he liked the Americans and he was sure the other people in his village would too if given time. The lieutenant asked if there was anything we could do for him, and he told us about the goats in the village. A couple of them were bloated and wouldn't stop drooling. Lieutenant Caius had me write it down and assured Hasheem that a veterinarian would be sent to look at the herd. Hasheem held his arms out and smiled like he wanted to give our platoon leader a hug. The lieutenant grabbed his hand and shook it instead. I thought that would have been the perfect time to kiss the man on his cheek, but Hasheem didn't seem to mind. We thanked him and he thanked us back sincerely, with bows and hand clapping. He even hugged me, excited by our offer of help to him and his village. We posed for pictures together. He gave me a saw so I could pretend I was fixing something in one of the pictures. We left their village feeling like we had just been visiting with old friends and continued to patrol Rodeo Drive, happy for small successes.

The next day there was no mortar attack, the birds chirped, we slept in a little bit, and we had the day off. It was like winning the lottery. I didn't know what to do with the free time. After breakfast

I made sure the squad cleaned their rifles and the machine guns. It took a couple hours, but after that we had the rest of the day to explore the FOB. Simon and I walked to the PX. Even though neither of us needed anything, I thought a can of BBQ Pringles and a Coke would be nice. The place was a giant cement cube with a ceiling probably forty feet high, filled with all the comforts an American boy could need while fighting in the desert. It was like a Walmart on the moon: rows of beef jerky, sunflower seeds in multiple flavors, Levi's jeans, alarm clocks, Coca-Cola and Pepsi products, Lays potato chips, *Playboy, Penthouse, Club Magazine,* Xbox and PlayStation consoles, television sets, Nike running shoes, Gatorade sports drinks, pop music CDs. To top it all off, they had novelty T-shirts: *Some days are Sunni, but most days are Shi'ite; I went to Operation Iraqi Freedom and all I got was this lousy T-shirt; Baghdad Brew Pub.* My favorite had a caricature of a big white soldier's head sticking out of a Humvee, with motion lines and slanted oval tires making it look like it was driving a hundred miles an hour. Over the Humvee it read: *Who's your Baghdaddy?*

I turned to Simon, "Is this war? I don't remember my grandfather telling me about *Who's your D-Day Daddy* T-shirts.

Simon smiled and walked over to the kitchen appliances section. I followed him, listening to the American Top 40 music lightly playing from overhead speakers, not knowing if we should have a sense of humor about these things. Shit, maybe the T-shirts were one small part of the bigger joke, the joke you can't tell people who weren't there. It just wouldn't be funny, which is a shame because that's the exact reason it is funny.

Simon bought a coffeemaker and grinder from the Filipino cashier and I grabbed my Coke and BBQ Pringles. We headed over to an Iraqi barbershop on base and got haircuts. The place still had holes in the walls from shrapnel, but there were three barber chairs and new mirrors. I paid a bald Iraqi man with a huge nose five dollars to shave my head, while an old television console in the corner played Turkey's version of MTV. The songs were obvious rip-offs of Western pop songs with Arabic-style singing running over them. At the end of the haircut, the old man massaged my neck for five minutes.

We walked over to the movie theater and went inside, but it was still being remodeled. The building had been some sort of banquet hall for the officers back when it was an Iraqi base. Crystal chandeliers hung in the lobby, and the trimming was ornate. The decadence continued into the bathroom. When I went to take a shit, I found a fancy bidet right next to the toilet. Everything had the gaudiest gold fixtures. I had never used a bidet before that day in a semi-bombed movie theater in Iraq. It was a glorious experience that I will hold dear for the rest of my life.

With nothing else to do, we headed back to our trailers. Being inside the wire felt weird. Not being on patrol made me feel itchy, jumpy, and nervous. I could have played on Simon's Xbox, written a letter home, or found a hundred other things to do to occupy my time off, but I decided to have Simon and Private Walken help me work on the truck. I wanted to make sure it was ready for the next time we went out. We hammered six-inch nails through the plywood walls into the metal bed of the frame, because the whole "hardened" box was sliding off the truck. I added another cargo strap around the outside of the damned thing to hold it together.

Then we drove it over to the tank graveyard by the North Gate, searched through the rows of blown-to-shit tanks, and pried off pieces of armor plating to stick between the plywood. We had to be careful about putting too much weight in there because the suspension was bottoming out, but it was at least an attempt to give the guys in the back a little more cover.

When that was done, I headed back to my trailer and sat on my cot staring at the blaring white walls. Under my cot I had a box from Amazon that I hadn't opened yet. There were three books in there. I knew what they were: *Twilight of the Idols* by Nietzsche, *American Psycho* by Ellis, and some political science textbook. Religion, culture, and government. The problem was that I had lost my motivation to read them, to write anything, even to scribble small caricatures of the people around me like I always did. I didn't want to be reminded that there was a world outside of the missions. My little brother Vince was the only person I'd spoken to during that first month, and I'd only called him twice. Blocking out home and family made it easier for me to be in such a shitty situation.

After a few minutes I reached down, pushed the box further under my cot, picked up my shotgun, and cleaned it again.

Mortars started landing around our trailers at around 0500 hours. I jumped out of my cot with only my PT shorts on, grabbed my flak vest, rifle, and helmet, and ran for the shelters. They landed close enough for the light of the explosions to cast my shadow on the sand behind me. The shitheads were really letting it rain, making up for not hitting us the day before. Once in the shelter, I called out orders between blasts for Baldwin and Melvin to make sure their teams were accounted for. All of Double Deuce stood there leaning against the cement walls of the bunkers smoking cigarettes—all of them except our machine gunner, Specialist Tully Patterson. Mechaiah O'Brian was his roommate so I asked him where he was. O'Brian said that when he ran out of the room, Patterson told him he would be there in a few minutes but never got out of his cot.

I sighed, put my helmet back on, and waited for the next round to land before sprinting to his room. The door was unlocked so I flung it open and flicked the lights on. Patterson was sleeping through the attack.

"Get the fuck up!" I yelled at him. When he didn't react, I shook him. He turned over, annoyed, but when he saw it was me, he jumped up.

"Sergeant?"

"Get your shit and get to the shelter." I stood up.

"Aw, come on, Sergeant, it's over. I just got to sleep."

"Get the fuck up."

The light and shadows danced around us as we ran back. One of the rounds had landed two feet from one of First Platoon's Humvees. It blew the fender out and caught the rubber of the wheel on fire. This was only twenty feet from our bunker.

"Run faster, Patterson!"

We got to the bunker, and as soon as I caught my breath I borrowed a cigarette from Simon. We laughed about Patterson wanting to sleep through the closest mortar attack yet. After ten minutes without another explosion Schofield ran from bunker to bunker to get a head count for the entire platoon, but not every platoon sergeant did it like this: one of the Arkansas National Guard platoon sergeants held his accountability formation in the open. A second wave of mortaring started, and the first round landed almost on top of them. We all jumped when that first round came down. It was only two hundred meters away. The screams started before we heard the second round whistling.

The first voices we heard weren't the wounded. They probably didn't even feel their injuries yet. The first voices were the people yelling orders for everyone to get back to the bunkers, to help carry the ones who couldn't make it themselves, to do something. The next sounds we heard were the loud, angry voices of the wounded. They screamed strings of obscenities that echoed through the bunkers. This was when I thought I should help, but before I could do anything the third wave of voices came. The badly wounded finally started to feel the pain of their injuries. These were high-pitched screams, and they passed right through me leaving a never-ending echo. They were pleas for help. I heard people calling to God and to other soldiers running around.

I started to run out with my squad, but Schofield stopped us. He said only people with EMT training would go. It was too dangerous to run into a mortar attack, and he didn't want to lose any of his men. Then Schofield put Cederman in charge and went to see if he could help, since he had medical training. I watched Schofield poised to run, stooped down at the mouth of the bunker, pausing to search the sky for falling mortars with the fire from the Humvee tire lighting up the one side of him. I remember thinking something that doesn't make sense out of the context of that night. I remember thinking that there is no such thing as heroes, not like those created by popular culture — there are only men who choose to do what needs to be done.

Three soldiers were killed instantly that morning, four were in critical condition, and another twenty-one were injured.

That mass-casualty-producing event changed things. Two Kiowa observation helicopters took off minutes after the attack, probably trying to use their infrared to find the mortar crew, but this was only the first step in a mission the whole battalion would soon be pulled into. While the brass in the TOC were planning this giant mission, my platoon and I went back to bed. But an hour later, an operations order came down from the colonel himself to do a cordon and search mission. The colonel had decided to surround an entire city with tanks and armored personnel carriers and have the infantry search each house for weapons, large amounts of cash, or anything else suspicious.

He picked the most populated area within thirty miles to siege. We called the place Hamtown because no one could pronounce the real name. The houses in the middle of town were nice, which is to say the windows had glass in them, the doors had knobs, and they probably had electricity and running water at one time. The outskirts of town had small farming quarters, and farther out there were hovels made of mud. Railroad tracks and dirt roads made up the borders of the town, and outside these borders were miles of dried-up fields filled with clumps of dirt, shriveled plants, and small, dying trees.

We had patrolled through Hamtown a few times before and never had any problems. The people there weren't friendly, but no one shot at us and there were no IEDs. From what I saw they used to be rich, and they still lived in luxury compared to the small farming villages that made up most of our area. Still, imagine you're upper-class one day and then overnight all of your money becomes worthless, your water is turned off, and the power is out. Then imagine living like this for months with little improvement. Iraqis are proud people, as prideful as Americans. I don't think I would have suffered through that forced humility any better. I'd stink-eye the troops I saw as responsible for my mess, too. I may even feel resentment, and that resentment wouldn't have anything to do with politics or religious jihad.

The indignant and close-to-hostile feelings of the people in the town were only one part of the equation. This giant mission would be the first time many of the soldiers from other units would set foot outside the wire since they had arrived in country and convoyed up to Taji. The majority of these heavily armed soldiers hadn't placed any importance on learning the culture or language; most of them had never interacted with Iraqis at all. The colonel's operation would probably be the worst way for them to do so for the first time, but "the hammer was coming down." It actually said that in the battalion operations order. There were going to be dozens of men and a dozen tanks with heavy machine guns and chainfed automatic grenade launchers sent to a place they'd never seen, surrounding people they either feared or strongly disliked.

Sergeant First Class Schofield knew it was a fucked-up mission. He told us that we were given a shit sandwich and we needed to either eat it or starve. I was starting to see the big joke, and I knew we were building toward a punch line.

The Shit Sandwich

Our new battalion commander came from a long career in the regular army. He encouraged all the officers and upper-enlisted men in his command to grow neatly trimmed triangular mustaches just like the perfect one he displayed to the world above his own top lip. To his way of thinking, a mustache instilled confidence and reminded a man that he was, indeed, a man. The lieutenant colonel and his mustache commanded our cavalry battalion and all the units attached. Bravo Company was one of those units. I heard that every time he briefed the platoon leaders he would pontificate on the rich history of the Seventh Cavalry Regiment, especially its exploits during the Black Hills War between General George Armstrong Custer and the Sioux Indians. He commented many times on the incredible and undying loyalty of Custer's men.

The morning of the mass-casualty event, he scrambled helicopters and ordered the cordon and search of an entire city. He also had the artillery units start to register the howitzers dangerously close to River Villa. Normally, artillery registration meant practice fire in order to get a better accuracy for the 155-millimeter cannons, but doing it in the middle of the night without eyes on the target did absolutely no good.

We called the howitzers 155 cannons because the round it fires is a steel bullet 155 millimeters across and 600 millimeters long. That is a little over six inches wide and about two feet long. This giant bullet weighs one hundred pounds, and the HE (high explosive) rounds have roughly fifteen and a half pounds of TNT inside. They are painted gold-and-olive drab and have a point-detonating fuse that blows when it smashes into something. When detonated, the round produces about two thousand pieces of shrapnel. The kill range is within fifty meters of the blast and the shrapnel will fly at least one hundred meters from the impact zone.

The lieutenant colonel had our howitzers firing into the farms directly adjacent to villages we had walked through, the villages we had promised to help just days before. Maybe his thinking was to show some muscle and scare people into telling us where the mortar teams were hiding. Vietnam veterans would call this tactic H&I

(harassment and interdiction) fire. Of course, no one on today's modern battlefield would call it that, since the US government outlawed H&I fire in the early 1970s. Whatever the case, our howitzers registered their cannons every eight hours for the next three days. The cannons started at six thirty in the morning while the squad leaders and I huddled around a map on the hood of the lieutenant's Humvee. I breathed into my hands, hugged myself, and rubbed my arms. It was probably only in the mid-sixties, but that is cold as hell when you're used to triple digits. We smoked cigarettes and followed Caius's finger scrolling across the map. Everyone jumped at the first explosion like the ground had disappeared underneath us. The shock wave crashed into us, followed closely by the boom. I ducked and grabbed my helmet. We all started to run for the bunkers until Schofield shouted, "Outgoing!"

Lieutenant Caius continued to brief us on the mission between cannon blasts. Compared to the operations we had done before, I would say that this one lacked complexity. Not that simple was bad, but "get the bad guys" was just so vague. Once the tanks had surrounded the village, I was to take my squad and kick down doors to search for shitheads. Of course, the shitheads looked identical to the people we were there to help, and this would make the mission very difficult. I hoped maybe the terrorists would be wearing novelty T-shirts to identify themselves.

Sergeant First Class Schofield stood with his arms crossed, the light of some far-off floodlights outlining the right side of his face. The cherry from his cigarette bounced around inside his silhouette. "A platoon and a half to clear a town with a population of around a thousand. It'd take a fucking week if we knew the place. The op order says we need to do it before dark." Another blast sounded in the distance. No one spoke for a while. Schofield exhaled and his cigarette smoke caught the light as soon as it left his black outline. "Go do your PCIs, and be ready to head out when the lieutenant gives the word."

Every house in the middle of the village looked like a box. Because it never rained, there was no need for a pointed roof. Most people had a terrace or at least a storage area on top of their house. Sometimes, during the hotter days, people slept up there. There were a few mansion-sized houses right in the center of town for what must have been affluent people.

We parked our trucks at the edge of town and waited for the order to run in and start searching. We waited like dogs testing the strength of the leash until the clinking of the tracks and the roar of the tanks' engines stopped, letting us know they were in place. The word to go would come down in seconds.

The bigger picture faded away and the only thing I could see was my small part in it. I stared a hole into the front door of the first house we would search. I didn't care anymore about the mortaring every morning. I didn't care about finding caches of weapons and money. I didn't care about home, or family, or the world. The present moment was all that was real; nothing else existed before and nothing would exist afterward. The adrenaline from the danger and fear made every second longer and lifted me from mere mortality. At that instant I was an instrument in a beautiful orchestra performing an epic symphony. History would forgive a couple of the notes being out of tune. I had the sting a scared person gets in the back of the neck, and then up the spine, turning fear to courage. Every nerve and cell cranked to full blast, every sense taking in more than what seemed possible. I felt every drop of sweat, the weight of the sunlight, every molecule floating around me. I saw everything, heard everything. I was weightless, strong, and kill-proof.

The word came. We sprinted across a dirt road to a large adobe shack surrounded by a fence of tin siding. I smashed the gate in with my foot and ran to the front door. I kicked it and it flew off the hinges into the house.

I stood there in all my terrible glory, ready to fight Satan himself, but instead I found myself face-to-face with a horrified old woman whose hunch made her barely five feet tall. Her gnarled old fingers covered her gaping mouth. The wrinkles on her face stretched around wide eyes.

A sixty-year-old grandmother in crusty black robes was the first occupant I had to deal with in my house-to-house search for terrorists. The smell of baking flatbread filled the front room, barely covering the odor of soil and feces. This frail old woman was the worst thing I could have found behind the first door. Training had prepared me for men with AK-47s, insurgents planning terror, or mercenaries with RPGs. I could have handled a firefight with al-Qaeda; I was ready to zip-tie Osama bin Laden; but this small, terrified lady with tears welling up in her eyes totally defeated me.

My war face fell off. In the span of a gasp I stopped being an infantry squad leader on a mission to uphold democracy and fight evil and became just some asshole who'd kicked in an elderly woman's front door. I looked over at it, looked back to her, and apologized.

Her breathing returned to normal after she realized I wasn't going to kill her. I think that became obvious to her when I bent down to examine the door, seeing if it was reparable. When she decided I didn't mean her any harm, all her fear turned to anger. She started screaming at me in Arabic, her voice a hoarse croak that sounded like a cinder block being pulled over concrete. Her arms started flailing at me, smacking my arms and flak vest.

"Jesus, lady. I said I was sorry." I let my rifle hang on its sling behind my back and put my arms up to block her slaps. Her curses flowed loud and steady. I could barely hear anything else.

In the meantime, the rest of the squad did what they were supposed to do: they flowed from room to room, from the front to the back. Between the old woman's squawks, I heard Baldwin yell that he'd found three more women in the back room. Simon walked out from behind a corner and gave me a half smile. "I thought you were killing her."

"Get her off me."

He stayed where he stood and shrugged. "You kicked her door down."

She stopped slapping and started pulling my arm and pointing at her door. The rest of the squad walked back out to the front. Baldwin told me that the house was all clear. They all stood there like some sort of chorus, laughing. The woman screeched and rasped without a pause.

I ignored her for a second and looked at the guys. "All right, on to the next house."

The squad filed out, which made her angrier. She yelled louder. All five feet of her was determined to not let me go without some sort of retribution. Finally I backed out of the door and grabbed my wallet. I took out a twenty-dollar bill and held it out. She stopped talking and eyed it suspiciously.

"The door was plywood and two hinges. Come on, lady, take the money. Shit, buy some windows too."

Baldwin called from the side of the house. "Sergeant, which house next?"

When I looked over to him she snatched the bill out of my hand and backed into her dark house that now smelled like burning bread. I jogged toward the squad, leaving her calling for her daughters and standing over the broken plywood. "Holy shit. Knock on the next one."

The people were okay with us searching their houses, like they expected armed strangers to go through their personal belongings. Most of the places were the same: no couches, no chairs, no beds, no television, no desks—just a knee-high, homemade table, or the occasional dresser. On top of those were dozens of folded blankets, pillows, and foam cushions stacked up. As far as I could tell, they threw all the blankets and pillows on the ground when they wanted to sleep, sit, or smoke a hookah.

The old woman in the first house may have killed my bloodlust, but I still enjoyed my job. It was difficult to be the one who made the decisions on the ground, especially when the higher-ups didn't give us all the resources we needed, but it was still the most exciting thing I've ever done. A translator, or some intelligence on the town we were searching, would have made my job a thousand times easier—not to mention some up-armored Humvees, or squad radios that I didn't have to buy myself at a sporting goods store. The language barrier was the biggest obstacle, but when I treated the Iraqis with respect and at least attempted to speak their language we found a way around it. I asked the occupants of every house if they could help us find the bad men. Every single person told me the same thing: "There are no bad men here."

I knew they had to see and hear the mortar rounds being shot at us. It took me a while to understand why they'd lie. They were tribal people like us, just part of a different tribe. Their countrymen meant more to them than we did. I wouldn't have given up even the most ate-up, broke-dick soldier in the battalion to an outsider, even if I knew he was dead wrong, so how could I blame them for not giving up a few of their troublemakers to armed foreigners? Plus, I had never met a group of people more full of pride. If they admitted to bad men living in their town, it would shame them. Once I realized this, the mission seemed impossible, both the specific mission of that day and the bigger mission. I stood in some stranger's living room while my squad ransacked their house and asked myself what the hell we were doing. Why were we there at all?

Hours went by with no shitheads found. The colonel must have started feeling frustrated, because the tanks began moving around the perimeter of the town like tigers pacing behind zoo bars. The lieutenant colonel screamed over the radio at all the officers and sent the command sergeant major out to kick young lieutenants in the ass.

The army is a beautiful institution filled with courageous men willing to give their lives for their idea of America and for each other. I know this because I've seen it firsthand. The ability to make quick decisions without caring about their real-life impact on other human beings is a strength in war, but a great leader also factors in the welfare of his men and the innocent people on the battlefield. Maybe the battalion commander was a good leader at one time in his military career. I was just a squad leader so I only dealt with the man indirectly, but even then I saw that he started to lose his composure and professionalism in River Villa. I wanted to think that maybe it was the pressure of leading so many men in combat—maybe he felt too much, or maybe he felt responsible for all the dead and wounded of the mortar attack that morning.

When the search part of the mission didn't come up with any shitheads, the lieutenant colonel must have decided to come in and search the houses himself. My squad had just finished clearing a house on the perimeter, and we stepped back into the street to behold the lieutenant colonel and his mustache in all their glory. He stood half out of the turret of an M1 Abrams tank with his long, naked, erect cavalry saber glistening in the sun, held out before him like a divining rod meant to find evil. The sight of him using the seventy-ton, jet-fueled battle tank as a chariot would have been funny if it weren't real. He looked like the caricature on the PX T-shirts: *Who's your Baghdaddy?*

Staff Sergeant Cederman's squad finished with their row of houses right after us, and they were leaving a house just as the lieutenant colonel pulled up. They were one block closer to the lieutenant colonel than my squad. Having a tank on the inside of the cordon attracted people who wanted answers. They hadn't been told that their town would be sieged and searched by strangers carrying automatic weapons. I'm sure they wanted to know why. I'm also sure they believed the lone tank carried the man they could ask. I started to put together the pieces: our battalion commander, lead man, played by a mad, mustached lieutenant colonel now stopping his tank to randomly take out his frustration on some hapless soldier; Cederman, the ever-faithful NCO wanting to suggest a better way to go about the search; the angry and scared townsfolk, confused and desperate to know why the soldiers were inflicting this humiliation upon them.

The heat coated us all with sweat, and the battalion commander's tank kicked up enough dust and sand to sugar cookie all of us. Cederman took off his helmet in order to readjust the radio headgear the army issued us. That radio only worked half the time so none of us wore it except for him, and he wore it only because he stuck faithfully to the rules. Staff Sergeant Cederman was the last person in the world who should have been reprimanded by someone like the battalion commander for being out of uniform. But from the lieutenant colonel's point of view, he had jumped down off his tank into the middle of a failed operation, and this dirtbag soldier out of uniform represented everything that was wrong with the world. The mob of villagers was screaming demands before the lieutenant colonel had even descended from his chariot. This pissed him off even more, so by the time he stood in front of Cederman he was furious. The lieutenant colonel grabbed Cederman's helmet and drove it hard into Cederman's chest. "The day I've been having, you're lucky I don't drop-kick this fucking thing across this shithole."

Cederman was completely surprised by the battalion commander's actions. His mouth dropped open to reply, but he didn't say anything.

"You know what, fuck it." The lieutenant colonel grabbed the helmet back from him, and he did kick it. He kicked it hard, and it went rolling away with Cederman chasing it.

Meanwhile, a squad of soldiers had filed out of the tank and surrounded the lieutenant colonel as his personal security. The colonel must have left his saber in the tank, because he walked toward the rabble with a puffed-out chest and an empty sheath. He reached down and pulled the pistol from his hip instead. "Which one of you motherfuckers knows where the worms who killed my soldiers are hiding?"

Heavy drops of sweat ran down my face and neck, stopping at my collar. I felt every ounce of the weight pulling me down, and the heat burned at my willpower. The phrase "don't make any sudden movements" ran through my head. There was not one thing I could do to stop the situation if it got ugly. A squad leader's authority stopped outside the lower enlisted, but despite all that I walked over to where the townsfolk had surrounded the colonel and his tank.

"I know you know. You have to know. Who's in charge here? Where's the imam?" The colonel paced the line of angry faces with his shining pistol in hand.

The mob of angry men recognized the word imam. The imams were a mix of holy man and mayor, the ones most respected in the village. The crowd parted and an old man in his sixties with unusually straight posture stepped forward. He wore dusty black robes with a red-and-white headdress and stood a full five inches taller than the lieutenant colonel. The men of the village gestured wildly and yelled their complaints, but the battalion commander ignored them and walked up to this tall man.

"So you're in charge, huh? Where are the bastards that killed my soldiers?"

The tall man looked down at the colonel and kept his mouth shut tight while the men on either side of him waved their hands in the air, spit on the ground, and screamed curses.

The lieutenant looked right into the imam's eyes and said in a flat voice, "You need to tell me right now where the mortar teams are."

The tall man didn't react. I had no idea if he understood or spoke English.

I was too far away to hear what the imam said, but I saw the lieutenant colonel's reaction. In a quick motion he holstered his pistol and with two fingers he struck the imam hard in the middle of the chest like some playground bully. He struck the imam again with every word he said to emphasize his point: "You will tell me where to find the Mujahedeen or I will bomb this fucking village back to the Stone Age."

The last push on the imam's chest sent him falling back. Some of the crowd closed around to protect their holy man; the rest exploded with riotous anger seeing someone they respected so much treated so badly. The lieutenant colonel immediately turned his back on them. He must have believed himself kill-proof, and maybe he was. His personal protection squad drew their rifles to their chests and pointed them at the crowd.

I ran.

"Lyl byet! Fadlak, lyl byet! Go home! Go home! Please, go home!" I screamed. The fact I was speaking in their language gave everyone pause, but they only stopped for a second and then focused their outrage on me, believing I understood them. The lieutenant colonel turned, surprised as hell to find an infantryman who could speak Arabic. "You know Iraqi, son?"

"No, sir. Only a few phrases." I kept my attention on the crowd.

"Good, tell these sons-a-bitches to give up the men who killed my soldiers." He had pulled his pistol again and used it to point at the Iraqis as if it were a finger.

"Please. Danger here. Go home," I said in Arabic. I couldn't remember the words to tell them what I wanted to say and I couldn't say it in English because the lieutenant colonel would think I was undermining him. My words tripped and stuttered, which only made the mob angrier and louder, all of them screaming at me. I understood only a few of their words: Allah, weapons, family, American soldier, go.

The colonel started laughing. "You need to brush up on your Iraqi, son. All you did was piss them off." He patted me on the shoulder, walked over to his tank, and called to someone inside, "Where's my goddam 'terp?"

A staff sergeant in his personal security squad with a nicely trimmed triangular mustache turned and said, "You told him to stay at the traffic checkpoint by the railroad station, sir."

"Hell, that's 'cause I can't trust the fucker. He's a raghead too." They shared a small laugh and then the colonel looked at me. He walked real close and put his right hand on my right shoulder. "Listen, son. I want you to take your squad and go that way." He pointed due west, away from town.

"Sir?"

"I got a feeling. Don't come back until I call for you. Search every house along the way and brush up on your Iraqi."

I looked down the road leading out of town and then over to my squad. "Sir, you want me to head due west?"

He pointed at an auto-repair shop on the edge of town. "Start with that fucking building right there."

"Yes, sir."

"Come on, now, time's wasting."

"Yes, sir."

I ran back to my squad as the colonel called after me, "And don't skip one damned building, I'm going to check on ya!"

We ran to our Humvees and loaded up. The first building we came to was the mechanic shop: just an ordinary small business with an office on one side and the roll-up door of the garage on the other. We knocked and knocked, but the place was empty. I thought about skipping this building on our way west, but the lieutenant colonel had pointed it out specifically. I told the squad to stack behind me. I lifted my shotgun at a 45-degree angle, turned my head, and blew the lock. The men filed past me into the empty front office.

A tactical search of the premises revealed a filing cabinet with business invoices written in Arabic, an empty water cooler, and a desk that leaned slightly to the right. On the desk was a nonfunctioning telephone and a couple framed pictures of what must have been the owner's wife and children. A search of the garage revealed tools and a few empty barrels that used to contain oil. We lifted the roll-up door and filed out, leaving the building unsecured.

We searched the next house and didn't find anything. The same went for the next three houses, but we kept heading west on some road the battalion commander had picked at random. I quickly realized that this small mission was a microcosm of the entire war.

The people who lived outside the town cooperated much more than the people inside the town did. They were all farmers who worked hard growing crops and who didn't have the mob mentality. I find groups are a funny thing; the more people there are, the quicker they are to express anger and indignation.

The farmers were very poor and were used to having their privacy violated. They didn't care who was in charge of the country or who was making the rules as long as they could keep working their land.

After almost two hours we came to a house that was different. When I knocked on the door, a man wearing brown slacks and a sleeveless sweater over a long-sleeve blue shirt opened the door. He had round wire-frame glasses and looked to be in his forties. I told him in my best Arabic that I needed to search his house.

"That's pretty good," he said.

This surprised me. "I'm sorry?"

"Your Arabic."

"Thanks."

He told me that he had lived in America for six years. He had studied architecture at the University of Illinois in Champaign, but had moved back to Iraq a few years ago when his father's kidney failed. They were on their way to a hospital in Baghdad for dialysis.

He stepped aside and let my squad file in and search. With his head low he leaned toward me and, almost in a whisper, told me there was a rifle in the kitchen. He said they used it only for defense. I asked him, "Defense against who?"

He shrugged and said, "These are crazy times, my friend."

We stood there, only a few feet apart, with his father in a wheelchair behind him. The fact that we could understand each other made what we were doing feel ridiculous. I wanted to apologize, but instead I told him the reason we were searching all these houses, the reason we'd sieged the entire town. My posture relaxed, I took my helmet off and slung my weapon. I asked, from one man to another, if he could help me. I asked him to please tell me anything he knew about the mortar attacks on our base. He hesitated, but I told him people were dying. I told him that he knew as well as I did that in this war there was nothing to die for. I told him that, from what I had seen, none of it made any sense at all.

His eyebrows came down heavy on his forehead, and he turned to look at his father for a second before turning back to me. "You know, it really wasn't a bad place to live under Saddam, not for us. He had his favorites, but he left most people alone. Unless you were a Kurd, I guess." He paused a while in thought, then continued, "In the middle of town there are a few big white houses, three stories high. The one with three white pillars in front was the house of an important officer at the Taji base. I heard he died when the base was bombed, but his sons and nephews live there. I would believe they don't like you."

"Thank you," I said.

"Is there any way you can speed up the search? We will be late."

"Of course. We're done." I called Baldwin and Melvin to stop the search and we headed back out to our Humvees.

I called Lieutenant Caius to tell him the news and he asked me where the hell I was. He had somehow received similar intelligence and was already planning the raid. My squad met the rest of the platoon at the garage we had searched. The aimless bullshit we had been doing all day had just gotten focused. Lieutenant

Caius and Sergeant Schofield had turned this into a real mission now that we had a target house. Caius sent Sergeant Zabat's squad to do a quick drive-by, to locate the house and get eyes on it. Once he reported back, the lieutenant told Cederman that First Squad would be doing the initial breach. My squad would filter in and search the bottom floor. Once the bottom floor was secured, Zabat would take Third Squad up the stairs to the other two floors.

Cederman and his Alpha Team hung off the right side of Lieutenant Caius's up-armored Humvee while Bravo Team hung off the left. The Humvee sped up to the house and stopped in front of the door, and the guys jumped off. Cederman blew the lock with his shotgun and the squad poured in like water.

My squad sprinted across the front yard. From inside the house we heard a woman screaming, and then a baby crying. I could hear Cederman call for Lieutenant Caius over the radio, asking what he should do about a distressed woman. The lieutenant told him to give her a quick search and let her go, keep searching the house. This old, wailing woman came out the door just as we were about to go in. She looked ancient, with deep wrinkles cutting across her crying face. Her long black robes and black headdress hung heavy with dirt. Baldwin pushed her to the side and the squad filed past her into the house. I stayed back to secure her, thinking maybe she had a weapon or a bomb. I didn't know. Simon stayed with me and we watched the old woman crumple and sit cross-legged on the dying yellow grass, yelling prayers to Allah, bending at the waist so far that her forehead almost touched the ground.

Then a baby ran out on unsure legs, a little girl who couldn't have been more two years old, wearing nothing but a dirty cloth diaper. The old woman ignored the child and prayed to her god instead. The baby stumbled toward me. Tears filled the bottom half of her eyes and her mouth gaped so wide I could see down her throat. The deep pools of water in her sockets spilled down her cheeks, clearing her vision. When she saw what I was, she froze and screamed in terror.

Third Squad sprinted past us and took off up the stairs to search the floors above. I stood in the doorway watching my squad search through piles of blankets and pillows. Baldwin called out that he had found two AK-47s and a barrel magazine that held a shitload more tumbling rounds than a regular clip. Melvin's team found at least a dozen stacks of one-thousand-dinar bills, all with Saddam's face on them, as well as some US currency. My squad flowed through the other rooms, trying to catch anyone hiding. Then I realized Simon wasn't inside with us.

I told the squad to keep searching and hurried back to the front yard to find Simon holding the kid. The baby sobbed uncontrollably, her face pressed up against his flak vest. Her tears made a dark spot in the center of his chest.

I shook my head and looked at him. "What the fuck, Simon. What if there were armed men in there?"

He gave me that goddamn half smile. "You guys would have taken care of them."

"You are a fucking infantryman, Specialist Scott. I need you to do your fucking job, and that's not cuddling war orphans." It killed me to be so hard on him, especially since he was only acting like how I felt. I guess that's what pissed me off the most. Simon was my reflection, and the pity, mercy, and common sense he brought to the battlefield I saw as weaknesses in myself. I also wanted to hold that baby and tell her everything would be okay, but that's not what an infantryman in the middle of a combat mission does.

"Sean, come on."

"God-fucking-dammit, Simon. Don't call me Sean. Look around. This is a fucking combat zone. We are on a mission to capture or kill the men responsible for the deaths of US soldiers. I am your squad leader. I need you to do exactly what I say, or someone could get killed. And, goddammit, you will call me Sergeant Davis."

He didn't answer. There wasn't anything to say. We were both right, but looking at that baby girl clinging to his chest I wished I were wrong.

I left him and the kid and walked over to Lieutenant Caius to give him an inventory of what we had found on the first floor. He stood outside of the passenger seat of his Humvee with the hand-mic from the truck's radio in his ear. I was about to open my mouth when Staff Sergeant Zabat took the butt of his rifle and smashed out a window on the second floor. He poked his head out, looked down at the lieutenant, and yelled, "We have at least a dozen mortar rounds up here, sir. Maybe more."

There were cheers from inside the house. Lieutenant Caius held a finger up between us and looked around dramatically. "The battalion commander is on his way over here. If you tell him we got this intel by him sticking his finger in the wind and sending you off on some bullshit mission, I will personally hamstring you, understand?"

"Yes, sir. We have three AKs, a sniper rifle, a shit-ton of ammo for each, and more stacks of money than I've ever seen in person."

"Saddam bills?"

"Yes, sir." I hesitated. "Also, American money."

"US, huh?"

"Stacks of Ben Franklins. Also, we have a baby, maybe three years old."

"A baby?" The battalion commander's squawking on the radio pulled Lieutenant Caius away from our conversation. I felt myself blush. Maybe I shouldn't have brought up the kid. I just wasn't prepared for these situations. While training for combat, the idea that there would be babies never crossed my mind, and now they were everywhere. They should have put that in their speeches to the new recruits: today's modern battlefield, not your grandfather's war, linear danger area at every alley, sniper at every window, and you can't do a fucking mission without stepping over at least one teary-eyed orphan who will break your heart every time you look at it.

"Where the hell did you find a baby?" Caius asked.

"She ran out of the house."

"Not our problem. Let it go."

"What about the old lady?"

"Did you search her?"

"Sergeant Cederman's squad did."

"Not our problem." Then he was lost to the radio again, calling in the cache we'd found.

I walked at a brisk pace over to Simon, slung my weapon across my back, and motioned for him to give me the kid. He held her tighter.

"Goddamn it, Simon. What do you want to do, bring her back to base, enroll her in school, and raise her between missions? Just give her to me. We're running out of time, the Mustache is almost here."

He handed her over even though she fought against it. I carried her, kicking and screaming, to the old woman still sitting there—cross-legged, eyes closed, begging Allah for a miracle.

"Hey!" I yelled down at her. She prayed louder. "Hey." I pushed her shoulder, and when her eyes didn't open I lost my patience and slapped her across her wrinkled face. That did the trick. "Your prayers are answered. Take the kid, go."

I dropped the baby girl on her lap. She grabbed ahold of the woman tightly and buried her head in the folds of the dirty robe. The old lady stared at me, confused.

"If you stick around here you'll be detained and interrogated by a madman." I searched my brain for any Arabic phrase but with all the shit going on I couldn't find one.

"Lyl byet!" Simon called from behind me. He made a shooing motion with his hands. He was telling them to go away. "Lyl byet."

The old woman put her hand on her knee and tried to push her way up. I helped her, and she shuffled away thanking Allah for her miracle. The lieutenant colonel showed up ten minutes later and thanked the Christian God for his miracle. He had finally found where the shitheads lived. We pulled security around the house and its cache of weapons, rifles, and ordnance. Everyone took out their digital cameras to snap pictures of real-life RPG rounds, artillery shells, AK-47s, even a Russian Dragunov sniper rifle.

The 'terps showed up in the late afternoon and, after talking to the Iraqis who lived around the general's house, got names and descriptions that led to the capture of what we categorized as insurgents, terrorists, the enemy.

I couldn't stop thinking about what the English-speaking man out on the road had said before taking his father to the hospital in Baghdad. Were these "terrorists" just fatherless sons wanting revenge? Now that we'd taken them into custody, would others avenge their arrest? Were there any real political motives behind their actions? Or did they bomb us because we bombed them? I squinted my eyes tight and in that darkness I saw Goya standing on the banks of the Manzanares painting *Saturn Devouring His Son*.

The lieutenant commander never found out where the intel had come from, but he took credit for it anyway. We got some credit for it, too, and because of it we were given harder missions. The two-star general decided to finally start using us for his air assault QRF, which meant we would be flying around in helicopters for a few weeks. Looking down at the houses I realized that each one held a family, each one was a home, each home had children, mothers, fathers, grandparents. That wasn't something I thought about in training and now it was something I couldn't avoid thinking about.

Tea at the Baghdad Zoo

The lieutenant colonel, our battalion commander, the Mustache, was relieved of duty in country a week or so later. He had worked his entire life to lead men in battle against a foreign enemy, trained long hours, went through the hell of Ranger School, and finally made it, but for only seven weeks. Being removed from command in theater is a career-ender. I could only believe that he took the loss of his men too personally. Maybe he felt too much, and that is what motivated the erratic behavior. That's how I looked at it. How I had to look at it. I hoped it was his humanity that motivated his inhumane actions, but in the end I had no idea and little time to reflect on it. He was removed for a long list of complaints filed against him by his soldiers, Staff Sergeant Tom Cederman's complaint being one of them.

The war went on, and the loss of the lieutenant colonel showed me that one man, even a battalion commander, didn't make much difference. War is a machine designed to lose its pieces while plowing through lives, lands, and history. Hell, it could lose its engine or steering wheel and it would make no difference.

One night I was sent to the TOC as the QRF liaison officer. From the title of the detail I suspected I was the middleman between the battle captain and my platoon on QRF standby, but nothing happened that night. I drank from the bottomless TOC coffee pot and watched some European bikini channel that one of the privates found. At some point in the night, a story broke on CNN. Some reserve unit from Virginia had taken humiliating pictures of Iraqi detainees in Abu Ghraib Prison. The photos were on high rotation, and the story was big enough to for some TOC private to turn off the bikini channel and wake the officer on duty. I sighed, watched, and thought, *Now they have another reason to attack us, so we can detain more of them, so they can attack us, so we can detain them.* The war caused the chaos that fueled it.

For the next few weeks we kept up with the patrolling of the perimeter around Taji, and we kept up with our shifts securing the bridge down south, but we also flew to the Green Zone whenever the general had an emergency. These weeks passed in a haze of sleeplessness and adrenaline-fueled intensity. Stories filtered in from other patrols, other platoons, or from the occasional visit to the chow hall. These stories would just break your heart. A six-year-old boy was playing in the middle of his village. He chased his soccer ball into the street, and a US Army five-ton truck ran him over. Not one truck in the convoy stopped. How did this happen? Maybe they didn't know they'd hit the kid, or maybe they did and were too afraid to stop. The boy's body was run over by most of the other trucks in the convoy, left in the dust, shrouded by the exhaust.

A nineteen-year-old National Guard soldier from the South mistook a pistol-shaped cigarette lighter for a weapon and gunned down a family, the first and last time he would ever pull a trigger in combat.

Our company flew out to another town for another cordon and search, but this time in the middle of the night. A terrified young mother tried to run out of the cordon. A woman carrying a baby and a terrorist trying to escape look the same from a distance through a night vision scope, and a machine gunner opened up on her. A couple of soldiers in our company who were medics in real life tried to help, but the woman and child died.

Machine-gun fire, mortar rounds every day, explosions, and the world ended sometime in there—or if it didn't, I couldn't tell. Days of living without sleep, chasing triggermen, firefights, and a growing intimacy with the dead and dying.

More orphans, more enemies, more fuel for the war machine.

The only downtime came from being on QRF standby. The rotation schedule was easy: one week MSR, one week on call. This meant sitting in a big, empty warehouse without electricity, thirty seconds from the flight line. If the call came down we grabbed our gear, jumped in a couple of Humvees, drove to the flight line, and waited for the Black Hawks to pick us up. The whole process took less than five minutes, although many times we waited hours on the tarmac for the birds.

The QRF standby warehouse was a bunch of aluminum siding welded to a gigantic steel frame over a cement pad the size of four or five basketball courts. We were afraid to sweep the place because if someone sneezed from the dust the damned thing might collapse on us. Since there was no power we didn't have much to do other than kill flies and catch up on badly needed sleep. We draped mosquito nets over our cots, and while they kept most of the exotic insects out they did nothing for the incredible heat. The first day there I thought I'd sleep for twelve hours, but my body was stuck on the continuous operations pattern: two hours off, one hour on.

The giant tin shack smelled of rodent feces and was stale as a crypt, but being in the direct sunshine was worse. Even without my flak vest, I wore a thin coat of my own sweat at all times. A sane person would think that a week of downtime would be a luxury during war, but it was intolerable. Time moved slower than it ever had before. I would write a letter home, read a book, listen to music, and play a whole card tournament before noon, and dread the empty hours after lunch.

One day Baldwin found a ragged, malnourished calico cat with a missing ear sneaking around the giant shed, probably looking for hedgehogs. There were a lot of hedgehogs in Iraq. The wretched little cat looked like it had survived a bout with a meat grinder. For the first couple of days she was only a blur, but after she ate the food Baldwin put out for her the first time she would let us know she was around with a pathetic growl that sounded like a death rattle. Whenever he heard this, Baldwin would jump up, even from a dead sleep, and call to her, rubbing his fingers together with a "here, kitty, kitty." And, contrary to all the laws of nature and common sense, the cat would stop and rub against B's leg until he pet it.

Soon every man in the platoon went out of his way to care for that thing. These steely-eyed infantrymen turned to baby-talking mothers over this wretched cat. The men in my squad called her Kujo and worked together to build her a house. Mechaiah O'Brian gave up his own pillow to make a bed for her. Simon made her a scratching post by wrapping an old length of rope around a two-by-four he pulled from the wall of the warehouse. Patterson would pick through the boxes of rations to find the spaghetti-in-meat-sauce entrée because he believed it was Kujo's favorite, breaking Schofield's number-one rule during combat: Thou shalt not rat-fuck the MRES. No one broke Schofield's rules, but this was an exception that even Schofield was okay with. I couldn't help but love that goddamned cat, too, because those feelings filled the void I caused when I blunted my emotions.

We started one QRF mission with a recon flight above Baghdad, riding in Black Hawks, to get us familiar with the layout of the area we would be patrolling. Helicopters from the Green Zone landed on the flight deck in Camp Cooke at 0500 hours so Lieutenant Caius, Schofield, the other squad leaders, and I could load up and fly above the city all morning.

That helicopter ride was our first one during the daytime. I never expected to see so much life. Rows of lush palm trees grew on either side of the green-brown water of the Tigris River. The sun sparkled and danced on thousands of palm fronds rising and falling in the wind like ocean waves. I imagined how many times this terrain feature had been scrawled on papyrus, drawn on paper, or updated on Google Maps. History rolled along underneath me, the stage for so many stories and myths. The patterns, colors, and symmetry of early Persian art turned before my eyes like a kaleidoscope.

All the patrolling on the ground had me seeing only the obvious signs of wartime—blown-out buildings, craters, bullet holes, wreckage. People drove their piece-of-shit cars, walked the garbage-filled streets, sat in their dying yards, and shopped in the makeshift markets. The place was just as full of life as it appeared from the sky, but not as beautiful as it was from the windows of a Black Hawk.

The pilots took us so low over the city I worried about people firing on us, but hardly anyone even looked up. Then they flew us to where we would have our mission the next day. Second Platoon would be tasked with conducting a movement to contact through the Baghdad Zoo and the adjacent parade grounds. The operations order said to clear out anyone there. The elections for a new Iraqi government were being held at the State Agricultural Building, and we needed to clear the sector of any possible mortar men or insurgents who might want to keep these elections from happening.

At the very beginning of the war, the Pentagon had planned what size armaments to use in the bombing campaign and which objectives should be decimated, devastated, or completely destroyed, and during all that shock and awe they spared the State Agricultural Building because it wasn't a very exciting target. Maybe they thought that Saddam and his sons wouldn't lower themselves to hiding in a building that auctioned livestock and smelled of manure. Flying around the city we saw it still untouched, the most official-looking building left. By default, it had been picked by the US to house elections for the temporary Iraqi government. It made me laugh to picture a bunch of confused, hopeful Iraqis in their least-dirty suits standing knee-deep in soiled hay, ink staining their right index fingers, with a vague notion that they had somehow just experienced democracy.

The next morning my squad jumped out of the helicopters right as they touched down at 0300 hours by the Iraqi Tomb of the Unknown Soldier, a magnificent memorial to the men who fought in the Iraq/Iran War. Each of us scrambled out of the bird, ran ten feet, and threw ourselves into the prone position, ready to shoot anyone who might have thought the helicopter was a target. The rotor wash pounded us and then the birds were gone. Without a word we stood up and started our patrol through the parade grounds, the same parade grounds I'd seen on the news the year before. The ones in the bigger-than-life picture of Saddam firing a shotgun into the air with one hand while his army marched below him. On either end of the grounds was a giant statue of two hands coming out of the earth, holding sabers crossed to form an arch.

We marched in the dark. Night vision devices cover only one eye today, so that if there is a sudden explosion it won't blind a person in the naked eye, but since it was pitch black my naked eye didn't see anything, and the whole world was monochromatic green. Forget depth perception or detail; the night vision goggles enhanced the light reflecting off the moon just enough to let me see the ground fifteen feet in front of me and not much else. We walked, light-footed, our weapons at the ready, through a broken-down amusement park. The children's toys around us were grainy lumps with exaggerated smiles and cartoon eyes. We patrolled in a loose wedge, like geese flying in a V, far enough apart that if a single grenade was thrown or a mortar landed in our formation it would kill only one of us.

Shoot anyone in your sector. It kept repeating in my head. You don't get too many of those orders in the military. Of course the ROE was in effect, but protecting the new Iraqi government was top priority. The operations order said that all friendlies were evacuated and no one was allowed in our patrol area. If we saw anyone, they were to be treated as a threat.

At 0430 hours we crested a small hill, and there sat five men with AK-47s around a campfire. We all dropped on our stomachs and stared at them. There were really armed men and we were really going to have to kill them. I lost my breath and the bottom of my stomach dropped out. We were really going to have to kill these men.

Army doctrine states that your unit should not engage the enemy unless you outnumber them three to one. I counted them a dozen times; they were five men and we were seven, but we had two squad automatic weapons and a couple grenade launchers and our rifles. We could take their lives in the span of a yawn. Patterson quietly unfolded the bipod to his SAW on my right, and Walken did the same on my left. We had the higher ground and they didn't even know we were watching them from barely fifty feet away. It seemed that hours went by between heartbeats.

Two men squatted by the fire, where a teapot sat on a small grill. Two others stood and smoked, and the fifth man spoke to all of them—maybe telling a joke, maybe planning an attack.

Finally Baldwin leaned over. "Sergeant?"

Jesus, I almost dropped my finger. In another second I would have, but one thing caught my eye that didn't make sense; they all had on black slacks and blue shirts. The enemy in this war didn't wear uniforms. Was that enough? I looked into Baldwin's face. He didn't want to do it anymore than I did, but the orders…

I turned to Melvin and whispered, "B and I are going to talk to them."

"What?" Melvin asked.

"Something's not right. We're going to go down there and talk to them. Light them up if things go to shit." I turned back to Baldwin. "Let's go."

My body didn't want to listen to me when I told it to stand. Hell, Baldwin probably didn't want to listen to me, but he followed me down that hill knowing that they could open up on us at any time.

They didn't see us until we were ten feet away, but when they did they went for their weapons. My eyes went wide and I lifted my rifle and felt the seconds grow impossibly long. The men moved in every direction. My ears prepared for the loud machine-gun fire I knew would come from behind me. I thought, *They are all going to die and there is nothing I can do.* The two who were smoking cigarettes had their AK-47s on the ground a few feet away. The rest had them slung on their backs and fumbled for them. I screamed in Arabic for them to stop or I would shoot: "Awgaf te-ra ar-mee!"

And a miracle happened. They stopped. They all stopped and looked at me. Then they smiled, big fucking silly smiles. There was no machine-gun fire. No one screamed in pain. The oldest one there put his hands out and walked toward me. He said in broken English that they were zoo security. They had taken it upon themselves to help out the US Army, which they admired so much. They were only going for their weapons because they wanted us to be proud of how they were securing a perimeter even while making tea. He shook my cold, almost numb, hand and asked if I wanted a cup.

I said yes, and smiled and laughed low. By the time I finished shaking all of their hands, the rest of the squad was walking down the hill. We called them in to Lieutenant Caius and resumed our patrol. The sun came up, and with it car bombs around the city went off. We'd see the twisting black smoke in the distance, then hear the explosion. I'd gauge the distance and call it in. Five hundred meters west of our position. Then we'd run that direction until we were called off. Four hundred meters north of our position. We'd run again and be called off again.

"Stay in your sector," we were told.

Finally, we found an open building and climbed onto the roof to watch the explosions going off in the city. I was witness to the end of the world, or how it would look: columns of black smoke rising into the sky and the sound of automatic fire bouncing off city buildings.

Two Kiowa observation helicopters zipped around from one smoke pillar to another. We took turns eating lunch, pulling security, and getting an hour of sleep. When it was my turn to rest, I sat down in a small piece of shade and ate pistachios my mom had sent from home like popcorn while I watched the symphony of war. I had front-row seats to the apocalypse, or the closest thing to it I'd ever see.

The world didn't end. Neither did our mission. We left the building to patrol the zoo, and to my complete surprise we found it was still open. We walked down the path from cage to cage in formation, and passed a young couple and a small family there to look at the remaining animals. How were there people at the zoo in the middle of all this violence? Why would they come here? Half the cages were empty, and the other half held malnourished and starving animals. Bombs went off around us in the city, elections were being held for a new government, and people still came to the zoo. I paused to look at a camel. Why the hell did they have a camel in their zoo? I thought it was hilarious. It was like us putting cows in our zoos.

Smack in the middle we found a broken-down hamburger shack manned by the head Iraqi zookeeper. He spoke fluent English and told us that when the bombs had started to drop all of his staff fled for their lives, and he never saw most of them again. He loved the animals so much that he risked death and dismemberment to stay and look after them, and would stay as long as he had to. War had cut off any financial help, and the entire infrastructure of the country had gone to shit. Even when the US came to rebuild, the zoo had been such a low priority that his pleas were ignored. Left alone with dozens of animals, he had to make some hard choices in order to save as many as he could. After a few weeks he started feeding the small plant eaters to the bigger meat eaters. That worked for a while, but when we ran into him he was five months in and had run out of small animals as well as all of the emergency pellets for the plant eaters.

He stood grilling the meat, telling us the story with tears in his eyes. We sat around the small shack listening to him while eating his gamey burgers, knowing there was no possible way they could be made of cow.

We returned to the pickup zone later that day with our bellies full and without anyone getting killed or blown up in our sector. I can't say what happened in the city with the car bombs, but the birds came and picked us up on time. I sat in the door seat and let the wind cool me down. The sky was so blue and clear I thought maybe it could reach all the way home. Holy shit, I had just saved five lives by having tea; maybe it was all that easy. The votes were cast for a new government and it was such a beautiful day that I thought the worst of it could be behind me. All I had to do was help where I could, save a life or two, and coast through the nine months we had left in country.

After our week of QRF standby was over our first patrol mission took us back to River Villa, where I had made friends with Farook and his father Hasheem. River Villa was the place where we had joked around and taken the picture of me pretending to saw something in his carpentry shop. I looked forward to this mission, but as soon as we walked into town the streets emptied. Parents called their children inside. None of the stores were open to us. We walked almost the whole way through town before we got to Hasheem's shop. I knocked on the door while the rest of the platoon waited on the road, spread out in road-march formation.

The doorknob turned, and before the door was all the way open Hasheem was yelling at me in Arabic. I asked him to please calm down and to speak slower. I couldn't understand him. I thought maybe he didn't remember who I was, so I reminded him that his son Farook and I were friends. This sent him into a fit of hand gestures and indecipherable screaming. Lieutenant Caius walked up behind me to see if there was a problem.

I began to worry. "Is Farook okay?"

I stopped trying to understand the stream of words and watched his motions. He looked at the sky, reached up into the air with a balled fist, and then brought it down. He opened the fingers of his hand when they struck his other palm to illustrate how the artillery rounds blew up when they hit.

"Hasheem, English, please. Is Farook okay?"

He repeated my question, mocking my sincerity. "Is Farook okay? Your bombs damage my son. His *friend's* bombs." Hasheem also reminded me several times of our broken promise to have his goats looked at. He said it didn't matter now because the artillery barrage had killed half the stock.

I couldn't meet his eyes as I gave him my empty apologies, but that didn't keep him from staring at me. The image of his small boy mangled in a bed kept me locked there on that spot, and I don't know how long I would have stayed if Lieutenant Caius hadn't yelled for the platoon to move out. Hasheem walked out to the front of his house and stared at each man in the platoon as we filed past him. He remained there, staring, even after Schofield's Humvee passed him, alone in the middle of the road.

Chicken Coops and Movie Stars

The war pressed on. We caught one mortar team, but trying to keep order in Iraq at that time was like trying to build a sandcastle while the tide came in. The fight for law and stability was a losing battle, but the chaos eventually became just one more thing to get accustomed to. One afternoon Simon and I found ourselves inside the wire during lunch hours, so we walked to the chow hall. Halfway there, mortars started falling from the sky around us, but we just kept walking while all the pogues ran for cover. One brave mechanic ran out to us and screamed at us to take cover, but we just looked at each other and started laughing. He looked so funny, all squatted down with his hands over his head like he might be able to block or deflect a mortar should it come his way. Before he ran off he yelled, "What the fuck, you two kill-proof?"

We laughed harder and kept walking.

Our platoon had become the go-to unit for the two-star general; we were one of the best infantry companies in theater. The difficult missions and the continuous operations for months on end somehow gave me a kind of apathy when it came to death. Not all death: some ways to die still scared the shit out of me—clearing tunnels, for instance. When we were sent down to clear a tunnel, it horrified me to think that I could get gut-shot by some shadow and fall down bleeding in the filth of an Iraqi underground pipeline. Even after the mission I had nightmares about dying that way, but walking to chow and getting hit by a mortar didn't faze me. If it was my time, it was my time.

Later, while out on a patrol, we found Garbage City: a whole village's worth of people who'd migrated into the middle of an old city dump and built houses from the trash. I saw an entire shack made of cooking-oil cans with Napoleon's face on the side. They cooked rats on spits over open flames. No shit, the whole place was like something out of *Mad Max*.

One time I drove Schofield's up-armored Humvee through a prison wall. The prison was deserted and we were tasked with checking it out, so I told young Private Walken to drive through a hole in the wall left by some explosion. It put scratches and chips up and down the sides of the truck. Inside, I dismounted with Baldwin's team to look around. A water main had busted weeks ago. There were cells in the ground filled with dark, murky water, and the whole place smelled like rotted death. I swear I almost felt the ghosts in there. It was creepy as hell and put me on edge.

There was a flickering light at the end of one dark hallway. I called the guys over and we quietly inched toward it. At the very end of the hall we stacked on the open doorway, with me in front. I took a deep breath and made my move. When I entered the room I almost shit my pants: I was face-to-face with a horse. A fucking horse. I found out it belonged to some refugee family who had set up camp in that side of the building.

Another mission took us to the old Iraqi Olympic training grounds. The grass on the soccer field had died, and every couple of hash marks there was a black crater from what must have been carpet-bombing. The only place the grass actually grew was out of the dark, stagnant water of the Olympic-sized swimming pool.

At the power station north of Baghdad, American contractors with American contract security struggled to get everything working again. We would stop there as often as possible while on patrol, because they had such an amazing cook. I found out he had actually been Uday Hussein's cook, but Uday had shot him in the foot years before so he had fled the country. After Saddam was captured, the chef returned to his home and started cooking for the Americans. The funniest part about it was that, because we were American, he believed it was a necessity to have French fries for every meal, even breakfast.

Our biggest mission came from the intelligence section in Baghdad. We were told of a factory that created vehicle-borne IEDs on an island in the middle of the Tigris. This mission had tanks, helicopters, infantry, explosions, machine guns, everything any halfway decent war movie would have, plus we were told there was a one-hundred-percent chance of contact. We were given satellite imagery, and each squad leader was given their area of operations.

My squad was given the biggest building, the building in which everyone believed the car bombs were being made. Oh, and it went off perfect. We could see the tanks assault the only bridge to the island as we flew in from the south. They fired their big guns into a summer palace Saddam had supposedly used, sending chunks of wall flying in all directions. The pilots stayed as low as possible and dropped us off on the other side of the island. They didn't even land. We jumped out the doors, fell about five feet, and just started running. We sprinted with the sounds of machine-gun fire in the distance and stacked on the first door of the factory while the weapons team got into a good position to cover us. We waited only a few minutes before the lieutenant gave the word to breach the factory. I blew the fucking lock off the door. The boys poured past me to clear the place. With cordite still in my lungs from the shotgun blast, I turned the corner to find a large empty room with two inches of dried chicken shit caked to the cement floor.

Not a single chicken. Not in the coop, not even within a ten-mile radius. The entire island, including all of the buildings on it, was completely deserted. This was a fact; we knew this because we cleared every square inch of that island. After four hours of walking in circles searching for shit that wasn't there, our platoon came together in an orange grove to sit in the shade and smoke cigarettes until the mission was deemed a success by someone in an air-conditioned building in the Green Zone.

The oranges were small and bitter, but the shade felt good. I nudged Simon with my elbow and called to Lieutenant Caius, "Hey, sir."

Caius looked over.

"Hey, so, since no one is using this island, well, can we have it, sir?" I asked.

He smiled big. "Yes, Sergeant Davis. Yes you can."

So that was how I became half-owner of an island in the Tigris River. Simon and I named it Davis Island.

The QRF missions didn't stop, but many of them were delayed or bumped back for reasons we were never told. Sometimes we would spend eight hours on the tarmac waiting for the birds; sometimes they came, sometimes they didn't—and when they didn't, we walked back to the giant tin shed and slept or played with Kujo. We spoke about so many different things while we waited, but, inevitably, the conversation would gravitate back to one subject: who would play our roles in the movie that Hollywood would surely make about us.

We leaned back on our rucksacks, sitting on the cold cement, talking hours about which star would play us. Then we'd pick each other's movie star and laugh. We would start with the leading men from all the recent blockbusters, but end up with any actor from any era. Many agreed that Simon would be played by David Duchovny because of his dimples and perpetually smiling eyes—not to mention the fact that there was something weird about both of them. For me, some said a young Tom Hanks, or John Cusack, or the guy from *Reservoir Dogs* who cut off that one dude's ear. I didn't really care who would play me, but I did indulge in that dream because it allowed me to be a character like Cyrano de Bergerac or Jean Valjean.

The care packages from home were amazing, but we gave most of what we got to the children of the villages. That June, Simon and I would drink good coffee sent from home and listen to music in his room. Sometimes we would watch pirated movies we had bought from the bazaar in the Green Zone, movies still in the theaters back home. We bought alcohol from the Iraqi kids while on patrol. Five dollars would get a single beer or a pint of whiskey. They were Muslim and their culture didn't involve drinking, so they didn't know the difference. I usually stuck to a beer or two, but one time we bought a pint of Ghost Whiskey. The label said it was from Turkey, and it featured a picture of a skinny girl in cutoff jeans and a blond perm. She was bent over, washing a Cadillac from the early '80s. It tasted worse than what we used to clean our rifles.

While on bridge duty, my squad made friends with a man and his family who lived nearby. He and his wife would cook us big meals whenever he knew we were going to be there. His name was Qaes, and he never accepted any money for the meals. The flatbread was amazing, as was the rice, the falafel, the tabouleh—all of it was amazing. Qaes would eat with us and then bring out tea. We all drank, talked about family, and smoked cigarettes in the moonlight by the river.

Qaes mentioned that he had children, so one day Simon surprised him by bringing out a television set with a built-in DVD player. He had bought a new one at the PX, so he gave this one to Qaes and his family. Qaes started crying immediately, and gave Simon a huge hug. They looked at each other for a couple seconds and then Qaes turned and gave me a hug, too. To my surprise, he also kissed me on one cheek and then the other. I breathed in the smell of date trees upriver, watched the reflection of the moon dance on the surface of the water, and smiled.

The Worst of It

Lieutenant Caius and Sergeant Schofield told the platoon—with great enthusiasm—that our new battalion commander was a real soldier who they had full confidence in. Great things were happening in the upper echelons, but being a squad leader didn't make me privy to any of it. We still worked continuous operations, still worked on hardly any sleep, and still did the most dangerous missions. The tanks started patrolling the main supply routes and this was great because it took some of the pressure off of us, but they didn't know the area like we did. One day, my squad was tasked with guiding them in a patrol, since we had pretty much lived outside the wire from day one. Caius gave the mission to Double Deuce; we were to meet the tanks at the North Gate the next day. But that night, Second Platoon was given a FRAGO, or fragmentary order. This meant a change to the overall mission, and we were instead sent out on helicopters to set up a traffic checkpoint on some farm, in the middle of the night and in the middle of nowhere.

We were told that a special operations team was in the process of raiding some high-value targets, looking for big players. Looking for the type of people that they put on our playing cards, the deck that made Saddam the ace of spades. They were doing this in the next town. If any of the terrorists escaped they might try to get away by driving down the road, and hopefully be flushed right into our checkpoint.

The birds dropped us off at 0100 hours and, like every time, we ran ten feet and jumped down into the prone position, ready to shoot anyone who thought the helicopter would make a nice target. None of us moved until the sound of the rotors faded away completely and was replaced by the soft buzzing of insects in the fields around us.

Weapons Squad and Lieutenant Caius were with us that night. Weapons set up their machine guns off in the distance so any bad men who tried shit wouldn't even see or hear what killed them. My guys set up the checkpoint on the bottom of a small incline so the cars wouldn't see us until they crested a hill, which would be too late to turn around without looking incredibly suspicious.

The lieutenant walked back and forth between the two positions with his RTO.

The first car was filled with drunk guys heading back from some soccer-watching party; we didn't see anyone else until early that morning. The next three cars were farmers going into the city or to another farm, but after that we saw a pair of truck headlights cresting the hill. It stopped as soon as the driver saw us. The sun was close to rising and the horizon was lit up, showing us the silhouette of something that looked like a five-ton or a garbage truck. I told the men to get ready.

The engine revved and then labored before the truck started moving our way again. There was nowhere to turn around for this guy. He had to go through unless he could drive backward.

Simon walked up next to me. "What do you make of this?"

"No idea, but he's coming this way. Get ready."

The giant jalopy pulled right into our makeshift checkpoint, and the driver smiled and waved. The first thing I noticed about the truck was how low it sat. The axles nearly scraped the ground. Someone had painted this antique dump truck blue fifty years ago. I told him to turn the engine off and get down. He hopped down one side of the truck and was joined by another man from the other side. They both wore stained, ripped overalls, and neither spoke English.

It took O'Brian and Patterson ten seconds of searching to discover why the driver had acted so suspiciously. O'Brian screamed when he found mortar tubes in the back of the truck. The two men were thrown down instantly. Baldwin planted a knee in the driver's spine and Walken pinned the other.

I walked around the truck and immediately saw what O'Brian was yelling about. There was no denying a very large tube stained with ordnance residue in the back, sticking out of the debris. The men were zip-tied, and I called Lieutenant Caius.

For two hours we talked with the men, called in their names and descriptions to be checked, and waited for instructions. Finally it came down that they were scrap-metal sellers. Since the war, there were tons of scrap materials littered across the country. They recycled it. The tubes in the back had at one time belonged to a couple of Iraqi tanks. I apologized while cutting their zip ties and let them go. As they drove off, I turned to Simon and said, "The training back home never told me I'd spend most of this war deciding which people not to shoot."

Being out on the overnight checkpoint didn't excuse us from our obligation to escort the tanks on patrol the next morning, but by the time we got back to base, unloaded our gear from the helicopters, and loaded it into the trucks, we were already a half hour late to meet the tank patrol. As we hurried to meet them at the North Gate, right about the time we started to pass the tank graveyard, there was an explosion louder than I'd ever heard. It was so loud that a person couldn't help but fear that the world was ending for a second.

The North Gate of our base was a smoking black crater when we pulled up. The road was just gone, replaced by broken slabs of concrete and flaming car parts for a quarter mile in every direction. The whole time in country I'd been surrounded by destruction on a massive scale, but the fact that it had happened just seconds before made it surreal. Why would anyone do this to another person, or group of people?

Thick smoke swirled black, gray, and white. I could barely make out the black outlines of the gate guards who'd escaped injury. They were statue-still, poised to shoot any threat. We parked our Humvee and I jumped out, but had no idea what to do. Flames leapt from the windows of a small white car. I saw two charred bodies still sitting inside, but with their arms pulled up to their chests and their hands curling back into their wrists. The heat burned at my cheeks even from fifteen feet away.

Screams behind me. A pile of bloody bodies and rags. The ones able to crawl dug their fingers into the earth and pulled themselves away. Sirens from field ambulances moved closer. A few medics were on the scene, tending to the wounded. I needed to do something to help, so I moved toward someone grunting, my right hand tight around the grip of my rifle, the inside of my left forearm pressed against my mouth. The smoke was incredibly dense and tasted poisonous: flaming plastic, burning fuel and body parts. I tripped and fell, coughed, retched, and spit the smoke out of my mouth. I slipped again. I caught myself with my hand. The ground was warm and I felt something soft give under my weight, so I pulled back and lost my balance again. My knee hit the ground, then my side, and I rolled until I stopped, flat on my back. I stayed there for a couple seconds watching the currents of smoke cross in front of the muted sun, so pale, so small.

The clank of the tank tracks pulled me back into the war. I jumped up. Some voices now were shrill, some too calm, others moaned low or called out, but none of the words made sense. I ran to where I knew US soldiers sat while controlling gate access. The guys who always told us to stop our truck, get out, and dry-fire our weapons into barrels full of sand. I saw a young man, almost a kid, sitting against the sandbags with his eyes shut tight and his left hand holding his stomach.

His face had a layer of soot or carbon so thick I thought he was black.

"What's wrong?" I asked.

His eyes opened wide, and the contrast between the white and the black made them glow. "Are you okay?" he asked in a Southern accent.

"What, why?"

He pointed at my face. "Blood."

I had smeared it across my mouth and chin from my sleeve. It wasn't mine and I had no idea where it came from.

The kid said, "I caught something in the fucking gut. The woman in the Datsun. She parked right next to the goddamned dump truck, jumped out of her car, and ran off." The kid's eyes moved like he was watching her. "Then everything was on fire."

He had some blood coming from under his flak vest. I didn't open it, afraid that it was holding something in. I yelled for a medic then turned back to him. "Hey, listen, you're going to be fine."

"Shit, I know. It just hurts like hell."

I could have left him there and gone to find others who needed me more. I wish I did, but I didn't. I should have, but I didn't.

When the smoke had dissipated and the wounded were taken away, only the tires of the cars still smoldered. Dave Zabat and Third Squad stood around their Humvee, smoking cigarettes without saying a word to each other. I nodded. We locked eyes for a second; no one spoke. Third Squad had been coming back in from MSR patrol and stopped to try and do whatever they could to help. The medics were there, the ambulance was there, the fire trucks were there, and the tank patrol had come back to pull security.

Simon, Baldwin, and Walken wandered back to our Humvee like zombies, one at a time. None of us had slept in over twenty-four hours. Baldwin and Walken climbed over the plywood wall into the back of the Humvee. Simon opened the driver's side door, I sat in the passenger seat, and we drove back to our trailers. We unloaded our equipment and weapons, and by the time I finally walked into the shower trailer there was Zabat standing in a stall, fully dressed, letting the blood wash off his uniform and swirl down the drain.

The command of Camp Cooke hired a limited number of Iraqi men every day to do menial tasks around the base. These men lined up outside North Gate every morning, hoping to be chosen to dig a hole or move rocks in order to receive five dollars for the day. When the car exploded, the blast cut through the dump truck, sending all the gravel meant to improve the roads on base into a line of thirty or forty men trying to fend for their families the only way they could. Zabat told me that when they got there they didn't realize they were driving on body parts. I could see in his eyes that the war was taking a toll as he told me about the man he had struggled to put out because his fat had caught on fire. What were people dying for? Five dollars? The price of a latte or a super value meal?

Two days later, June 12, at ten o'clock at night, I sat in Simon's trailer playing Xbox with him and his roommate. We felt good, relaxed. We had just gotten off two consecutive missions and we had the next day off. Simon laughed while schooling me on some shoot-'em-up game, and we sipped that god-awful whiskey cut with chow hall sodas. I outranked them both and was a noncommissioned officer. This meant I shouldn't have been fraternizing, but that rule was made back in the real world, and there, in country, Simon was my best friend. Drinking in theater was forbidden, too, but we did our jobs and never got shitfaced.

Suddenly, the door opened and Lieutenant Caius leaned in. He scanned the room until he saw me. "I knew I'd find you here. Come on—FRAGO."

I followed him out and lit a cigarette while we walked to his Humvee, where Schofield and the other squad leaders already stood along with two new additions. They were FOS, forward observers. They were attached to infantry platoons when the mission required artillery rounds. I shook my head and threw the cigarette down.

Lieutenant Caius told us the obvious: our day off was canceled. Then it got worse. The platoon would be split in two, in order to do three missions at once. The lieutenant would take our squad on an MSR patrol up north to a place we hadn't been before, and sometime during that patrol we would stage a fake checkpoint in order to observe a known terrorist's house. Schofield and the rest of the platoon would be on bridge security.

We were going out undermanned and with shoddy equipment, and all of us were still exhausted from the last five missions. Our truck was about to fall apart, the radios didn't work for shit, and before every mission I had to give someone up for a first sergeant detail. Now I had to tell the squad that our one day off in weeks was cancelled.

Seven hours later, my squad, Corporal Quinn's team, and the men in the lieutenant's Humvee sat waiting in our Humvees in the shade of some cypress trees. We borrowed Liam Quinn's team from Third Squad because we never rolled out of the gate with fewer than four trucks to a patrol.

We all waited for Lieutenant Caius, who was inside the TOC giving a roster that included the names and social security numbers for each person in each truck, along with a list of the weapons and ammo we were taking out. He was also checking for any last-minute changes to the operations order. We filled the time complaining about our shitty trucks. The plywood box in the back of Melvin's truck had been nailed so many times the boards had started splitting. The suspension in our rig was shot. Quinn pointed at a bullet hole in his truck's windshield that had been there for over a month.

We all laughed, smoked, and joked while assembled around the hood of my truck. Except Simon. He sat in the back of the truck behind the machine gun mount in the middle of the big plywood square. I used the rear passenger's side wheel to step up and saw him staring at his boots.

"What's up, man?" I asked.

"Nothing, just a little tired." He looked up with his half smile.

"No shit. How are you enjoying your day off?" I asked.

"When's the party start? Can we wear our Hawaiian shirts?"

"Insurgents wouldn't know what to think...what are you doing back here? Don't you want to see Liam's hole?" I laughed, thinking he'd do the same, but he just looked at the horizon. The sun was coming up.

"I got a theory about holes."

"Me too, especially after that last leave before heading over. Did I tell you my dad tried to buy me a whore?"

"Everything we do—drinking, drugs, girls, even going to war—is to fill one hole or another," he said, and I didn't know why he was being so serious. I wished he'd stop.

"A twenty-five-dollar Korean prostitute in downtown LA."

"That's why we're here, Sean. It fills some kind of hole."

"Shit, Simon, you can't say that around a bunch of infantrymen." I needed to lighten the mood, so I yelled to the rest of the guys. "Hey, Simon says we're only here to fill a hole."

The guys laughed and threw rocks at a stray dog waiting around for scraps.

Baldwin said, "I'll fill your hole."

Liam laughed. "Hell, I'd fill a couple holes over at the laundry. You see those Filipino girls?"

Finally Simon smiled and said, "See, it's true."

I heard the first sergeant come over the radio in the cab. Since the Iraqis had stopped being so eager to volunteer for the menial tasks around base, the first sergeant had started assigning more details to soldiers. I always tried to keep my squad from those shitty details, but that morning he caught me. Walken, Baldwin, and Simon were standing around the hood of the Humvee smoking cigarettes, laughing, and bullshitting, but stopped when I looked over at them. "He's not falling for it today. We have to send someone back to supervise a work crew."

"Make Bravo Team do it," Simon said.

"They sent someone last time," I said. "It's got to be Alpha."

No one volunteered. I pointed at Simon. "It's between you and Walken."

Simon crossed his arms and raised an eyebrow. "Come on, what about B?"

"Virtues of rank," Baldwin said, and laughed.

"Don't make me do it again, Sean. Please," Simon said.

Walken threw his hands up. "I always do it because I'm the lowest rank. It's not fair."

"See, he knows his place," Simon said.

"Come on, Sergeant," Walken said.

"Fine, I'll flip a coin. Walken, call it in the air." I pulled out a quarter and tossed it up, end over end. Walken called heads. I caught it, slapped it down on the back of my left hand, and uncovered it.

There was Washington's profile. He'd won, but instead I told him it was tails. "It's not the private's lucky day."

"Ha." Simon rubbed young Walken's helmet like he was mussing the hair of some school kid. "Don't worry; we'll be having more fun than you will, but at least you get air conditioning once in a while."

Lieutenant Caius walked up holding a couple pieces of paper. "What's the problem?"

"First sergeant's detail, sir," I said.

"Tell him you forgot," he said.

"Tried, sir," I said, and lit another cigarette.

"Guess you're fucked, Walken. Go tell the TOC to take your name off the roster. Okay, gather round." Caius walked to the hood of his Humvee and held up a piece of paper; on it were two faded black squares, three blue parallel squiggly lines, and two red straight lines. This was a printout from someone's PowerPoint presentation, the only map he was given of our objective. The squares were close together, one small and the other smaller. They represented the house and guesthouse of our target. The squiggly lines were the irrigation ditches in front of the house, and the straight lines were the roads. I looked around at the other guys, ready to laugh if anyone else started. There was no way that what he had just given us was the real op order. The only real intelligence revealed here was that one of the TOC printers was dangerously low on toner.

Assuming the coffee ring was an accident and didn't mean anything, I understood that our mission was to fake a traffic checkpoint about an eighth of an inch past the squiggly lines, about a thumb's distance left of where the red lines intersected, above what appeared to be an ink stain. From there, we would keep eyes on the two faded squares in hopes of seeing the real target: a gold-colored BMW that, hopefully, would have an arms dealer inside.

I stood with the expression of disbelief Picasso may have had if, after presenting *Guernica* to the Spanish Republican Government, it was used for pin the tail on the donkey at a child's birthday party. I started to believe the brass in the TOC had no idea people shot real bullets and RPGs at us. "What does this mean in reality, sir? Where are we going?"

Lt. Caius closed his eyes and grabbed the bridge of his nose. "About twenty miles north of Taji."

We had never patrolled that far north, and it seemed like a

dumb idea to try it now without satellite imagery, intelligence, or a guide. I didn't mean to, but I let my frustration slip. "The least they could have done was whip out the Crayolas. I mean, maybe some aquamarine between the squiggles and some burnt sienna to show where the land is."

I guess it finally got to Lieutenant Caius. Maybe he started to see the big joke, too, and didn't think it was funny being used as a punch line. He hit the hood of the car. "I'm sick of this shit, too. I'm sick of it all. Look." He turned and pointed at the TOC. "You see all of those up-armored Humvees parked around that fucking tent? That's all they do is sit there, or go to the chow hall, and we have to drive around in these fucking cardboard coffins. They sit in air conditioning all day, and we're expected to do a job with this shit intel my daughter could have drawn. I know it fucking sucks, but that's the way it is." He threw the papers down on the hood of his truck.

Caius walked off and pissed on a cypress tree, leaving us sighing low or kicking rocks around. "Okay," I said in my most confident voice. "Load up. SP in fifteen minutes."

We all loaded up without saying a word. I felt like an asshole for causing the lieutenant's outburst, but somehow I felt better knowing we were all in this together. War is hell, sure, but hell we can deal with. The stupidity of it all made it intolerable.

On our way up north we stopped by the marketplace for some chai with the old men. The meat seller had just slaughtered a pig and hung it from its hind legs on a little gallows-type rig. Blood ran down the body and out the neck into a plastic bag to be sold separately. It was so fresh that the blood smelled sweet, and the flies hadn't even started to land on its mouth and eyes yet.

The faded morning light slanted over the tops of the market buildings. Villagers and merchants haggled in Arabic over the prices of the vegetables, fruits, and other goods. We parked in front of the marketplace. Caius jumped out of his truck, and I got out of mine to follow him into the sort of open-air café. I ordered a couple of chai teas from a man behind the counter. The simple, small tables were made of wood and, just like the chairs, not one looked like another. Old men in dirty robes and headdresses sipped at their small cups and eyed us suspiciously.

About a month earlier we had started coming to the café for tea.

Most days the place would get all quiet when we walked in. When we would finally get our chai, Caius and I would sip at it, smiling like highly armed tourists, and nod at the old men. Every once in a while a conversation would start and we'd glean some useful information, but that day no one said a word to us. We finished our tea, gave the cups back, and continued the mission north.

The horrible maps were way off, and we didn't have grid coordinates. Every right turn along the MSR looked like it might be the spot. Simon called up every time he saw two houses together that might be like the ones on the bad PowerPoint printouts, but none of them seemed right.

After a few hours the lieutenant stopped us on a side road to call Battalion for more intel, and that was when Specialist Ford, the chicken rancher, saw the gold-colored BMW from the turret of Caius's truck. The whole mission was to pretend to be on a traffic checkpoint while watching the house from a distance. This was so we didn't spook the arms smuggler and IED-maker, but there we were, all four vehicles, parked in his front yard searching around with our binoculars. Unless they were complete idiots, they had to know we were looking for them.

"Son of a bitch," Caius said over the squad radio. "Okay, everyone move. We'll head south for half an hour or so, and then come back to set up the checkpoint."

And that's what we did. We headed back into familiar territory and did a quick patrol without a problem. On our way back up north, the lieutenant's Blue Force Tracker picked up a blip. The BFT is a radar-like device the size of a laptop screen that blips and beeps if it picks up the signal from a LoJack-like device attached to all friendly units. The blip he picked up was from an MP vehicle. Checking it against a list of stolen or destroyed friendly vehicles, he found that the blip and beep belonged to an MP Humvee stolen in the Green Zone two weeks back. It was coming from an abandoned quarry right off the MSR. He pulled in and we all followed.

The quarry must have been closed down years ago, and I had a hard time imagining anything productive happening in a place that looked like a county fair parking lot. For a quarry, the Iraqis hadn't dug too far into the ground. Three Iraqi men stood in the middle of this lot, in front of two small, gray buildings. They gave us the stink-eye but there was nothing unusual about that.

Each building had something in Arabic spray-painted over the plywood on the boarded-up windows. A long conveyor belt ran for a hundred meters from the side of one rickety building to a half-dozen piles of rubble around the dig site. The lieutenant told us over the radio that the blip had disappeared. He said that maybe the BFT had malfunctioned.

Caius then told us to Charlie Mike. This meant for us to continue the mission. He pulled back onto the MSR heading north, but I had this feeling in the bottom of my gut. I never really believed in intuition or hunches, but that morning, at that moment, I knew something bad was going to happen. I knew something was wrong.

"Give it another loop around," I told Baldwin, and then I yelled back to Simon, "Watch these fuckers."

Melvin's truck followed Caius onto the MSR, but Quinn's truck stayed with us.

His voice came over the radio, "Davis, this is Quinn—whatcha got?"

"I'm not sure," I told him.

I wanted to stop and question the three guys glaring at us, but I really didn't have a good reason, and the lieutenant was already so far up the road. He called over the radio for us to catch up. I told Baldwin to pull back onto the highway. I looked back at the men, and they started to walk fast toward the piles of gravel—maybe too fast. Caius's voice came over the radio again. He said the first two trucks had just passed a broken-down Toyota Land Cruiser with its hood up on the right shoulder. It was white with orange fenders, the way that all the taxis in Iraq were painted. He said we needed to give it plenty of room, make sure we skirted around it. We were already too close. I turned to tell Baldwin to give us some room. I had half the sentence out of my mouth when the car exploded five feet away from me. I was knocked unconscious instantly.

I opened my eyes and saw solid blue sky above me. The vision in my right eye was blurry, so I shut it tight a few times. Then Baldwin's head entered the frame of bright blue. He had my head cradled in his lap. We were outside the truck now. The inside of my mouth was coated with ash and tasted like battery acid. There was no ringing in my head like I thought there would be—in fact, I didn't remember hearing the explosion at all. I didn't hear anything for several moments until, slowly, sound came back: the burning of wood behind me, Baldwin screaming my name, gunshots all around us.

My body came back to me the same way, bit by bit. Blood slicked my skin under the right sleeve and right leg of my uniform. The heat from the burning Humvee was almost unbearable on the left side of my body. Then stings in the small of my back, like I was lying on hot coals. I sprang to a sitting position and pain shot behind the right side of my ribcage. I could see the muzzle flash from the triggermen coming from behind the piles of gravel. The three men in the quarry. Rocks popped up from the road, hitting me in the face and pinging off the fiberglass hood of the Humvee. I had no idea why, until I realized the bullets were hitting all around us.

In the Fade

All the details hadn't come to me yet, but I knew we had been ambushed. Baldwin's face was determined, but there was no way to block out the fear. I screamed at him, "Where is Simon?"

He turned away, looked at the ground, and shook his head.

"B, where's Simon?"

The back-and-forth movement became more exaggerated and he wouldn't answer.

"Goddammit, B."

"He's dead, he's fucking dead."

The ground popped with small explosions. A rock kicked up fast and hit me hard in the cheek, drawing blood. Out of reflex, I held out my right hand to block any more, and then I saw it was cocked all sideways. I saw it before I felt it. I had no idea I was hurt, but my fingers were as white as alabaster and the whole goddamn hand stuck out sideways. Under my tattered sleeve was a compound fracture, torn muscle, ripped tendon, jagged bone, and all that blood spurting from a four-inch gash, turning my sleeve dark red. I could see it leaking from between each layer of pink muscle—the deeper the wound, the darker the red.

I was sure I had lost my right hand at the wrist. In my mind I knew the doctors would amputate, but for some reason that I can't explain, I wasn't angry about it right then. I guess I had other things to pay attention to. The explosion had lifted the truck straight up and spun it. Baldwin dragged my dead weight out through the driver's side so I wouldn't get burnt up in the fire, but there we sat in the midst of the flaming wreckage, under fire from three triggermen shooting their AK-47s at us from the cover of the rock piles.

Baldwin pointed at them. "They're shooting at us." Their heads poked up, the barrels of their rifles flashed five to seven times, and then they dipped down again. Luckily they were firing from the hip and spraying, or they might have hit us. Baldwin went for his rifle to return fire, but I stopped him.

"We need to get to the other side. Help me." He pulled me to my feet and a bone in my right leg snapped on my first step. The pain

Sean's Humvee after the vehicle-borne IED on June 13th, 2004.

from my wrist came in waves—then my ribs, my knee, my leg. I pressed my right hand to my chest and threw my left arm over B's head. He pulled me up and I hopped around the truck, and that's when I saw Simon slumped in the back like he was only taking a break, the flames burning around him. I wanted to call out to him, to scream at him, *Get the fuck out of there!*

The plywood went up in minutes, and the heat was so intense I thought my uniform had caught fire. The rounds ricocheted off the metal frame and wheels with constant dings. The front driver's side tire went flat and the truck lurched away from us; Simon's body fell over. On the other side of the Humvee, Baldwin set me down. I don't know why, but I noticed how shallow I was breathing and thought that I needed to take deeper breaths, so I closed my eyes and concentrated on that for a while. The pain from all the breaks and cracks cut into me. Nothing else existed. I thought that if I opened my eyes I could find something to take my attention away from the terrible pain, but the first thing I saw was Simon's Kevlar helmet rocking next to me, the inside of it coated with dark blood.

It couldn't be. I didn't want it to be real. I yelled to Baldwin again, "B, where's Simon?"

Baldwin had rushed back into the flaming cab of the truck to pull out the radio and weapons. My question confused him. "What? I told you, he's dead."

"No, no, no. B, where's Simon?"

"Stop asking me, he's fucking dead."

We were pinned down behind our burning Humvee, but Liam Quinn's Humvee had turned around and parked maybe fifty meters away. The machine gun from his turret opened up on the three triggermen. Liam saw I was injured, and without hesitation he slung an aid bag over his shoulder and ran into the direct fire to help us. He made it halfway before the triggermen set off a second IED on the side of the road that had been hidden by trash. The blast hit him hard and sent him flying through the air, but I didn't see him land because Baldwin shielded me from the explosion with his own body. When I did see him again, he was flat on his back and not moving. I thought for sure he was dead.

Specialist O'Brian rocked the machine gun from the turret of Melvin's Humvee, really kicking up dust and keeping the fuckers' heads down. The other two Humvees in our patrol had looped around, and drove right into the kill zone to help us. Every round from the machine guns echoed in my broken bones. No other pain in my life had been so intense or so real. I held my arm tight to my chest. The blood wouldn't stop spurting out, and the world dimmed to the beat of my heart.

I woke up in the passenger seat of Lieutenant Caius's up-armored Humvee. I remember the steady voice of his RTO calling in the nine-line MEDEVAC off one of the laminated sheets Staff Sergeant Cederman had given him a long time ago. I took a deep breath, looked around, and, either because of denial or confusion from loss of blood, asked again about Simon.

The RTO waited until after he finished the MEDEVAC request, then turned to me with more of an inspection than a look. This reminded me that I had asked the question before. Then it flashed through my head, seeing him there, slumped over in the middle of the flaming fucking plywood armor they gave us. The fucking plywood armor with sandbags in between, as if that could possibly withstand a blast. I remembered his helmet rocking and his blood spilling. I started hitting the inside of the windshield with my broken hand, blood splattering and bones cracking with every impact.

"Sergeant Davis, you shouldn't be doing that. Sergeant. Sir, sir!" The RTO called to the lieutenant, who was standing against the hood of the truck directing the men's fire.

Caius leaned into the cab and grabbed me. "Sean, Sean, knock it off. Knock it the fuck off, Sergeant!"

Then there was nothing until the bright blue sky again. Someone had put me on my back in the road with my right arm wrapped in a couple of blood-soaked field bandages. The .50 cal still barked seven to ten rounds at a time. I heard Mechaiah O'Brian yell that they got one, cut the fucker in half. Then the ground shook with mortar rounds and everyone screamed, "Incoming!" but I didn't care. I didn't care about much at all. My helmet was off now, and I could feel a very slight breeze in my sweat-soaked hair.

When I woke up next, I heard the lieutenant scream into his hand-mic, "If you don't land that goddamned chopper, we will shoot you down ourselves. We have one friendly KIA and two critically wounded. We need transport, now!"

I didn't realize I was lying on a stretcher until four men picked me up. I shivered in the direct sunlight. The heat was gone, maybe from the whole country. I shuddered under the heavy rotor wash as the men loaded me into the helicopter. I had never been colder in my life than in that 120-degree heat. The crew chief made sure

I was tied down to the stretcher and it was secured to the helicopter. Liam Quinn was placed directly above me in his stretcher, with only a foot of space between us. At some point, I was given some morphine for the pain. My head rolled to the side when we lifted off, and I saw my platoon get smaller and smaller until they were gone.

The Punch Line

They hurried me into a room with more light than I imagined heaven would have. I felt each wobble of the gurney wheels in the fault lines of my broken bones and stared up at the unbearable white, letting it bleach my vision, hoping that would take my mind off the pain. I had lost too much blood, I had fractures, shrapnel wounds, breaks, and burns, but my wrist had been so badly damaged that it needed the most attention. The silhouette of a surgeon's head shadowed me for a second, while some assistant put a mask over my mouth and nose and swung my arm out on the right wing of the stainless steel table until it locked perpendicular to my body. I lay half crucified, and finally the anger set in. It washed over me as I considered the fact that I had no idea what I might die for.

Time stretched and bunched, flowed and stalled, to the unpredictable rhythm of a morphine drip. I woke again, not knowing how long I had been out. A single thought shook me. My eyes shot open and I looked down. I was relieved to find all four fingers and a thumb sticking out of the cast on my right forearm. They were discolored and swollen to the size of sausages, but all of them were there. Wires, tubes, and shiny metal rods stuck out of the bleached-white sheets on my bed. Machines surrounded me, beeping, humming. There was the low, muffled sound of air being released. The room was beige, with chipped paint in the corners, but other than that it was a hospital room like any I'd seen anywhere else. Small, no windows, white tiled floor.

Before I was completely awake, a pretty half-Asian nurse walked in and stretched on her tiptoes to change my IV. She smiled down at me like an angel.

"You're awake. Are you in pain?" Her words and smile were so full of pity and pride.

Everything ached, but I could feel the medicine had dulled it. "I'm okay."

I saw my boots, flak vest, and helmet in a pile in the corner of the room. She saw me looking at them. "We had to cut your uniform off and dispose of it, but we saved those."

I stared at that pile so long my eyes lost focus.

After a few moments she asked, "Would you like to use a phone to call home?"

Home. The word broke my trance. "A phone?"

"Yes, maybe you'd like to call a loved one?"

I nodded. She left the room for a minute and came back with a big black cell phone in one hand and a plastic bedpan in the other. "Do you need to relieve yourself before you call?"

Relieve yourself. She let the words roll off her tongue like it was the most natural thing in the world. She was really asking if I had to shit, because if I did it would be a two-person operation. There was no getting out of that bed with all the monitors, machines, and braces.

Blood rushed to my face. She must have seen it because she started talking fast about nothing, as if a constant flow of words could stop the embarrassment. The drugs they gave me for the pain usually caused constipation, but sometimes they took a while, she told me. She added that it was all part of her job. She did this all the time. It really wasn't an issue. I shouldn't feel bad about it.

Tears came and I hated myself for crying. I tried to hold it back, but I couldn't. The whole situation seemed so stupid, and there was really no reason for me to bawl like a baby, but I had this flash of anger with no way to do anything about it. Hours before, I was planning and executing combat missions; I'd led men, I'd had power over life and death, and now I couldn't even shit by myself.

I turned my head and stared at the pile in the corner while the nurse slid the bedpan under the covers. She told me about the success of the operation on my arm, how it was a testament to the world-class talent in the armed forces combat surgical teams.

The pile of equipment in the corner looked as if the soldier wearing it had suddenly disappeared, letting it all just fall to the floor. The boots, the flak vest, and the helmet on top.

She told me that not many surgical teams in any hospital anywhere would have been able to save my hand.

It felt so unnatural moving my bowels in bed. I could smell the shit.

The boots had the laces cut out, the helmet had black carbon stains on the right side, and the flak vest had small shrapnel holes running up the back.

The rods sticking out of my arm were there to ensure the bone healed correctly, she said. It had been splintered, so they screwed a piece of metal along the radial above and below the fracture.

"I'm done." I said it so quietly there was no way she could have heard me, so I repeated it louder. "I'm done."

The wipes she used were warm. I appreciated that.

"That wasn't hard. I don't think we'll have to do that again. Don't worry," she said.

Before she left the room she gave me the phone. I held it in my left hand for a while, thinking about whom I should call. Then I realized I didn't know anyone's number by heart except Jaime's and my little brother Vince's.

Jaime. I hadn't really thought about her in a while and didn't want to yet.

After a few minutes I pushed Vince's number into the phone. There were a couple clicks and hushed static before a constant clicking, which must have been a substitute for the ring. On the third ring Vince picked up. I could tell I woke him. "Hello?"

"Vince." It was all I could get out. I hadn't thought about what I was going to say.

"Philip?"

"I told you they couldn't kill me," I said, and laughed, mustering up all the bravado I possibly could.

"What?" He turned very serious.

"They blew me up, shot at me, and even mortared me. My truck was blown up, and a friend of mine..." My voice cracked at the word *friend*, and I had to stop for a moment. When I continued, my voice was lower, and grave. "There was an ambush. My friend Simon was killed instantly. I was hurt."

"Are you okay?"

The fear in his voice put a lump in my throat. "I'm fine. A couple broken bones. I'll call again later. Tell Mom and Dad that I'm okay. I gotta go."

I hung up before he could say anything else, closed my eyes, and pressed the phone against my forehead.

I slept for a couple of hours, until the two-star general's aide came to see me. He was a staff major with a sympathetic posture and a glistening, dough-like face. His whole body shook, either from nerves, lack of sleep, or caffeine. I screamed when his concerned and compassionate hand fell on the torn muscles in my shoulder. This made him jump as much as I did, and he apologized profusely before telling me that the two-star general was on his way to personally present me with my Purple Heart. He would be there in ten minutes, and the major just wanted me to know that there would be some journalists accompanying him, but that if I wasn't up to speaking to them that would be just fine. I should let them know if I became overstimulated, and they would leave.

I said, "Yes, sir."

The major bumped the bed as he turned to leave, sending me into a full-body convulsion. He shook his head and gave me his genuine apologies for the entire time it took him to back out the door.

I spent the next couple minutes trying to make the pain fade and get my pulse down by controlling my breathing. The jagged edge of a broken bone tears through muscle like splintered glass. When ribs are occupied with repairing their cracks, they forget they are supposed to move in and out with your lungs, and they complain with every breath. The right side of my body was so swollen that the tight skin felt like it might rip with any sudden movement.

The door swung open, almost as if by divine intervention, and stayed open while the two-star general walked in—a fine-looking, weathered man with hard eyes and well-earned creases around his sunburnt mouth and forehead. He had the steady, detached demeanor of Odin, and the barrel chest of some Norse warrior. His attention went to the machines around my bed. He only looked down at me when he was at my bedside. My eyes slowly moved to meet his, but right before I could, a photographer's flash forced me to blink, and then another, and another.

"We're all proud of you, son," he said, and I couldn't help but think about how many times he'd had to say that. I wanted to ask why.

The general's big hands glided like a ten-ton crane from the pocket of his starched DCU top to a foot above my chest. He opened a green plastic clamshell holder with gold trim, revealing my Purple Heart. He pulled the shining, heart-shaped medal out, letting the engraved profile of George Washington dangle over me.

My lungs emptied. I sucked in violently but couldn't get any air. The room spun. I didn't want to embarrass the general in front of his journalists and photographers, so I desperately tried to keep my shit together.

"You have brought credit to your unit, the army, and your country."

I tried to focus on his thin lips, but all I could think about was the profile of George Washington, the same profile on the quarter I used to kill my friend in a cheated coin toss. He talked about the Revolutionary War, and how the Purple Heart was the first medal ever given to the bravest soldiers. I was unraveling. The general flashed a look at his aide, stopped mid-sentence, then started again and skipped from a history lesson to specifics. "Son, you did a great job out there, and we all owe you a debt of gratitude."

He bent at the waist and pinned the gold-and-purple award to the woolen hospital blanket, above my heart. The camera flashes went off in quick succession. The general glided out of the room with his entourage buzzing around him while I drowned in the air like a fish in a dry creek bed.

After a few days, a doctor told me that they were packing me up and loading me onto a helicopter to be flown to Camp Anaconda in northern Iraq. There, I would be loaded on a plane and flown to Germany to heal up for a while, then back home. There was that word again: home. I didn't know how I felt about that. The soldier in me still wanted to fight. The soldier in me still had a fierce sense of duty, and going home seemed like abandoning the squad.

That afternoon, Lieutenant Caius came to visit. The nurses had just given me a healthy dose of morphine so I wasn't completely conscious, but he told me he was proud of me.

I felt like a faker. The painkiller loosened my tongue and I let some anger show: "For what? Really, why? I got blown up. I didn't do anything brave or heroic."

Caius was patient. "Your squad did a great job out there. We killed all three of those shitheads. We were the first patrol I know of that killed the triggermen who got them."

I didn't feel any better or worse after hearing that. Revenge wasn't something that ever crossed my mind. I could tell that the lieutenant didn't care for it either, but he was proud of how the men performed under direct fire. He said I should be proud of it, too, because it was a direct result of my leadership. I thanked him and he stood there at the side of my bed for a while. He told me Liam was heading to Germany with me, and Baldwin had taken some shrapnel during the secondary explosion but was fine. I looked away and nodded. He told me everyone in the platoon wanted to come visit and that they all wished me well. I nodded again.

"You're going home, Sean." He smiled.

"I know. I'm sorry, sir," I said.

"Nothing to be sorry about. Just get better."

The smiling nurse injected a syringe full of something into the bottom of my iv bag and turned the drip a little higher. The cool feel of the saline and morphine slid into every vein of my left arm and flowed all over my body. I breathed deeply with a smile and felt my steadied heart beat an easy rhythm, like a satin-covered drum. The real world gave way to the colors and lights behind my eyes, only interrupted by a few different faces looking down at me, asking if I was comfortable after a loading or an unloading.

The wheels of the Black Hawk hitting the helipad at Camp Anaconda woke me up. I turned my head to the side and saw four soldiers crouched down running into the rotor wash. I loved them for doing their jobs and taking care of the injured people. Hell, I loved everyone there. They unlatched my stretcher and carried me toward a big tent, but it took a little while to get there and in that time I got to look into a sky full of more stars than I had ever seen. Millions of them right above me—and the colors, my God. I saw little lines radiating out in circles, like a painting by Van Gogh or Cézanne. Inside the big tent, everything looked to be painted with thick brushstrokes filled with vibrant colors.

They barely had time to move me to a bed before I heard the familiar whistling of a mortar attack. All the staff jumped and rattled from patient to patient, checking monitors and talking to the hurt soldiers. The place was like a pinball machine.

"It's okay, they only hurt if they land on you," I called out, and meant it in the most sincere way.

The first explosion sent the hanging fluorescent lights swinging, making the shadows run all around the room. A black female lieutenant came in and yelled for all of the staff to run to the bunkers, God bless her. Reluctantly, all her soldiers filed out, leaving the bedridden patients. They had to. The lieutenant turned to leave, too, but as she hung in the doorway she saw me smiling at her. She paused, and looked so worried. I waved her to leave.

"It's okay. It's okay," I whispered.

Another explosion sent the shadows running again, and she

jumped like a spider had landed on her back. She was ready to go, but before she did, she found a flak vest and ran over to me. She set it lightly on my chest, like I was a child and she was tucking me in.

"Thank you," I said, and I loved her for the sadness I saw in her face, for her remorse at leaving me.

The rounds whistled and exploded, whistled and exploded again, but they didn't scare me. I loved watching the shadows run around the room. The explosions were the bass drums of the big symphony. What a beautiful and unending song, just a bit out of tune. I laughed out loud. I laughed until tears flowed down the sides of my face and pooled in my ears. I laughed long and heavy, until I could feel the pain in my ribs even through the morphine, because I finally, finally got the joke.

I Flew Over 2,000 Miles Completely Naked

The right side of my body had been so swollen and hard to move that no one ever put anything on me except a blanket. I didn't wear underwear in combat, and since my whole uniform had been cut off I was as naked as a baby being born. They flew me from place to place with only layers of blankets, and that's how I flew the two thousand miles to Germany. I thought that I must have set some sort of record for nude flying.

The flight from war to the real world only lasted a little over four hours. I flew from a place where mortar attacks sent everyone running for their lives every day to a warm hospital bed with a chunky male nurse leaning over me wearing scrubs printed with Disney characters, and, as far as he was concerned, I could have been a guy on vacation who broke his arm skiing.

"Germany?" I asked. My voice sounded rough and distant.

"Yes, you're at the 5th General in Stuttgart, Germany, and you're doing fine." He held a thermometer in front of my mouth until I opened up.

"What happens now?" I asked.

"Well, that's up to the doctors. I'm sure one will be in soon to let you know." He jotted down my vitals on a chart and smiled at me one more time. Then he left.

I was alone, lonelier than I had ever been before. This feeling took me by surprise. For the last year, I had spent every second of every day, whether asleep or awake, with at least one other man, and most of the time with eight to thirty other men. I needed to hear Patterson snoring, or Baldwin singing off key, or Melvin complaining. I had wanted a solitary moment for so long, but sitting there in that room by myself I felt like an amputated limb.

The closed door muffled the voices down the hall, but I strained to hear the nurses' conversations. I dreamed of Simon and me eating chicken and rice at the bridge with Qaes, with his kids running around us and laughing. Simon kept asking Qaes for the recipe for the flatbread that Qaes brought out with dinner. Simon fucking loved that bread, and was convinced it would be a great seller at the bakery and tattoo shop he and June were going to set up.

Qaes was blown away by the fact that Simon wanted to start a bakery; he had a hard time seeing us as anything but soldiers. I told him I was an artist, or wanted to be someday, and we all laughed. Simon said the walls of his shop would need a good mural, and I would have complete freedom to paint whatever I wanted. He would pay me in tattoos.

The drugs left me disoriented every time I woke. I wouldn't know where I was for a second or so, and then it would all come back to me, including the horrible feeling of the loss of my friend. It got so I didn't want to sleep anymore.

On the second day a short, stocky chaplain knocked on my door and poked his head in. He had a full head of dark hair that looked like it had never seen a military buzz, and when he sat at my bedside he didn't say anything at first. He only sat there and looked at me until he seemed satisfied with some conclusion. Finally he said, "I'm Rabbi Mizrahi. How are you doing? Not physically, I mean, I can see that, but…well, you know."

"I'm fine, sir."

He slapped his knees and straightened up. "I understand you lost one of your men. Do you want to talk about that?"

I was glad for the company but a little embarrassed. "I'm sorry, sir, but you said you were a rabbi."

"Yes."

"I'm not Jewish."

He shrugged and moved his hands around when he spoke. "I know. You don't have to be to talk. You know, one of your dog tags said Voodoo and the other said Zoroastrian. The other chaplains probably think you don't take our job too serious, but I thought you still might want to talk."

That had been my standing joke for the last couple of years. Every time I got a new pair of dog tags I had a new religion stamped into them. I'd heard once that if you died on the battlefield the army absolutely had to find the appropriate holy man to do your last rites. I thought it would be funny for them to kill a chicken or try to find a Sumerian priest if I died. I had laughed about it, but now it was real, someone had actually read them…well, it was still a little funny. I smiled. "I'm sorry, sir. That wasn't professional of me."

"No, it was funny as hell. So we know you have a sense of

humor." He leaned forward and smiled like we were good friends sharing a joke.

"And I'm agnostic," I said.

He leaned back in his chair and raised his chin like this was a revelation. "Ah, agnostic, the lazy man's atheist."

We laughed at that for bit. When the chuckles stopped we sat not looking at each other.

The rabbi sat up and straightened his top. "I heard that somewhere, but it's not true. It is better to have some faith than none at all."

"Yeah." We sat there across from each other for a while, listening to the muffled voices down the hall. I very much enjoyed having him there next to me, but I had no idea what to do. The whole incident seemed so big in my head, so chaotic. I had no idea where to start. "It just doesn't make sense."

He nodded and set both hands on his lap and looked at the tiled floor. "No. None of it does."

"I don't understand why." My voice cracked and so did the facade. I broke down, covered my face with my good hand, and sobbed with clenched teeth. I closed my eyes and saw Simon so vividly. It was the night we walked to the Fox and Firkin on leave, right before I drove to California. I felt the sun on my face. I smelled the dogwood blossoms. Why did he die? Why did I live? Why did they attack us? Why were we there? "I don't understand any of it."

"I don't either," the rabbi said, and he reached over and patted my shoulder. He gave me a kind moment that I hadn't known I needed.

Two days and a surgery passed. They built some sort of erector set with metal wires sticking out of my soft cast to keep my wrist from turning until the bones mended a bit more. Rabbi Mizrahi arranged for a cell phone, but I didn't want to talk to anyone. Almost a week had passed, so Simon's family had been told a few days back. I thought about that a long time. I knew everything about these guys, from their shoe size to their dreams and hopes. Simon's mother had no other children. June dreamed of a wedding. I could see them crumpling in the doorways of their houses in front of two uniformed officers standing on their porches or front steps.

I thought it was probably expected of me to call my mom, so I had Vince give me her number. I tried to swallow down the lump in my throat and dialed. She answered on the third ring.

"Hey, Mom. I don't want you to worry or anything, but I was in an accident." The line went dead, like I lost the connection. I knew those words were wrong as soon as they came out of my mouth. There was nothing accidental at all about what happened.

"Vince told me. Are you okay?"

I stared at the small spots of blood that had soaked through the bandages on my right arm. "I'm fine. I broke a couple bones and got knocked around, but I'm going to be fine." I should have stopped talking right there in order to make her feel okay about the whole thing, but the words wouldn't stop coming, "One of my good friends was killed and another was hurt bad. Simon was only two feet behind me when the bomb went off. I saw him, Mom. I saw him dead back there, and I can't get it out of my head."

She kept apologizing to me like it was all her fault. She said she was so sorry, over and over again. Then neither one of us said anything for a long time. "I'm sorry, Mom. I'm fine. I'll be back in the States soon. I just wanted to let you know that I'm okay."

She told me she loved me and that she was proud of me. I thanked her and told her I loved her too.

Liam Quinn happened to be in the room across the hall from me. After a few surgeries he was able to walk around with his arm in a sling as long as he pushed his iv stand. He smiled and laughed while telling me how big the gash in his back was. Some shrapnel somehow smashed his shoulder blade and dug out a big piece of flesh.

In a few minutes I was cracking up with him. We told each other stories about Simon and roared with laughter until I couldn't see through the tears. I don't think I had ever laughed that hard about anything. Then we talked about how bad we both felt for leaving the platoon, but he told me they would be all right. I believed him.

We stayed in Germany for a few more days, and every once in a while I would see Liam either running from or chasing the pretty nurses down the hall and laughing. He wasn't depressed or feeling sorry for himself, and that helped me. He left a day earlier than I did. They told me he was flown to Fort Lewis, Washington, only a few hours from home. I couldn't wait to get back to the Pacific Northwest.

Purgatory Looked a Lot Like Texas

I landed in Washington, D.C., at 1:00 a.m. Eastern Standard Time, in a C-141 Starlifter, a plane big enough to carry 154 soldiers, 123 airborne soldiers with gear, or eighty guys on stretchers like me. My plane only held ten soldiers, including myself, and four of them were the flight crew. The rest were fobbits, soldiers who never went outside the wire, the ones who stayed in the FOB. They were coming back with allergies, back problems, or other complaints.

One of the crew walked my wheelchair down the ramp and onto the tarmac. I had thought we were going straight to Fort Lewis, Washington, but landing anywhere without blown-to-shit buildings was all right with me. A shuttle van and nurse's assistant met us at the airport to bring us to wait at a hospital until our next flights were ready to take each of us to our duty stations.

All the houses and buildings had lights, the guardrails were still in place, and the van's radio played music I could understand. There was no trash littering the roads and the grass was green. No more rubble. No more mortar attacks. No more continuous operations. I was back in the United States, in America.

We pulled in the front of a small hospital and I was helped into another wheelchair. Two World War II veterans who had to have been in their late seventies were waiting for us in the lobby. They were wearing hot-dog-vendor hats covered in small, military-themed ceramic pins. The fobbits stayed outside, huddled in the smoking area, but I was rolled in. The vets greeted me with smiles from behind a foldout card table piled with trifold pamphlets. The men stayed seated but saluted me. One handed me paperwork to join the Meritorious Order of the Purple Heart, along with a ceramic pin of my own and a phone card worth twenty dollars.

A homely middle-aged woman with tired, puffy eyes came from inside the hospital and said I was scheduled to fly out the next day. She also said that the hospital was almost full so I would have to share a room, but it wasn't that big of a deal because the other man in the room was comatose.

I didn't know what he suffered from, but I figured from all the machines and noises coming from his side of the room that he wasn't coming back from it. A nurse kept coming by throughout the night, asking me to rate my pain level between zero and ten. I was a steady seven before the pills. After the pills, when the pain was a high two or a low three, I drifted off, but my sleep cycle was still set to life outside the wire and I woke up every couple of hours. I spent most of the night listening to the dying man's phlegmatic breathing and the beeps of his machines. This left little else to think about besides death and dying.

A few hours after the sun lit up the room, a big black woman pushed a wheelchair in and told me to hop on. She gave me a couple more pain pills, then took me to a plain white room with rows of tan plastic chairs and a podium in front of a dry erase board. In the chairs sat four other newly returned soldiers. One of them was missing an arm. Another had an eye and half his face bandaged. The other two wore casts like me, but without the erector set. The large nurse addressed us all with a big old smile and told us that after the doctor talked to us we would be taken to lunch in the cafeteria, then loaded onto buses to the airport and flown home.

"All right, honeys. The doctor will be in soon." She lumbered to the door without turning around again and shut it behind her. The other soldiers didn't look around at all. As far as I could tell, they didn't know anyone else was in the room. These men were out of sync with the world. They stared at the wall or the floor like they were watching a movie. I thought that maybe they were stuck somewhere else.

The morning sun shone in through the open Venetian blinds, projecting the shadow of a fly onto the podium. I poked my left index finger as far as I could down the cast on my right arm and scratched. Five minutes went by as I sat in silence and watched the shadows move down the wall. Only then did I start to wonder what the doctor was going to say.

A small, bald man with thick glasses and a long white coat walked into the room and stepped behind the podium. He held a metal clipboard about a foot away from his face and started reading aloud without saying hello or introducing himself. "Many returning veterans will find that they may be suffering from deep depression or thoughts of suicide."

The shadow of the fly crawled around the podium.

"These may be symptoms of post-traumatic stress disorder. If you find yourself with unexplained feelings of loss…"

I couldn't help but look at the soldier missing his arm and think, *unexplained.*

"If you have any thoughts of harming yourselves or others, you should seek help immediately." He continued to explain in a very clinical way how to restructure our mental health, like he was telling someone how to put together a piece of furniture bought at IKEA. He gave us permission to have these surges of pain and episodes of emotional chaos. He told us that the human brain wasn't wired to have that much adrenaline pumping through it for such a long time, and how this can have lasting effects, but that the military's top doctors were researching these effects. "Don't give up," he said. "There is help out there."

At the end of his speech he pulled some handouts off his clipboard and took a few awkward steps around the room to put them on the laps of the other soldiers, and then handed one to me.

On the paper was a topographical map of Iraq with the silhouette of a soldier squatting down in the foreground, his head in his hands, and beside him the words, "PTSD: The Invisible Wounds of War."

I read through the couple pages of the pamphlet. When I looked up next the bald man was gone, and had been replaced by the big black nurse. She wheeled me to the cafeteria. She told me how lucky I was that it was Tuesday, because on Tuesdays they had meatloaf.

That night I took a C-130 filled with soldiers, first to Ohio, where a few got off, and then to Illinois to drop off a couple more before finally arriving at Fort Hood, Texas. The last stop. After we landed I was taken to Darnall Army Hospital, where I asked yet another nice female nurse when I would be going to Fort Lewis. She said the doctor would be in to talk to me soon, and she helped me into the bleached white sheets of another hospital bed.

Half an hour later, a stocky Asian man came in wearing oversized glasses and blue scrubs. He told me I needed at least one more surgery on my arm and that he would schedule it as soon as possible, but it would be at least a few weeks out.

"What the fuck?" I couldn't hold in my frustration. The loud and angry words would not stop coming out of my mouth. The doctor wouldn't look at me, but kept telling me to stop talking and calm down. I did the opposite. No one had told me I would be stuck in Texas. I was supposed to be going home. They all told me I was going home. Finally, he lost some of his cool and threatened me with legal action if I didn't listen to him as a superior officer.

In my mind, they had promised to take me back to Portland, to the Pacific Northwest. I may not have had a physical address, but I needed to get back to what I considered my home. Then, out of nowhere, they tell me I'm staying in Texas? Texas was just another flat, hot desert. I roared, asking if this was how they treated all the combat-wounded. All I wanted was a straight fucking answer about when I would go home. Why wouldn't anyone just tell me what the fuck was going on?

The doctor must have had a horrible day, because he lost it, too, and screamed at me to shut up. He kept saying it: "Shut up, shut up, shut up." Then he left.

The first thing I did the next morning was use the phone card the old Purple Heart vets gave me to call the armory in Corvallis, Oregon. I talked to Sergeant Stimpson, who had stayed behind. He shared my outrage about the situation and said Liam Quinn had been flown to Madigan Medical Center at Fort Lewis. No one knew why I was sent to Fort Hood, but he would do what he could to get me home.

Three days went by, and in my world only three other people existed: the day-shift nurse, the swing-shift nurse, and the grave-yard-shift nurse. I saw each one twice a day when they checked my vitals, brought my meals, or issued pain pills.

Every meal was cold without exception and came with a lima bean and vegetable medley and a tasteless, gelatinous cube in a primary color. I tried to pass the time by watching the small television mounted in the corner of the room.

One day, on the local news, the anchorman reported that three Fort Hood soldiers had been killed in Tikrit, and then abruptly cut to a story on how Halle Berry's husband was challenging their prenup. I changed the channel and landed on an entertainment news show talking about how Paris Hilton had spent some ungodly amount of money on a sweater for her dog. Every channel reported nothing, and the only mention of our men and women in combat came in the form of one or two sentences spoken out loud or just scrolled across the bottom of the screen. The war and its casualties had become a footnote to pop culture.

When I slept, I dreamed about people being burned alive, with their guts blown out, screaming in pain. When I was awake, episodes of rage or sadness came without warning and occurred with increasing frequency. Frustration, anger, and depression came at random times and for little reason. I could barely keep from throwing a tray of food across the room one hour, and then the next I lay weeping into my blanket.

Just like someone learning to walk again after losing control of their legs, I had lost my ability to contain my emotions. They rolled around inside me, too big and too sharp to ignore. I needed help, but there was no way I could ask the doctors in the army. I didn't care if they thought I was crazy, but I didn't want them to see me as helpless. The army had built me to be strong my entire adult life. Finding weakness and rooting it out made a good soldier a great one. No, the army wouldn't be where I would turn for help.

I called my little brother Vince with my Purple Heart phone card, but when he answered, the whole rehearsed conversation about these emotional fits disappeared and I went back to being the big brother. I told him I was fine and would be in Texas for a while for a surgery, but that I expected a full recovery. We talked about family and events but stayed away from politics, war, and, especially, feelings. Before we hung up, he mentioned something he thought was odd. Jaime had called him and asked about me. He said I should call her because she sounded worried out of her mind.

Jaime. I hadn't thought about her for so long, but now that I had I couldn't think of anything else. She was the missing piece, the person I could talk to about my problems. With her I could be the artist again, and wouldn't have to be the soldier. She was the connection I needed to get back to normal. I had no idea how she had found out, but she was worried out of her mind. I needed to call her. Vince gave me her new number, and my clumsy and shaky left hand wrote it down, slowly, on a napkin.

There wasn't much left on my phone card, but it had to be enough. My fingers shook when punching the numbers in, and I didn't breathe while the phone rang.

Her first hello was generic, but when she heard my voice she almost started crying.

"Hey, Jay," I said, trying to be calm.

We talked like we did back in my little one-bedroom apartment on Hawthorne. She told me she had a breakdown when she heard

I was almost killed. It made her think about how badly she had treated me. She apologized for standing me up, for not writing, for everything. All of the pain and frustration poured out of me while talking to her. She very quickly became my only outlet, and she listened.

She said she had finally realized how important I was to her when she told her political science class she knew someone who was almost killed in the war. In the middle of her report, she stopped and broke down. They all gathered around her in support.

I imagined her with swollen eyes and tears streaming down her face, falling to the floor and cursing herself for standing me up at Big River. In one of my favorite scenarios, she clutched an old photo of us to her sobbing chest. It was great. Our long and happy life would start the day I limped off the plane in Portland. All I needed to do was get home.

Attempted Murder

After a week, they let me out of the hospital and assigned me to a company of soldiers unfit for combat. They were regular army soldiers stationed at Hood that, for one reason or another, couldn't be sent to war. Some women had become pregnant immediately before their units deployed—some openly admitted they did this on purpose. The men complained of chronic injuries that kept them from being sent to war. In a few cases these recent injuries were real, but many others were faked. I was the first combat-wounded soldier assigned to this company. My room was on the third floor of one of the barracks without elevators, and with my broken leg it took me almost twenty minutes to climb the stairs. My roommate was a light-skinned black kid in his early twenties who looked as healthy as a horse—in fact, he looked like he could have bench-pressed a horse—but he couldn't go to war due to frequent migraine headaches.

On my first night in the barracks, I woke up in a panic because I heard the familiar sounds of rounds flying through the air and exploding. I jumped out of my bed and scrambled around the room, feeling for my weapon and flak vest in the dark. My thrashing and thumping woke up my roommate. He asked what the hell I was doing, a bit of fear in his voice. I half knew I wasn't in combat, but I also knew what I heard. I told him to listen. He plopped back down on his bed and said the artillery firing range was a half mile down the road. It was only a training exercise.

Three or four times a day I called Sergeant Stimpson back at the Corvallis Armory, hoping he had found a way to get me the hell out of Texas. Two more Bravo Company soldiers had been injured a week after my ambush and had been sent to Fort Lewis, Washington. The anger came back. I was glad no one else was sent off and kept away from home, but, goddamn, why did they leave me in Texas? They stuck an infantry squad leader who was wounded during violent combat operations in a company of broke-dick fobbits who were either too weak or too sick to go to war or, even worse, faked being too weak or too sick to go to war.

My new platoon sergeant was a skinny black man in his forties with yellow gin-drinker's eyes who chain-smoked. Between
fits of coughing he spoke in a high-pitched, nasally voice. I limped
around and saw the rest of the soldiers in the company trying as
hard as they could to look pathetic, sick, or weak. I pictured some
of them on an off-ramp of some highway in ten years, behind a
cardboard sign reading, "Iraqi era veteran, anything helps, God
bless."

My surgery had been bumped back a few weeks. Really, this
was because more wounded had been coming in from the war, but
in my mind it was because the doctor was trying to get back at me.
I filled the days limping to doctor's appointments. They saw me
for my arm, my leg, my back, my nightmares, my PTSD, my dizzy
spells, and everything else.

I was given drugs—so many drugs.

They prescribed Ambien, Vicodin, Percocet, OxyContin, ser-
traline, fluoxetine, and multivitamins, and I took them all. I found
that if I washed the pills down with a bottle of red wine, sometimes I could sleep up to five hours at a time. I saw no other way
to pass the time, so I would try to sleep three or four times a day.
Weeks passed in a narcoleptic, narcotic blur.

One Thursday in late July, five weeks after Simon was killed
and I was injured, a military criminal detective knocked on the
door of my barracks room asking for Staff Sergeant Philip Sean
Davis. I was immediately apprehensive since it was eleven in the
morning and I was wasted. He wore a cheap reddish-brown suit
the color of an Alabama mud puddle and gold-rimmed aviator
glasses with lenses so dark I couldn't see his eyes. His thick hair
and big gut made me think he was a civilian, but with a synchro-
nized and highly practiced motion he produced identification to
show he was an officer in the military police. I was in boxer shorts,
drunk on duty, and abusing prescription medication.

I took an unsteady step back and, with a grand gesture, asked
him to come in, but told him to talk softly since my roommate was
sleeping off one of his chronic migraine headaches.

"It would be better if we went to the station," he said with a
thick Southern accent.

"Sure, sure. Let me get my wallet…and my pants." The nerves
came back. My wallet seemed like something I should have on me
while talking to investigators at the CID station.

CID stands for Criminal Investigation Command; the letters

don't quite match up—the D isn't used for anything but the acronym. Some say it once stood for department; others say division. We got in his unmarked late-model baby-shit-brown Ford Crown Vic and took off.

I kept trying to ask him why he needed to talk to me, but he was on his cell phone the entire time, talking about a robbery at the Class VI that must have happened the day before. I asked anyway, in the lulls of his conversation, but he would just hold up a giant finger.

We pulled into a single-story building that looked like a strip mall. He badged us into a back door, then led me through the incredibly busy station filled with desks, filing cabinets, and framed pictures of different generals dating back to the creation of the CID. I took short breaths because I was convinced he would smell the wine on my breath, and I kept my lips pursed because I knew they were probably stained with merlot. He pointed to indicate I should sit down in a chair that looked like the kind one would find in a high school classroom.

Before he sat down at his messy desk he took off his cheap brown suit jacket, showing a holstered Glock 17 pistol hanging off his straining belt. Then he took off his aviator glasses, revealing a lazy eye. He shuffled through some paperwork and didn't say anything for a while. I sat there listening to the keystrokes of the computers all around me, the phones ringing, the general buzz of office activity.

"I understand several armed men detonated a device near a vehicle you were riding in. I've been assigned to your case."

"My case?" I had no idea what the hell he was talking about.

"Attempted murder. I'm going to need you to remember what the men looked like." He put the point of his pen on his pad of paper, showing me he was serious.

"Attempted murder? In war?" I took a second to process that. "How many of these cases do you have?"

With his pen still poised and without looking up he repeated, "Can you describe any of the men?"

I rubbed my forehead and tried to remember. "Sure, there were three of them. They were all about five foot eight to five ten, all had black hair, all had black mustaches, all had AK-47s…are you going to go over there and try to arrest them?"

The detective dropped his pen on his desk and looked up at me, sending his lazy eye floating in its socket. He explained to me in a very defeated tone that he understood the futility of his actions. "Listen, for reasons beyond my control the inspector general is having me chase around you boys, and I don't know or care why. I was told to fill out the paperwork on these incidents, so that's what I'm doing."

"You must be very busy."

"Hell, I ain't fucking the goat. I'm just holding the tail."

I liked that very much. The thought of painting my own masterpiece protesting the war, protesting war in general, popped into my head. Goya, Picasso, Golub, Davis. The canvas would be three stories tall and painted like an American flag, and in the foreground I would put a very dignified-looking goat with a subtle smile, staring with a deep satisfaction at all who gazed upon it, while a determined yet compassionate Uncle Sam in top hat, tie, and patriotic jacket mounted it from behind with his pants around his ankles. There, on the right side, a young private in desert camo looks away from the act in disgust while holding up the tail between two fingers.

The whole thing was so damned funny and ridiculous until the story started coming out of my mouth, and then I realized I hadn't told it to anyone else in detail. I paused at the hard parts and swallowed down all the words that got stuck in my throat. I looked up and blinked at the ceiling to hide the tears. For his part, the detective was very patient, and subtly found a box of tissues for my running nose. I rubbed my forehead to hide my swollen eyes, and coughed to hide my breaking voice, but finally I got through it. When I was done, the big man offered me a ride back, but instead we went to a doctor's appointment for my leg.

He pulled up slowly in his big boat of a cop car, and I opened the door to get out. Before closing it, I turned around and asked, "So, will I hear anything about this?"

"No, probably not, son."

"Okay then. Thanks." I closed the door and limped to the office.

Army Ants

I didn't have much to do other than experiment with different drug combinations, and this made it entertaining to lie spread out on the thin carpet of my barracks room and watch hundreds of ants march in two lines across the cracked paneling nailed to the wall. I tried desperately to think of a reason they would scurry back and forth, but since neither line was burdened or better off than the other I had a hard time thinking of one. Whatever the purpose, all of them, without doubt, believed it to be very important.

Someone knocking at the door broke the trance. If I had been expecting someone I would have let them knock all day, but since I wasn't I got up and limped to the door; finding a reason for the troop movements would have to wait.

The skinny black master sergeant stood there with his yellow eyes, his forehead a wrinkled mess. "All right, Davis. You won. Your wife went to some congressman, and the base commander called yelling at me to get you home."

Standing up and walking to the door got my blood flowing and made me feel I was filled with crumpled tinfoil. I stepped back and leaned against the door. I was pretty messed up, but I knew I didn't have a wife.

He walked around the barracks room looking at everything but me and said that shit was coming down on him and it was my fault. "Hell, you think I wanted you here? Shit. You're not even regular army. I just deal with the shit they give me."

"You're not fucking the goat, you're just holding the tail," I said, and laughed.

"Shiiiiiiiiiiit." He drew out the word until it faded away, looking me up and down like he was trying to decide if I was worth yelling at. He told me I needed to get my ass to the company office and pick up my clearing papers. If I got to it right away, I could be home in a couple days. "You so short you can eat here and shit in whatever hillbilly, tree-hugging place you came from."

I watched the door close behind him and sat there for a while longer without moving. This news didn't feel like I'd expected, and I wanted to know why. Going home should have made me all excited and happy, but there I was, still thinking about ants marching back and forth.

Fuck, I have PTSD. Those words echoed inside my head repeatedly. I had no idea if PTSD was the sort of thing that you self-diagnosed. None of the doctors would officially diagnose me. They seemed scared of even saying the words, but I did know that since getting back I'd felt either too many of the wrong emotions or none at all.

They had me on alpha blockers for my nightmares, antidepressants for my moods, and heavy doses of Vicodin for the pain. I was self-medicating with wine, beer, and whiskey, too, all to stop the pain: the physical pain of my injuries and the mental pain of blaming myself for the death of a friend, for leaving my platoon at war, for surviving. I wouldn't let myself have a clear-headed moment because I was so afraid of that pain.

I pulled out my new cell phone and called Jaime. I thought that maybe if I acted normal I would feel normal again, and the normal thing to do was to call my girlfriend to let her know I was coming home. She picked up right away and without letting me say a word she told me how she'd pretended to be my wife at a Bravo Company family support meeting. Oregon's fourth district congressman had happened to attend this meeting. With tears in her eyes, she asked why the US Army sent her combat-injured husband to Fort Hood, Texas, while the other Bravo Company soldiers had been sent to Fort Lewis. She described how the people all erupted in rage over this, and how the congressman vowed right there to do something about the injustice of it all.

My attention floated to the cracked wall paneling. I noticed that the wood grain was actually a sticker over pressboard nailed to crumbling drywall.

Jaime babbled on about the reactions of the students and faculty in her political science class, and how they said she'd actually taken a stand and acted. She was a political *activist* now, and though this accomplishment was a small victory against the war machine, it was a victory nonetheless.

I gave her the appropriate affirmations during the lulls in her monologue, but the sincere pride she felt made me want to laugh. She still had all the same qualities I couldn't stand but had forgotten about while pining over her. This was the same Jaime who always needed to pick the next big cause so she could be on the cultural and moral high ground. She had a long career of saving things: the whales, Tibet, the environment, and, now, a combat-injured soldier from a bullshit war. I was just a blue fin tuna, a giant panda, or a great white shark to her.

"What are you laughing about?" she asked.

I reached out and smashed a couple ants with my thumb. The little lines stopped for a moment, but when I took my thumb away the troop movement resumed. "Nothing. Just funny how life works."

The Blast Supper

When I told the lady at the airline ticket counter I was a combat-wounded veteran on my way home, she found her manager. The airline gave me a free ticket at the front of the plane along with a signed card from every crew member. Before we took off, the captain made an announcement welcoming Staff Sergeant Davis home from Iraq, where he was wounded by an IED. He said that he spoke for everyone when he said welcome home, and the entire plane cheered.

On the flight, I couldn't pay for a drink and could barely keep up with the ones that were bought for me. People came up to shake my hand and thank me for my service. By the end of the flight I was half in the bag and believing the world was a pretty fucking cool place. I was going home, goddammit. Home to my girl. I put all doubts out of my head completely.

My plane landed under the gray clouds of the Northwest on a Friday. I usually walked slowly so people wouldn't see me limp, but I couldn't contain my excitement and the alcohol hid the pain. I looked like a power walker with one leg a half a foot shorter than the other as I made my way past the security checkpoint. The bright blue of Jaime's dress would have caught anyone's eye, but the way it was tight in the right places and loose in others put me in a trance. I ran to her and felt kill-proof again, like I was storming an objective or kicking a door down. All emptiness disappeared and I was whole again. I swept her up with my left arm and buried my face in her hair, breathing in the smell of exotic fruits I could not name. I'd made it home.

Maybe I was wrong about being broken. Maybe I did love her, and maybe she even loved me back. Whatever I'd thought in Texas was bullshit. I was wrong—wrong about me and wrong about Jaime.

Then there was a bright light. I saw it even through closed eyes. When I opened them I couldn't see anything but the camera crew. Jaime had called the news so the local population could see an injured soldier coming off the plane surrounded by her and her friends from the political science class at OSU. I looked around and tried like hell to blink my eyes normally again. The after-image stuck in my vision, making everyone around me face-less. Dozens of voices called to me, but I couldn't make out the words. Everything moved around me, but there was nothing I could focus on. My stomach dropped and my breath left me like I was banking hard in a Black Hawk. A woman's fist flew at me and I flinched before realizing she clutched a microphone with a news logo. She asked me how it felt to be home.

I squinted, smiled without showing teeth, and said, "Feels great."

She turned and talked to the camera for a bit about how Bravo Company was from Corvallis. Jaime started squeezing my left hand when the news lady mentioned osu. Jaime's face glowed with pure rapture.

The lady turned back around and asked how it felt to have so many great friends there to welcome me home. I didn't want to say I didn't recognize any of them. "Feels great."

The news lady's smile didn't fade, but it faltered a bit. I guess both of us knew I wasn't acting properly for a returning soldier. She redoubled her enthusiasm and asked, "Now that you're home, what's the first thing you want to do?"

She stuck her microphone out. This was my cue to grab it, jump up and down, and scream to the viewers at home, "I want to go to Disneyland, eat fast food, worship Jesus Christ, and buy American!"

Hell, I didn't know what to say. Maybe I was boring and fucked up in the head, but I didn't want my homecoming moment tele-vised. I didn't want to share it with anyone, and all I did want was a fucking well-done steak, a pint of microbrew, and a blow job. That was the god's honest truth.

I could only smile, so the news lady immediately broke eye contact, letting me know that wasn't the proper thing to do while being interviewed. I stared into the camera for a while, not mean-ing to let the awkward energy build. I had to say something. "I'm just happy to be home with my loved ones. It feels…great."

She thanked me sincerely for my service, my time, and my sac-rifice. Then the light on the camera went out, and before my eyes adjusted, the entire crew was gone. Jaime drifted away to her class-mates to talk about their small victory, leaving me alone to won-der what the hell had just happened. That's when I saw Francisco Cabra and Mike, my old art school buddies. Francisco and Jaime had remained friends this whole time. He found out about my injuries through my brother Vince and told Jaime.

It was so good to see them again. They each gave me big man-hugs and asked how the hell I was doing. I hadn't seen either of them more than a couple times since leaving Portland for the state job. Francisco's long and curly hair had gotten longer, and he still stood only a couple inches over five feet with his boots on. Mike was just under six foot, and the only thing new about him was a bushy, lumberjack-looking beard. They both wore holey jeans and had on T-shirts that had been washed a hundred times too many.

We exchanged run-of-the-mill pleasantries. Smiles, nods, and a gap in conversation followed before Francisco leaned in and whispered, "You wanna get stoned?"

Back in art school, I was probably the only person who didn't smoke out, including the faculty. Francisco knew it and had stopped asking me back then, but I'm sure he figured that since it was a special occasion he'd ask one more time. I said yes, and that surprised me as much as it did him.

The freethinking socialists of the OSU political science class came to a consensus and decided we would eat dinner at a nearby German restaurant. I thought this was a wonderful idea; being high made so many ideas wonderful. Before I knew it, I was sitting at a big table covered with a blue-and-white cloth that had a diamond pattern, just like the Bavarian flag. The table was in the back of a room, with wooden eagle sculptures arranged on the bar and bolted to the walls. These weren't the lifelike eagles one would see flying in the Northwest, but more like the type you would see on a soldier's collar or in a propaganda film.

Mike and Francisco sat to my left, Jaime sat to my right, and the small party of scruffy-haired college students surrounded the rest of the table. Most of them had facial hair and glasses and wore thrift store clothing. The whole scene reminded me of da Vinci's *Last Supper*, and I guess since I was the center of attention that made me Jesus. Again I thought, *How wonderful.*

I smiled a lot, laughed, and ate at least a bite of every dish in reach, but I ignored the barrage of questions. The college kids needed to know what I thought of the war. They needed to know my stand on all of it and asked over and over again until they got the question through my cloudy brain.

I knew how they wanted me to feel about war; it was the same way Jaime wanted me to feel about it, but I didn't hate it and I couldn't put into words why. War killed thousands of men, women, and innocent children. War killed some of the soldiers I served with, including a dear friend. War nearly killed me and left me broken, but I didn't hate it. This wasn't our grandfather's war. This wasn't *Band of Brothers* or *Slaughterhouse-Five*. The infantryman of today desperately tries to make friends just as much as he tries to make people dead. I spent more time saving children and deciding who not to shoot than shooting and getting shot at. I'm sure some rich asshole was making another mint off the whole thing, but I know we tried to make people's lives better. Why were these kids so angry? I wanted to tell them there were good people over there in uniform, learning the language and culture. I wanted to express to them that, while I tried my best to be a good soldier, being a good person was my priority, but it came out all stoned. Instead I blurted, "I learned how to speak Klingon, for fuck's sake."

Francisco and Mike started laughing, but no one else knew what to say to that so no one spoke for a while. After a couple minutes of listening to the bustle of the restaurant, someone wanted my opinion on whether or not the US should police the world. Another wanted to know if I thought the UN inspectors had been acting under the Bush administration's orders. Someone else asked if the Iraqi government would be able to stand on its own once we left. Was Bush the Devil?

They all looked to me. I was the expert on the subject.

"The Iraqi government is a little kid with a bunch of older brothers. They're all starving little desert rats. All we can do is sit there and make sure they finish the fucking Skittles and give them a few bottles of water. And Bush seemed all right. He ate his spaghetti with a spork."

No one asked me another question after that, but that was okay because I was thinking about how wonderful the person who invented fondue was. I was happy when the dinner ended. I couldn't wait to take my beautiful girl back to a hotel and have extra-kinky porn-star sex.

Jaime rented a cheap motel room close by just so we could be alone and as noisy as we wanted. But when she pulled her blue Dodge Neon into the Motel 6 parking lot, I lost it. In the next parking spot over idled a Ford F250 Super Duty pickup truck, like a grass seed farmer would drive. The smell of diesel fumes

reminded me of the war, and a dark guilt, mixed with my intox-
ication, made me spiral out of control. My arm and leg started to
ache and my mouth went dry. The temperature must have gone
up ten degrees, and I started breathing faster.

Why did *I* survive? Why was I here after a big meal and drinks,
back home, ready to be with my girl? Why was my life worth saving? What was June doing right now? I knew why Simon wasn't
alive. He was killed because I told him to stay in the back of that
fucking Humvee and the top of his head was ripped off. He was
dead.

I remembered that time I was out with June and Simon at the
Fox and I told June I didn't know what I was doing. I blew off her
question with some stupid remark. Such a dumb, small comment
said on a drunk night, but it fucking stabbed at me. I don't remember regretting anything more in this world. The sobs started with
a gasp and the world got blurry. I looked away from Jaime and
bawled uncontrollably in the passenger seat. A very awkward couple of minutes ensued, and an uncomfortable silence settled over
us before she reluctantly reached out. She pushed my head down
to her chest like I was a kid with a nightmare. I hated it; I didn't
want to need her help, but I let her do it. We stayed like that for a
while, her not wanting to comfort me and me not wanting to be
comforted. After a while she patted my head and said, "You're
probably not used to drinking yet."

I never asked to live with Jaime and she never offered, but that's
how it ended up. She shared a giant brown house right off the
osu campus with an ever-changing roster of roommates. When
I moved into her downstairs master bedroom, there were three
other students and one dog on the lease of the four-bedroom
house. The basement had an occupant and so did the breakfast
nook, with a curtain instead of a door. And there were three cats,
a gerbil, and a python spread throughout the house too. All these
animals lived in peace as long as they weren't in close quarters.

I was on a week-long leave, and my main intent during this
time was to find the artist I used to be, to get rid of all this anger
and crying bullshit, and to not think about the army at all. Of
course, this was impossible. Television, radio, the Internet, newspapers—all had daily stories of suicide bombings, dead troops,
and ieds, even if they were buried under trivial pop culture shit.

I couldn't help but read and listen to them all, in case someone I knew had been hit.

Then there were the conversations with the roommates while making coffee, waiting for the bathroom, or reading the newspaper in the living room.

I had no idea how the hell I could be expected to settle in and reintegrate into society. The guilt never left me; I blamed myself for Simon's death constantly. I thought about his mom and how I should go and talk to her and June. The idea that I was responsible for his death hit me every day, along with how I had let down my squad, my platoon, my company. I needed to block it all out.

The VA made it simple to get my pain pills and sleeping pills refilled. Drinking and other recreational drugs always seemed like a wonderful idea.

The Life of the Party

Trent lived in one of the bedrooms upstairs, but he took care of every plant in the whole house. His thick brown hair was always in a ponytail running halfway down the back of a T-shirt showing how he had worked or volunteered for some sort of nonprofit organization. He spoke with a lisp, but I could never see if he had a harelip because of his perpetual five o'clock shadow. In our first conversation, he ambushed me while I was making my morning coffee in the beautiful kitchen with the vibrant blue ceramic-tiled counter. The sun hadn't come up yet, but it wasn't dark outside, either, and the early morning light made the white curtains in the front windows glow like the room was haunted.

Trent told me he majored in civil engineering but had a strong inclination for politics. He begrudgingly admitted he had never been in the military, like this was a secret and not readily apparent from his posture and the way he moved and spoke.

Trent told me that his grandfather served as a quartermaster in World War II, commanding the Red Ball Express. When I didn't react, he told me that was a convoy system used to get supplies to the troops on the front lines in a hurry. I could tell by the way he told me this that it was supposed to mean something special to any man who ever wore a uniform. In his mind, this somehow made us kindred spirits and thus gave him permission to ask blunt questions like, "What the hell are we doing over there?"

I struggled with the childproof top of my Vicodin. "I could tell you what I did, but it wouldn't make you feel any better."

"It's a war for oil. We are trading American blood for Iraqi crude. Doesn't it piss you off that you were used as a pawn?" He pulled the trigger on his squirt bottle and misted the broad leaves of a houseplant on the counter.

I visualized grabbing Trent by his ponytail and bouncing his head off the beautiful blue ceramic tile.

Trent's thin fingers darted around the base of the plant, picking the dead leaves from the red clay pot. "This whole war was started because of Bush's daddy issues. He wanted to show up

Bush Senior, and a bunch of warmongers jumped on board because they saw they could make money off it."

I poured cream into my cup and stirred. "You can't blame the Romans for the potholes in the roads."

I don't know why I said it and didn't know what I meant by it, but Trent paused for a while and nodded like it made sense to him. He moved to the sink to throw away the dead leaves in the garbage underneath and said it was good talking to me. We would have to pick it up again later, he said, because he needed to hurry off to his first class. I watched him walk out after grabbing his book satchel made from environmentally friendly fabric. When the door shut, I poured my entire cup of coffee into the red clay pot and went back to bed.

The Big Brown House had a reputation around campus. None of the kids who lived there had to work for a living while going to school, but some, like Trent, volunteered between classes for Greenpeace, Children International, the Jackson Street Youth Shelter, the United Way, et cetera. When the weekend rolled around, the kitchen, living room, or porch would fill up with all types of naive but passionate college kids wanting to save the world and drink to excess.

That first Friday night, everyone wanted to talk to me. Knowing a veteran made the war personal for people, and because it was a portion of our culture many of these people felt they needed to be a part of it. After talking to me, they could tell their friends, family, and acquaintances they knew a guy injured in the war, and that gave their opinions more credibility. The more a person knew me, the bigger their role in the giant comedy.

Jaime stood next to me and held my hand and smiled when I first started to tell my stories. Once I had a couple of beers in me the war was all I wanted to talk about, and the more I drank, the more graphic the details became. At the end of the night I was talking over everyone else in the room. By that time I had told all my stories and had started to retell them with bigger exaggerations, the no-shit-there-I-was types of stories. I was saying it was Saddam's daughter who detonated that car at North Gate and mutilated over fifty innocent Iraqis. No shit, I saw her with my own eyes right before I was knee-deep in everyone's guts. I talked about the time my squad was cut off from our unit in the middle of the unbearably hot desert with a hundred starving orphans swarming our Humvees and desperately fighting over what little food and water we could give them. Then I told them my favorite story: early in the deployment, Sergeant First Class Schofield let me borrow his up-armored Humvee and I drove it through a prison wall. All the prisoners had escaped, but the place wasn't empty. Lawless nomads had made their homes there and Battalion decided they might be a good source of information, so they told us to go in and arrest them. We dismounted from our Humvees and flowed from room to room, from cell to cell. At the end of the day we pretty much had the whole damned thing cleared, except for the offices. I was on point even though I wasn't supposed to be. The squad leader's place is in the middle, to keep full command and control of his men, but I liked to lead from the front, and when I turned the corner at full speed I found myself nose-to-nose with an old gray horse that looked beat to shit.

I started laughing, but no one else did. The people closest to me forced a smile, but they didn't get it. They didn't get it because they didn't live through it. Then the story became funnier to me because I really had sunk low enough to become a cliché. They didn't know; they weren't there, man.

That Saturday night I chased people around to make them listen to me. I would corner a group of partygoers in the kitchen, living room, or porch and tell the stories again. I saved the story about Simon's death and the ambush for last. No grotesque detail was omitted; I told almost the entire story of that morning, only leaving out the coin toss. I never told anyone about that part, ever. The party ended when the story did. After a story like that, there was no way to go back to having fun. The people who didn't leave started talking about politics, religion, death, and the futility of war.

On Sunday night I found myself sitting alone, sipping my beer in various rooms of the house while the party was going on somewhere else. The people had gotten enough reality, or at least my version of it. Wanting to be reminded of the ugliness of war and having it ruin your entire weekend were two different things. Unfortunately, my stories weren't disposable for me. I couldn't take them or leave them. If I didn't pull them out and fill a room with them, they filled the smaller space between my ears until it almost burst.

Even in the weekdays that followed, I couldn't control myself; whenever my mouth opened, war stories spilled out. If someone complained about their life, I had a story a million times worse about poor Farook, or Mustafa, or a little kid we called Oh-My-Shit because that's what he always said when selling us cheap cigarettes or Turkish whiskey.

By Wednesday I was spending most of my time alone, sitting on the end of Jaime's queen-sized mattress in my boxer shorts, staring at the wall. On Thursday I wouldn't leave the room. Empty beer bottles and old fast food bags spread around me like ruins of little buildings in an empty city.

I think Jaime was ready to throw me out by Friday, and I couldn't blame her. She hadn't slept right for the last couple days because I woke her up three or four times a night, checking that the bedroom door and windows were locked. I hadn't showered or shaved all week. To me it wasn't a big deal because in the field sometimes I went close to a month without a shower. I never cleaned up after myself and I alienated all her roommates, but what really pushed her over the edge was a milk jug half full of piss.

One morning she came back after classes, put her book bag on the floor, and with quick and sudden movements began to organize all the little pieces of jewelry on her dresser. She spoke into the mirror with quick and cold words. "So, what did you do today?"

I scratched my five-day-old beard. "Nothing. Grabbed a burrito from the corner."

"Listen, Sean. I'm trying to make something of myself, okay?"

I had no idea what she was upset about. "Of course you are."

Without turning around, she slowly raised her left arm and pointed at the piss jug in the corner. This perplexed me for a moment, because I couldn't make the connection between her future and a half gallon of my urine. "I don't need this," she said.

"Oh, shit. I meant to throw that out before you got home. One of the roommates was in the shower and…" I pushed myself off the bed, picked up the jug, and started for the bathroom.

She stepped in front of the door, her eyes looking down at the beer bottles but not at me. "Think of what I'm going through. I can't be your crutch right now. I have my senior year coming up and I need to be focused."

We stood a foot apart but didn't look at each other.

"You want me to leave?" I said it without emotion. I had nowhere else to go, but it didn't bother me. I genuinely didn't care.

She paused. Maybe she loved me? Or maybe she was going to take another political science class this year and needed a test subject. I didn't know. All I really wanted was a pint of beer and a shot.

Her posture softened. She was almost tender. "I think you need more than I can give."

"How about I disappear for a couple days? Give you some space. Then we'll go from there." I walked around her to the bathroom down the hall and poured the piss down the toilet.

Self-pity, frustration over an obviously bad relationship, hell, even melancholy—I had all these emotions, but they were under glass, buried and not working right. I knew I didn't belong there. Maybe I didn't belong with people at all, not normal people. The unit was still there for me, and they had help available if I would just ask for it. But I didn't want help. I didn't deserve their help. The piss splashed into the toilet, sending little drops onto the flowery rug and my shins. Fuck. I needed to do something and I knew it.

I called Liam. He had been back from Fort Lewis for a while. I should have called him earlier; I knew he could help me, but I was in my shell. He picked up on the first ring, excited to talk to me for the first time since we'd both gotten home. He insisted that I come out to Suds & Suds, the pub across the street from the Corvallis Armory.

I threw my clothes into the same white Toyota Corolla that held my books and art supplies and headed down. The bar was connected to a laundromat on one side and a pizza place on the other—a hugely successful enterprise in a college town—and it always kept an open corner for the military guys. The taps of close to fifty different microbrews were lined up behind the polished wooden bar. Cards were given to repeat customers, and you'd get a stamp for each type of beer you drank. Faded Polaroids were thumbtacked to a corkboard to commemorate the patrons who had drunk all fifty types of beers, but there hadn't been any new pictures put up since Bravo Company deployed, despite several attempts.

I walked into the joint and my eyes took a couple seconds to adjust to the dark, but when they did I saw Liam sitting in the corner with Sergeant First Class Leroy Williamson and Sergeant Jason Hosford. Liam waved at the bartender for another pint glass, and before I had sat down my beer was poured.

Leroy and Jason had been wounded in two separate events. An IED hit Leroy up near Taji, and Jason had been shot through the knee on a patrol ten miles out of Najaf. Hugs all around. The bubbles in my pint floated to the surface, and for the first time in too long the world made sense. I loved these men instantly, not because of their charming personalities but because we shared something no one else in the world could understand. This feeling had nothing to do with words; it was fully realized by proximity alone. We were war-injured mutts from the same battles, and we immediately drank to our brothers who didn't make it.

We started talking about our wounds, as if the stories were seeds that with care and cultivation would grow into something fantastic. Williamson showed us a pressure sock covering the lumpy, burn-scarred skin. He would have to wear it for the rest of his life. We all smiled and hit him in the shoulder. It was a scar he could be proud of.

Jason rolled his right pant leg up to his thigh, showing us a shiny pink patch of skin where a bullet had entered his knee after it ricocheted off a wall and then tumbled through his leg behind his patella. Then he showed us the exit wound: a bigger shiny pink patch with white lines radiating out like a crater on the moon.

Without a second's hesitation, Liam pulled his shirt over his head and turned to show the five-inch purple gash across his back. With a giant smile, he craned his neck to see the reactions on our faces. We laughed and nodded. I had never seen anything so grotesque and yet so beautiful.

"They're going to put in a prosthetic shoulder blade next week. You know, so it doesn't indent in so much," he yelled, more to the bar than to the three of us. He knew that women love scars, especially scars on a wounded soldier, and there were a couple coeds in the room.

My turn came up, and I showed them how when I moved the thumb on my right hand I could make the tight skin over the missing muscle in my forearm dance back and forth. I said that maybe I would get a hula dancer tattooed there. The four scars on my arm and a silver-dollar-sized one on my knee were big and ugly enough to be proud of, but my best scar came from when the back of my uniform had caught fire from the engulfed Humvee. I wouldn't have shown them sober, because it happened to be right above my ass crack, but since I had already drunk a couple pints I stood on my chair and pulled my pants down a couple inches. The burnt skin had been torn away when B dragged me over the hot asphalt to the stretcher, leaving a shiny dark-brown patch of scarring the size of a claymore mine in the center of my back. The jagged brown skin was surrounded by a series of shrapnel wounds from the second blast. Tiny pieces of red-hot metal had torn through the skin of my lower back below my flak vest.

I stood on my chair with my pants halfway down my ass, looking back at the three of them. They busted up laughing. "What? What is it?"

None of them could catch their breath for almost a whole minute, until Liam, pointing at me, finally said, "It looks like you splatter-shit your pants."

I laughed harder than they did while zipping and buckling. I yelled across the room, "I went to combat in Operation Iraqi Freedom and all I got was this shit stain!"

Tears came to our eyes and ran down our cheeks. We laughed hard and loud, maybe to defy death, maybe because we were scared of it. The bartender came over, but instead of asking us to keep it down he brought us a pitcher of beer on the house and told us some OSU student in the ROTC program had already bought our next one.

The conversation came around to the guys who were still over there, and how we should do whatever we could to help them out when they got back. Leroy leaned forward and said we should call ourselves the Blasted Bastards. I agreed. I agreed to most everything they said all night, even when I realized that because Leroy was a sergeant first class, he had the connections to actually make our little club more than just drunk talk at the pub.

The more we drank, the grander our plans became. We would start a website and talk to business owners about getting the guys jobs, and talk to schools about getting the guys enrolled, and talk to renters about getting the guys places to live. Before we knew it, we would be on *Oprah*, starting programs to memorialize all our fallen brothers. We dreamed about skate parks, fire engines, high schools, and college scholarships named after our fallen brothers. We would make sure no one forgot their names, and we would make damn well sure the returning soldiers were fixed up right.

Then we talked about the problems we were having. We came to the conclusion that real life was harder than war. In combat you have two things to worry about: the welfare of your men and completing the mission. Back home we had to deal with work, rent, bills, and relationships. We all agreed it was a shame that a relationship couldn't be fixed by shooting someone, and laughed. No one gets us, we said. Civilian life is shit and no one can understand that, no one but the Blasted Bastards. I told them about the piss jug ending my relationship and they all took my side. Not one of them could even fathom her argument. If I wanted to piss on the couch and then light it on fire, well, that was my right as a combat veteran. Liam told me there was an extra couch in his basement and I would stay at his place. We talked and drank for another hour, until Vinnie's wife called and said she was coming to pick him up. She announced herself with a honk from the parking lot, and Jason left with them. I watched Liam smile as he talked to a coed he must have already shown his scar to once or twice. After fifteen minutes, the four of us started back to his place. Liam and Williamson hung on each other and spoke in low, familiar words that I paid little attention to since I was having a hard time working my legs.

I had lost my equilibrium and my car keys, but still barely held on to my pride until I started retching in the bushes in front of Liam's house. I went at it until my stomach was empty, and then a bit longer. My thoughts flowed from one subject to another between fits. I thought of how nice my body was for getting rid of the poison I had fed it all night. Then I imagined what Oprah would say if she saw me on all fours in my buddy's yard, yakking up bar pretzels and craft beer.

Liam stood on the lawn only a few feet away. What a great guy. He was tending to me again instead of to the coed he'd brought home. He sent her inside to the kitchen for more beer. "You okay?" he asked.

"Sorry," I said.

"Ah, I'll spray it down in the morning. Let's go inside. Cold as hell out here." He gave himself a half-hug with his good arm, rubbing the triceps of his bad one.

I stood up, swayed a bit, and wiped my mouth with the sleeve of my sweatshirt.

"Better?" Liam asked.

"Got a headache and my arm hurts." I looked at the clear sky and thought of the stars back at Anaconda coming off the helicopter. "You ever feel guilty for coming back?"

"I've got pills for that inside." He patted me on the back to move me in the direction of the front door.

I didn't know which condition he had pills for, and he never clarified. He disappeared into his room with the girl. I moved slowly and deliberately down the stairs to the basement. The extra couch sat on the cold concrete between the Ping-Pong table and the washer/dryer set. I shooed off a sixty-pound golden retriever so I could lie down.

A Bright, Shining Star Is Born, Then Fades Out Completely

Inside a week, the Blasted Bastards became more than drunk talk at the pub. Leroy had spoken to some high-ranking staff officer at MILDEP, the State of Oregon Military Department, and this great idea spread like fire after an artillery attack.

Who didn't like the idea of becoming a celebrity while helping the civilian population of our state support the troops? The hole that 9/11 left in people had changed into a need to support the troops, a need that could not be met by magnetic yellow ribbons and bumper stickers.

I had my own emptiness from the shame and guilt over Simon's death, and traveling around the state talking to small-town business bureaus, city councils, and high schools seemed like it would help. Plus, there is no worse existence than that of an infantryman with no mission and no troops to look after, and as much as I didn't want to be an infantryman anymore, I had no choice until Bravo Company came home. The Blasted Bastards deployed all over the state, flying in the governor's personal helicopter only a week after their drunken inception.

Three weeks into our tour, Liam, Jason, and I had just spoken to the chamber of commerce of the city of Burns, Oregon, population 3,020, explaining the benefits of employing veterans. Leroy couldn't make it to this appearance. He was busy trying to further our cause by talking to the big brass and meeting with a historian who was writing a book about our battalion. After our presentation, I stepped into the helicopter, sat down in the plush, comfortable seat with a homemade quilt on my lap, and waited for the pilot.

We were each given a quilt made by a group of army wives in the Harney County Women's Club. Mine was stitched in a pattern they called "crazy." This meant each square was made up of different-sized scraps of all kinds of shapes sewn together, with only the color of the scraps creating the pattern. Across my lap lay a blue field with white stars next to stripes of white and red, made especially for me. It was entitled *The Crazy Patriot*, it had my name and rank sewn onto it in the corner, and it was by far the best gift I had received from anyone for going to war, including the medals the army had given me.

My cell phone vibrated in the pocket of my desert camouflage uniform. I pulled it out to look, but I knew who it was. Jaime wanted to know how the talk went and what newspaper the article would appear in. She had started a scrapbook for me. How cute. I ignored her call and put my phone back in my pocket. Then I pulled out a flask from another pocket and an orange pill bottle from a third. I washed down a couple ten-milligram oxycodone tablets with a swallow of Johnny Walker Red.

A week and a half later, I sat in the turret of a Humvee for the first time since Iraq. Liam sat next to me and Jason drove, the head of a long line of floats and classic cars. We were the grand marshals of the Philomath Frolic Rodeo Parade. The Humvee had a shiny coat of red, white, and blue paint that displayed shooting stars and a wind-whipped flag. Big yellow-and-red letters on each door read *Oregon National Guard – Defending Freedom* over a giant 1-800 number. The Humvee was up-armored.

Jason coasted down the main street at five miles an hour. Screaming, smiling children ran alongside waving small American flags. I stared into the upturned helmet on my lap that was filled with red, dark blue, and purple Jolly Ranchers.

Liam nudged me with his elbow and said with a big smile, "Throw some candy to the kids — you'll feel better."

A week later, I stood just offstage behind a giant brown curtain that smelled like Elmer's glue and gym socks in the auditorium of Walker Middle School, the third stop on our tour of the Salem-Keizer Public School circuit. The principal had wanted to drag out our talk for a whole period, so they had Liam, Jason and I speak in succession. Liam was onstage talking about how hot it was in Iraq and how much he missed his family back home while he was over there.

I pulled the curtain back just enough to peek out at the schoolkids in the theater chairs. The first twenty-five rows were filled with third, fourth, and fifth graders, and to my surprise many of them were actually paying attention. Sure, some were pulling lint out of their belly buttons or sticking fingers in different holes in their heads, and others laughed with the kid in the next seat, but just about half watched Liam walking excitedly back and forth onstage, giving his spiel. I was up next and only needed to talk for five to seven minutes, but I didn't know what the hell to tell these kids. I never did. At the other two schools I stood in the background and let Liam and Jason do the talking, but this time I was up next.

Major Donald Stern stood next to me, looking sharp in his Class A uniform, his perpetual smile, and his perfect hair, nodding periodically throughout Liam's speech. He was the conductor of this orchestra, the host of this game show. He was the guy who booked our gigs. Leroy had handed Major Stern the ball, and Stern was scoring touchdown after touchdown with the media.

Jaime loved the whole thing. She said that I could use this opportunity to talk about how I really felt and what I really thought. Her naiveté was cute, but I knew she really wanted me to use my platform to say what *she* thought about the war. I wasn't against the war. I knew the men in my unit were trying to help people over there.

I felt like shit. The one thing I had accomplished in my life was my most painful memory. My day job now was to smile, nod, and display the medals on my uniform. The one people wanted to see the most, of course, had the same profile of George Washington as the quarter in that goddamn stupid coin toss.

Major Stern's whisper startled me when he leaned over. "They love Liam, huh?"

I sighed and squinted like I was looking at Liam from a great distance. "Yeah."

"Jason did a great job too."

I nodded while staring at the reflection of the stage lights around Liam's desert combat boots.

He put his right hand on my shoulder. "But the thing is, neither of them really touched on a subject these children probably want to hear about. I'm sure their parents want to hear about it too."

I looked at him because I knew he expected me to. "What's that, sir?"

"Well, when you go out there, try to talk about the good points of war. You know, the camaraderie, the fun." He smiled.

"Sorry, sir. What?"

He doubled his well-meaning enthusiasm, and in a loud whisper that turned to a yell over the growing applause, he said again,

"Listen, all they and their parents see are the bad things on the five o'clock news. Tell them about the good things. You helped people, right?"

He walked onstage as Liam walked off, and I kept staring at where he had stood. I couldn't do it. Even if I weren't so hungover or so clouded with drugs, or feeling so much self-pity, my mind still wouldn't have been in the right place.

Major Stern introduced me and I shuffled out under the bright lights, feeling the heat on my cheeks and forehead. I limped to center stage and took the microphone from the stand, surrounded by a near-silence broken only by a sniffle here or a cough there. Hundreds of pudgy little faces focused on me with wide eyes, and the scene struck me. Suddenly, I knew I was standing in the middle of a memory I would never forget: those little faces that hadn't even grown out of their baby fat, looking to me for something. Little empty vessels desperate to be filled with whatever anyone poured into their heads. That was the moment I made the connection. Infantry: the root word is *infant*. We send our children to war and when they come back they are something else. Not children at all.

I stood looking down at the lights reflecting off the stage under my combat boots. I heard the snickers and low whispering slowly growing. I took a deep breath and spoke directly into the microphone with a low voice, which erupted into feedback before my words came booming over the speakers. "I wanted to be an artist when I grew up."

Their laughter took me completely by surprise, but after a second I chuckled a bit too. "I did, really." I let them laugh until they were done, it was such a beautiful sound. "You know, wars happen for reasons no one understands. Not even the people fighting them know why. I mean, I sometimes they think they know, but…" I trailed off, and for a while there was only the low buzzing of the PA system.

I looked up and scanned their faces. "We should be kinder. If you ever find yourself in a very bad place, make sure you do what you can to try and make people's lives better. I guess that's my message, if I am supposed to have one: be a good person…ah…" My mouth hung open and no more words came out. I didn't know what else to say. "Ah, fuck. I'm sorry."

I fumbled putting the microphone back on the stand and then walked offstage. I made it behind the curtain before one of the teachers started an awkward, unsure clapping that led to the children's applause. I walked past Major Stern and mumbled into my chest that I couldn't do this anymore. When I pushed open the double doors to the parking lot, the light burned my eyes. I walked to my white Toyota Corolla and drove away.

Half of *60 Minutes*

Jaime had been so encouraging of my media tour; she saw it as a sign of maturity. In her eyes I was serious about putting myself back together and fixing our relationship. I was tired of sharing a couch with a golden retriever, so I moved back into the Big Brown House.

I had driven there from the middle school fiasco, only stopping at the liquor store for some cheap whiskey. Later that night, when Liam called me with our next week's schedule, I told him to win the hearts and minds without me. If anyone else had a problem with that, he could give them my number. A week went by and I didn't hear from anyone.

Since I was still convalescing and going through physical rehabilitation a few days a week, the military still paid me like a full-time soldier. Leaving the PR tour meant that I should have answered phones, filed paperwork, or swept floors at the armory Monday through Friday, but since quitting worked so well, I decided not to go there either.

Jaime didn't talk to me for a few days. I wasn't the smartest guy around, but I saw the pattern: our relationship seemed to hinge on my public speaking engagements or newspaper articles. Damned if I knew whether we loved each other or not. If we did, it was an unhealthy type of love. She always remarked that I never showed emotions and that she might as well be in a relationship with a robot—an alcoholic, pill-popping robot. She said these things to make me angry, to get a reaction, but I didn't react at all until finally I would blow up. This brought out the worst in her—the venom-spitting, hate-spewing worst. Then I raged. These late-night battles resulted in breaking, throwing, and cursing, and once I even punched a hole in the wall, which caused a big stir with the other roommates. Both of us forgot what little thing we were fighting about and pleaded with the roommates for an hour not to call the cops. That exciting night ended with an hour of great sex.

I enjoyed her like I enjoyed drinking good whiskey to excess, smoking way too many of my favorite cigarettes, or any other luxurious poison. Even our fights were fun for a while. The arguing became an amusing game, with strategies designed to verbally beat the other into submission. She loved to throw my words back at me and I loved to hang her with hers. She had gone from being the only person I could talk to about my feelings to the only person who would let me treat her badly, and she gave it right back. I took it.

What we had was broken and neither of us wanted to fix it. For a while it didn't seem like anything could, so when a producer from 60 Minutes called me asking if I they could interview me for a story, I answered yes without hesitation. When the producer asked me if I had a girlfriend or a wife I said yes, I had a fiancée who had helped me get back home after I'd spent months in an army hospital in Texas. The producer said it would add a real human element, something the average American could relate to.

When I called them back, a female producer asked me if I owned or rented my home, and I told her of my transitory situation. She asked if there was a nice park nearby where the crew could meet us the next morning.

Ten minutes before the assigned time, Jaime and I sat in my Corolla with the windows down. A convoy of black SUVs with black-tinted windows rolled in and assembled around us like we were rock stars. A pretty, thin woman with short brown hair and a tight-fitting turtleneck told me the crew had been in Oregon for a few days and had already interviewed the general, the highest-ranking army officer in the state of Oregon. She said it without much respect attached, like it was just another day for her.

I shook her hand while half a dozen other people in tight sweaters or expensive coats buzzed around us. One of the guys clicked a small machine in the air and talked about how bright it was; another said any sound they got in the park would be shit. Television types moved fast and with purpose.

The woman spoke, and although her accent wasn't like a New Yorker's I could tell it was East Coast metropolitan. She said that we would do the actual interview at my house, but they wanted to get some film of my fiancée and me walking around the park with the ducks swimming in the background. She said she knew from the military department that I was injured, and told me if I limped that would be "okay, not a problem at all."

The lighting guy, producer, audio tech, and all her assistants swarmed around us off camera while Jaime and I walked through the park hand in hand for the first time ever. They told us to smile and talk about something warm and intimate. The people at home would see us and hear ambient sounds but not our words, so it was important for us to appear happy. So we did. And we were. All the bitter, ugly stuff melted away and Jaime let her guard down, and I saw her dimples again like I used to before heading off to war. And even though our conversation was faked, she would wait for my words to end without interrupting me. We made eye contact. At first it was only because the woman in the tight sweater told us to, but after a few moments I really did want to look into those big blue eyes.

Why had it been so hard before? It was so easy. Suddenly I thought it would be simple to have a beautiful relationship for years to come. All we needed was a small group of people with the proper instruments to keep all the conditions perfect while giving us directions and whispering encouragement as they crouched and scuttled beside us just off-screen.

I stopped and put my hand to her face, partly because I felt it would be a good conclusion to the scene, but also because I wanted to feel her smile. Our faces inched closer until I felt her breath on my nose and mouth and then we kissed, not like a couple but like strangers. The cold autumn wind carried orange and red leaves through the air around us, the ducks were really swans, the clouds disappeared instantly, the world balanced out, and I felt myself getting an erection.

No one said cut but the producer did tell the crew to wrap it up. Within a minute's time our audience was gone, and we went from the inspiration of Middle America to just plain Sean and Jaime. But not all of the magic had worn off. Jaime called her roommates and asked them to leave for a while so we could film the interview. We all loaded up and convoyed to the Big Brown House.

Steve Kroft was certainly treated like royalty. He didn't get out of the suv until everything was set up around the dining room table. This made me realize he had been there at the park, too. I wondered if he had been watching.

His eyes were filled with as much compassion as the Buddha's, and he had the weathered face of a pugilist twenty years past his prime, with vibrant brown hair feathered and parted down the middle. The second he sat down across from me, he stuck his hand out with a humble smile. He said he was happy to meet me and truly appreciated my service and sacrifice. His flattery worked perfectly, and in seconds I felt a deep need to not disappoint this man.

The interview started with small questions asking what unit I was with, how long I'd been in the military, how many deployments I'd had, and so on. The mood turned a bit when we started to talk about the equipment. Steve Kroft was very interested in the fact that we had to buy our own radios from sporting goods stores. He played out this tangent of disbelief for a while, and at its crest he asked me if Simon would still be alive if we were driving in an up-armored Humvee that day.

I hesitated to break up such a good conversation. I wanted to be Steve Kroft's buddy, and a real Humvee during combat operations should have been a no-brainer, but saying something like that could have gotten me into a shitload of trouble. Plus, Simon's head and shoulders would still have been exposed even in an up-armored Humvee. Saying yes to his questions seemed to me like turning on the boys still overseas. I couldn't do it, so I told him I didn't know.

He paused to let me know my answer caught him off guard, which is to say it was wrong. I sighed and swallowed while he steered the conversation back to something friendly for a while. Right when I got comfortable and thought we were buddies again, he asked if I had any issues with the deployment. Where to start? How about the fact that every FOB had a fucking Burger King but we had to steal machine gun mounts from other units? There was also what the army called our "intelligence," and don't get me started on PowerPoint maps. I had so much to say. I went into the story of how we couldn't test-fire our weapons before a mission because supposedly we didn't have enough bullets, but the wax bullets they gave us to use in Kuwait must have cost three or four times what a regular bullet would have cost. Then, of course, there was the air-conditioned trailer in the middle of the desert on a brand-new firing range. Every soldier can bitch about the army, but a great one doesn't. I was still depressed and feeling low about a lot of things. I shouldn't have done it, but I was on a roll. Then he cut me off and asked me again if Simon would still be alive if we had been in an up-armored Humvee.

This confused me greatly. Maybe he forgot he had already asked the question. I waited for a second or two and told him again there was no way of knowing. This time his calm demeanor buckled for just the briefest moment, and he looked over to his producer. He took a small breath and smiled, bringing the conversation around to how the army had stuck me in Texas. I went off, talking about the broke-dick platoon, the ridiculous attempted murder charge, and anything else I could throw in. I let it all out and Steve Kroft nodded with soft eyes throughout my entire rant. He understood. We were good friends. Then he leaned in, the definition of empathy, and asked me in a low, soft voice, "Do you think your good friend Simon would be alive today if you were driving in an up-armored Humvee?"

Didn't he know that every time he asked me that question I saw the image of my dead friend in the back of that flaming truck? "I don't know. Too many factors. Insurgents killed my friend Simon, not the government or my chain of command."

Steve Kroft thanked me for my time and shook my hand, and within minutes the television crew was gone. One of the producers gave me an email address and said they'd be in touch. He took down my address and told me they would send me a couple copies of the show, before it even aired.

I sat at the kitchen table staring at the dying houseplants on the blue tile counter with the producer's card in my right hand. Jaime leaned over and kissed the side of my head. She told me how proud she was, and then asked if I would I drink any tea if she made it.

The show would air around mid-November, and it would send me into a complete mental breakdown. But until that time, Jaime and I tried the best we could to live like the producers and the crew were still there, just off camera, telling us to talk to each other about trivial things, smile and make eye contact, pretend to listen, and act like we were happy.

I spent most nights at the pub, where I usually bumped into Liam and Jason, and amongst the college kids Jell-O-shooting their way to heaven we spoke about the latest places Major Stern had sent them. If they didn't have any girls with them they were on the hunt for a couple. One night they introduced me to Reanne, a short girl with sandy-blonde hair pulled back in a ponytail under a plaid Windsor hat, the type a poor Irishman would wear to go golfing.

She leaned forward when I took out a crumpled pack of Pall Malls and asked for one, so I put one in my mouth and lit it before passing it over. She leaned way back in her chair with full control over which way the curves of her body fell. Her breasts stretched the old logo of a soda company on her tight pink T-shirt. It said *Crush*. I coughed and sipped my pint. "How do you know Liam and Jason?"

The question changed her completely. She sat up and closed her coat, hiding the good parts.

"They were in Iraq with my fiancé."

"No shit."

She told me Alex Burkert had asked her to marry him before heading downrange. Alex was a rifleman in Cederman's squad. I told her I knew him well and started in on a story. Alex had this cherub-like face and golden locks. He reminded me of Ganymede in Greek mythology, the beautiful shepherd boy abducted by Zeus, and although the Iraqis may not have studied the same myths, they thought like Zeus did. Many of the Iraqi men flirted with him constantly. I told him it was a compliment, and he might have thought it funny at first, but after a while he felt he needed to do something to look manlier, so he started chewing tobacco. The problem was that he kept swallowing the juice and making himself sick. Burkert puked after almost every mission for a month.

We laughed and talked about him for a while longer. Before lighting her next cigarette, she asked, "So you were on *60 Minutes*. What was that like?"

"Yeah, it'll be on next week. Have you heard from Alex lately?"

Her eyes closed slowly for a second, then rolled over to the bar where Liam and Jason were ordering our drinks.

"Yeah. He said they're heading to some big city in the west to relieve some Marines or something."

"Fallujah?"

"Yeah, I think so." Her face scrunched and her attention flitted across the dance floor. "I hate the music here. Seriously, play one good song, huh?"

"Yeah." I smiled back at her.

She wasn't beautiful, but she wasn't unattractive, either. She didn't have any features that stuck out other than the ones stretching her T-shirt, but she had the confidence that came from being the center of our collective attention, and that was enough to make her sexy. And she needed to feel sexy. She told me later that night that all she had done for the last six months was worry about Alex every second of the day. Going out with Liam and Jason had made her feel close to Alex in some weird way, and at the same time it let her stop worrying. Liam and Jason told me it was like doing her a favor. Hell, in their minds they were doing Alex a favor, too, taking his girl out for a good time.

A few days later I was digging my fingers into the burlap-like fabric of the futon in the Big Brown House as all the roommates and some of their friends huddled around the television, excited to see someone they knew on a national show. The second hand on the big clock ticked away as the announcer talked over clips from the upcoming episode. The first half of the show was about Governor Arnold Schwarzenegger. I remember thinking that he was probably watching this episode and would end up seeing me on the television, which had to be some sort of irony since I'm sure the reason I went into the army in the first place had something to do with watching him.

All the roommates and their friends gave a kind of hurrah when my section of the show started. The story was about how our troops were being sent to war without the proper equipment. They interviewed the family of a soldier killed in combat, they interviewed John McCain, they interviewed the head general in Oregon, and then they interviewed me. By the time I was on, it looked like I wanted revenge for how the military fucked up my life and killed my friend. At the crescendo of the interview, Steve Kroft asked me, "Would Simon be alive today if you were driving an up-armored Humvee?"

The camera cut to me looking confused and not answering, then black — commercial time.

The sound bites they had used led the room of liberal college students to the conclusion that I believed some big American War Machine had wronged me. They cheered, patted me on the back, and threw around words like "war hero." All the girls looked at me with admiration, wiping away tears. Even Trent, who had by this time undoubtedly used his deductive reasoning skills to conclude that it was me who had purposely killed his houseplants, patted me on the back in a display of sympathy and solidarity.

At the end of the show, the editors had decided to roll credits over Jaime and me walking happily in front of a duck pond at the park on a fall day. The music played over the muted scene, but the viewers saw an all-American boy and his gal joking and flirting—fade to black.

I didn't say a word. There wasn't anything to say. I had let down the only people on the planet I was able to make myself care about. If I could have dug my fingers into my chest and pulled out my own heart, I might have. I wasn't anti-army. I wasn't anti-government. I didn't really know what I was, but I did know I wasn't that kid on the television with all those complaints walking through the park. That night, all the rigging in my head collapsed. Instead of believing I was caring too little for real life, I decided that my problems came from caring too much. I called Francisco Cabra in Portland. He and I had been roommates during art school, and I was sure he'd let me stay with him again. I didn't really have anywhere else to go. I hadn't called my parents or brothers since the first week I was back, and I had ignored their calls.

Francisco paused in thought for a while. He said it would be crowded, but he could use the lower rent. I could move into the basement of the house he was renting. In the time it took me to pick up my clothes off Jaime's floor and stuff them into my A bag, I was gone.

Committed

Francisco liked to say he lived on top of the only active volcano within a US metropolitan area. I don't know how true that was, but his house did sit only a few blocks from the park on Mount Tabor in the middle of Southeast Portland. The row of houses on Belmont and Sixty-Ninth were built in 1902 for the poor people who worked on the rail line that used to run from downtown all the way to Eighty-Second Street.

Before Francisco rented the small two-bedroom place, an old woman with a great fear of what lay beyond her walls had lived there. She'd had someone bar the windows, doors, and every other portal to the outside world. Once inside, it was easy to become cramped and to feel cut off from the rest of humanity. We called it the Asylum.

When I pulled up, Francisco and his roommate Andy were wrestling a five-foot Christmas tree through the door. Andy was around my age, clean-shaven and pale. He fought wildland fires for the state during the late spring, summer, and early fall, but lived on unemployment and sold a little pot or coke during the off-season. He stayed in one of the two small bedrooms connected to the living room. Francisco stayed in an even smaller room by the kitchen, so small he had taken the door off the hinges to be able to fit his bed in it. The close quarters made it so I couldn't sleep in the living room, but they did have a basement I could share with the water heater, insects of different sizes, and weeds that squeezed through the cracked foundation.

The two of them had rearranged boxes of old *Rolling Stone* magazines, engine parts, paint cans, and a bunch of other shit to make me a living space in the middle of the cement-and-brick basement. Then they helped me carry down the stairs a futon frame that I bought at the Goodwill. Since the living conditions were less than ideal, I would only be charged two hundred and fifty dollars rent a month. I wrote them a check and suddenly had a place of my own for the first time since my shitty apartment in Albany. I had no problem staying there, I told myself. I had slept in worse places.

The party started that night and became a lifestyle. The Asylum attracted all types, every night. They were the service-industry crowd, the shit-job crowd, the in-between-jobs crowd. Francisco decided that he and I would be artists, and Andy would be a DJ who sold drugs. Our house was filled every night. The rabble made the trek up the hill, with meager amounts of money, to buy plastic sandwich bags full of artificial happiness. Most would smoke in the living room or do a line in our bathroom. I found an audience that would really listen to my war stories no matter how many times I repeated them. Every once in a while a smackhead would show up, but we didn't socialize with them. Whenever we caught someone nodding off from heroin, we kicked them out and watched them stagger away until they were gone.

We all knew it wasn't the best existence. Shit, that was probably everyone's favorite conversation. But it wasn't bad, either. We shared the tendency to abuse drugs and alcohol, and there was a type of kinship there, a way to fill the hole. I let go and fell in with the freaks, the hipsters, the musicians, the underground artists, the street taggers, the lost, the forgotten, the absolute bastards, the metalheads, the stoners, the tweakers, and the strippers.

I was the only one with a constant stream of extra money. The army was paying me during this time of rehabilitation and convalescence, and I had no problem spending it on all on vice and debauchery. Because I bought the drinks, no one minded sharing the pot, the shrooms, the pills, or the coke. Days were replaced by cycles of consciousness that sometimes lasted two or three nights, sometimes only a few hours. I slipped outside of time and wondered why I had ever lived inside it. I dove so far into this flophouse lifestyle that I hardly recognized myself beneath the dark circles and patchy beard. The army hadn't called, so I must have fallen through the cracks. I knew sooner or later they would catch up to me, but I didn't do anything to change.

When the up-drugs carried me, we went to the store and bought tubes of oil paint, linseed oil, paint thinner, and giant secondhand masterpieces at the Goodwill to gesso over. We'd score a four-foot canvas for ten bucks, and all we had to do was paint over an ugly rendition of Monet's *Water Lilies* or some god-awful coastal scene. I bought many smaller canvasses as well and furiously painted them. I painted in the vein of Goya, Dalí, and Munch, except that what I painted was undisciplined, hastily applied, and honestly not very good. Most of my paintings were my representations of myths; I was hoping a girl would be impressed with how smart I was when I explained a piece to her. Sisyphus, Damocles, Icarus, the giant King Nimrod with half his body and one arm stuck in the ice floor of hell. None of them were great, but they were good enough to get me into some stoned chick's pants for a night or two.

Sex is a great way to forget your problems, just as good as the drink or drugs. I was doing all I could to avoid the nagging thought that I hadn't spoken to June yet. I hadn't spoken to Simon's mother or father. I didn't want to remember that I hadn't written a letter to my squad, who were still in the middle of a war. They had it so much worse in the months after I left. Then there were the Blasted Bastards. I hadn't talked to them in...how long?

One day in early December I sprang awake from a nightmare and found myself next to a small girl with orange hair and the flag of Ireland tattooed across her back. Cold light came down the stairs, so it was either morning or evening. I couldn't see her face, either in the physical world or in my memory, but her hair, my God, was tangerine-orange. My bladder was straining and I needed ibuprofen, so I slowly moved from under the covers to get up and immediately felt that I had shit myself. Not much of it made it outside my boxers, but what was there stuck to my ass and the back of my legs.

Vague facts came back to me about the night before. I had met the orange-haired girl at a seedy strip bar on Hawthorne Boulevard. She told me her name was Lylith, spelled with a Y. I couldn't take my eyes off the fangs in her mouth as she spoke. She told me that her uncle was a dentist and had given her the vampire teeth for only a couple hundred dollars. She felt she had gotten a great deal and repeated this fact many times.

I slowly and carefully moved from the bed to the floor. The concrete was so cold it burned my ass and calves. The shit had little smell, but the room had an aroma like alcohol and body odor mixed with the scent of acetone coming from a cracked and stained mason jar that sat on a table in front of an easel. On the canvas, a man stripped of skin floated above flames shaped like damned souls. He looked up at a blinding light he would never ascend to, his arms open wide.

Lylith said it reminded her of a mix between the album art on her Tool CDs and the woodcarvings for Dante's *Divine Comedy*. I took that to mean she wanted to sleep with me.

Sitting in a pain coma with my boxers filled with whatever poisons I had put in my body the day before, it seemed like a good moment to examine my life. I had no structure and no purpose. What was I doing, really? Would I decide to do something about this behavior or just keep hiding in bottles, pills, and strippers? Fighting in Iraq had given me an inflated ego, like I had done something important. The fucked-up part about all that was that I had done that job extraordinarily well. Back home everyone treated me like some sort of hell-broke hero. No one knew what to do with a combat vet unraveling right in front of them, not even the guys at the armory. Sergeant Stimpson would have been completely right to send the MPs after me and force me to come to drill, but I was taking full advantage of his kindness by simply not showing up. I was taking their money, but I was AWOL. My friends, family, and army brothers didn't know what to say to stop me, so I decided to see how far I could go with it. Fuck it—even if I killed myself from drinking too much, I figured I should have been dead already anyway.

Beams creaked overhead, letting me know that several people upstairs were awake. Carefully, I slid the soiled underwear off and used the outside to clean myself. I dug through a pile of clothes to find some cutoff BDU pants and hid my boxers behind the water heater. A second later, someone upstairs turned on some industrial metal. A couple people yelled, like a drink had been spilled. Lylith rolled over and blinked her black eyes open. She had a faded blue tattoo of a rose above her pink nipple.

"Hey," she said.

I sighed, but then smiled right away. "Time to get back to the party."

Dying the Hemingway

Every morning we collected dozens of bottles from every flat surface in the house and drove to the store for the deposit. We used that money to help pay for the next couple of twelve-packs and smokes. The party pushed food, clothes, and hygiene to the back of my mind, and soon I looked just like everyone else — scruffy facial hair, jeans with holes in the knees, dirty shirts, and dark circles under my eyes.

We celebrated Christmas Eve by sitting in the living room around our dying tree, more pine needles on the floor than on the branches. Andy had scored some mushrooms and we each did a few lids. Francisco and I set to work painting on our biggest canvas yet, a five-footer he stretched himself. This was to be our epic piece, a giant crucifixion scene with Papa Smurf nailed to a cross, but it unraveled when the drugs kicked in and ended up as different globs of colors with varying textures. I dragged my brush so slowly across the canvas, watching each combat mission I ever did unfold in the color trail; it was like creating a motion picture. In the top corner I painted a copy of the PowerPoint map we were given the morning of the ambush: the blue squiggly lines of the river, the roads, the two small squares. Then I started with a shark swimming through the entire piece.

Behind us the house filled up with people too broke or too disillusioned to visit their real families, but I didn't have time to mingle. My masterpiece demanded all my attention. At some point Francisco left the painting and joined the party, but I couldn't stop. When I painted on hallucinogens, I became convinced my color blindness went away, and I didn't want to waste this opportunity to see everything as it had really happened. I kept painting and going back in my life. I painted the man I saw kicked to death in Haiti, my minimum-wage life before the army, my father and mother.

Hours went by, and the drugs wore off at the same rate as my enthusiasm for the piece. Francisco walked up right as I decided to take a break and told me Jaime was coming to the house. He'd invited her when he found out she had moved back up to Portland after graduating during winter term.

"What? Really?" I asked.

"Is it a problem?"

I thought about that. I hadn't talked to her since I'd left, but didn't know if it had been weeks or months ago. Did I care about her? I hadn't thought about it much, but I didn't want her to see me all strung out and looking like shit.

"I guess not, but why didn't you tell me earlier?" Francisco handed me a bottle of High Life. "I did—a few times."

I looked at the crowd clustered in small groups in our dark little living room: talking, drinking god-awful cheap beer, smoking joints. Then I looked down at myself: three dirty socks on each foot, still wearing the cutoff BDU bottoms, a tight thermal with holes under a stained T-shirt, matted hair, and different colors of paint up to my elbows. With this many people in the house, I couldn't take a shower in the one bathroom. I set my beer down on a speaker and started for my basement just as the door opened. She came in looking more beautiful than I remembered. Her attention fell on me first and she smiled. I tried to avoid a hug by telling her I didn't want to get paint on her, but I really just didn't want her to notice how bad I smelled.

"Hi. So, how are you doing?" she asked; she was in such a good mood. I didn't know it was possible. She had to be faking it to get at me, letting me know she wasn't having any problems getting over me. We hadn't seen each other since I'd left. This meeting shouldn't be cordial. There should have been some anger involved.

"Good, good. I'm painting." When I turned to explain the piece, I lost whatever I had seen in it before. I might as well have fed an elephant food coloring and had it shit on the canvas.

"Nice," she said, with those full dimples. I tried hard to read into that one-syllable word, to find out what she was really thinking.

"Why aren't you with your parents?" The words came out forcefully, like an accusation.

"We're going to have a big dinner tomorrow. I'm up here because I just signed a lease on a new apartment. The landlord agreed to meet me. I know it's Christmas Eve, but I was so excited. The place is in Northwest, right over a sushi restaurant." She told me she'd found a job downtown with a national nonprofit organization that helped refugees and funded micro-entrepreneurs trying to make the world a better place. The people she worked with were creative and dressed sharp. They had team lunches in bistros and talked intelligently for hours about politics and world affairs, even after work.

"That's awesome." Each of her successes made me feel worse, and she told me about every single one. She'd found a great roommate on Craigslist; the apartment was eco-certified green, built in the '50s but newly renovated. She loved living downtown, sharing the vitality, watching all the young professionals like herself.

"So, what have you been up to? Are you still in the army?" She asked like the words had no weight to them, like she had forgotten my problems.

I played her game and told her I'd been focusing on my art again and was very committed. I created a whole relationship with Lylith, omitting the fact that we were a one-night (or maybe two-night) stand. I didn't tell her that I dumped her after she bit me. Instead, I explained that I had to cut the relationship short because I had finally found myself and liked being alone. Besides, I needed to concentrate on painting. Oh man, life was amazing. I told her Francisco and I were working like madmen to get ready for our big art show at the end of the month.

"Where?" she asked.

I picked up my High Life from the speaker and sipped at it a couple times. "I forget the name of the place. It's a new pub in Southeast. Brews free-trade coffee."

"I hope I get an invitation." She saw me searching for something behind her and turned to see what it was, but even I didn't know. When I saw Andy I waved him over. He walked toward us, a little confused but happy.

"Of course." I took another sip. "Hey, I'm sorry. It's been great talking to you again. I kind of have to go, but here's my buddy Andy. He fights wildfires, he's a DJ, and he lives here, too."

I cut through the crowd, out the door, and into the front yard to light a cigarette. The light rain on the grass soaked through all three pairs of my socks when I moved to hide at the side of the house where the porch light didn't reach. I squatted next to the garbage. The music, laughter, and conversation went on; no one noticed my absence. I kicked the chain-link fence between the Asylum and our neighbor's house. I kicked it over and over again, then grabbed the chain links on top and jerked it back and forth without accomplishing anything.

Pearls before Swine

The va hospital in Portland, Oregon, sat on a hill much like an old castle would have in the medieval days. The cement walls were the color of the clouds and the windows reflected the sky, so most days the ten-story hospital blended into the sky. Oregon Health and Science University's hospital grounds gleamed in the sun only a half mile to the north on the same mountainside, making the va hospital look weather-stained and antiquated, which wasn't too far from reality.

I had received a mandatory appointment letter for a mental health consultation every time I had changed my address. *Returning vets are given priority,* it said, and *the Department of Veterans Affairs is doing everything it possibly can to focus on helping the new generation of war heroes.* Maybe the word "hero" was why I hadn't gone before. Either the word had changed definitions, or it was being thrown around loosely to describe anyone who went over. I blamed myself for Simon's death. I wasn't a hero. I didn't charge any machine gun nest, I didn't fireman-carry a man to safety, I didn't even fire back. Many times before trying to sleep I would go through the event again and replay it all. In most of these waking dreams I fired back with my rifle in my left hand, hitting the men who shot at us. The second explosion wouldn't go off, and I would turn to see Simon. He was knocked out, but came to and took cover beside me with that same goddamn half smile.

For some reason, when I got this latest letter I followed the directions on the appointment notice and drove deep into the dark, low-ceilinged parking garage of the facility. The mental health clinic was detached from the main hospital, underground in the cavernous structure between the areas where the staff and the patients parked. I found a spot out front and watched people walking in and out of the sliding glass door. There was no other department accessible from that sliding glass door, so I knew that anyone coming through it was in need of psychological help. Old, fat men with shiny coats or hats announcing the names of the ships they served on. They had gray hair and braided ponytails. They limped out leaning on canes. They looked a month away from a full funeral service with honors, complete with the triangle-folded flag and a plot on the hill. And all of them lit a cigarette the second the door slid shut behind them. Maybe that automatic glass was a time machine. I waited, convinced I would see my future self stumble out at any minute and light up a Pall Mall.

I thought of driving back down the hill and grabbing a pint at the Triple Nickel, but the memory of an orange-haired vampire doing a bump of coke off the coffee table in the Asylum stopped me. Then I thought about the fights I'd been purposely getting into down at the Belmont Inn. I was lucky no one had called the cops, but there was little doubt I'd lost control too many times. Chauncie, the doorman, wouldn't even let me in the place anymore.

Control. That was one of the words in my head. A soldier needed control. A soldier *craved* control. Without it there was just chaos and irrational behavior. Then I busted out in laughter. The hole theory Simon was talking about: he was right.

Gradually, I realized I wanted to kill myself. This surprised me. I didn't think I had it in me to be so lost, but this life was empty and hard. I had abandoned a job I took pride in, ignored my family, and lived in an unfinished basement that looked like some prison cell out of a Dumas novel. *Yeah*, I thought, *I wouldn't mind just being gone at this point.* I only wished that I could have died in combat instead of Simon; that way, my brothers would have gotten to split the four-hundred-thousand-dollar insurance payoff.

My foot revved the engine. That would be one way. Just back out of the parking spot, put it in drive, and gun it into the fucking wall. I visualized the steam shooting out of the radiator, the crumpled hood, and my body hanging over the steering wheel. I scanned the garage for anyone who might see or hear the squealing tires and the crash. I pictured an old, toothless veteran on the news with some fucking lady shoving a microphone in his face, trying to get him to say the right sound bite.

I was afraid of looking weak by asking for help. Asking for help was the hard part. Killing myself would be easy. Unless it wasn't. What if I survived? How did institutionalization sound? And if I *were* able to kill myself, who would get stuck with paying for the funeral?

With quick and violent motions I turned the engine off, jerked myself out of the car, put my head down, and started walking to the clinic. Maybe the time machine worked both ways; maybe it could send me to a time when I was able to care about something.

The lobby only had old issues of either *Better Homes and Gardens* or *ESPN The Magazine*. This pissed me off. I sat between a Korean War vet drooling into his beard and a geriatric seaman who smelled of ashes and egg salad. This pissed me off. On the wall hung black-and-white portraits of smiling men and women who, according to their typed italic testimonials, had sought and received help in some VA mental hospital somewhere. This pissed me off the most. How the hell did they get their shit together when I was falling to pieces? They were all fakers. They probably didn't see any real shit.

A woman who could not have been five feet tall but was definitely over two hundred fifty pounds called my name. Her fat rolls stacked on top of each other and pulled at the buttons of her small blue pants suit. She stood there smiling at me, her face a giant, doughy sphere with regular skinny-person hair all sprayed up like she had been wearing it the same way since the height of the Reagan years. Small little sausage fingers covered in gold rings reached to shake my hand. Big gold dangling earrings and a pearl necklace made her seem like a small Christmas tree. Maybe a bushy, round Douglas fir.

She said she was pleased to meet me, and maybe she genuinely was, but I knew immediately that even if she had the cure to all my problems corked in a vial I wouldn't have swallowed it. I immediately decided not to let this woman help me, and to make this visit end badly.

I stared deep into the highly waxed floor while following her down the long white hall to her office. The shine reflected every fluorescent light in the place but wasn't deep enough for me to see anything of my reflection other than a blur.

Her office was bureaucratic in function and usage, right down to the decorated frames of family members propped up against office supplies on the desk. She motioned for me to sit in the ergonomic chair, complete with lumbar support. I plopped down under a motivational poster showing a man standing atop a snowy mountain peak. Under the picture was the word *Achievement* and a quote from Theodore Roosevelt: "It is hard to fail, but it is worse never to have tried to succeed."

Ha, I thought, *it is very easy to fail. I've been doing it for months now.*

I couldn't drag my eyes to look at her. Instead, I stared at the corner of her wooden desk, picked at a hangnail, or coughed into my shirt. She smiled at me and I resented her for it. Her kindness infuriated me. There was no doubt I had made a mistake by coming in. If this hack were halfway decent at helping people with brain problems, she wouldn't be morbidly obese. All I needed was some time—time away from the drink, the drugs, the girls. If I could plan and execute combat missions in a hostile foreign land, I knew I could fix whatever the hell was wrong with me.

She started in with her credentials and the highlights of her career, but I didn't hear them. It was more than not listening; this was an intentional erasure of every word. I deleted her name and qualifications immediately after they left her spit-glistened pink lips. I needed to get out of her office, but I wasn't in combat anymore; there were rules, rules I had to follow, rules that said I couldn't just spring up, throw the door open, and leave.

"Your file says you were in combat. I read you were injured. That must have been horrible," she said, her little hands resting like piglets in her lap.

"IED in Taji. Killed one of my best friends." I said it without hesitation. My words were meant to slap her in the face.

"My God, that's horrible." She turned to her desk and opened a thick manila folder. I wondered what else about me was in there. I hadn't seen any head doctor enough to have a folder that thick. Her gaze bounced from left to right as she flipped through the pages.

I continued in a loud, monotone voice, "The IED flipped my Humvee six feet in the air, killing one of my best friends instantly. Then the motherfuckers opened up with automatic machine-gun fire, pinning my driver and me behind flaming wreckage. I remember the bullets bouncing around me. I remember looking down at my blood-soaked sleeve and mangled arm." I said every word to punish her for not being there. I wanted to shame her for being a part of the society that sent me to die, sent my friend to die.

"There was a second explosion that tore through the muscle and bone of another of my friends, crushing his shoulder blade to nothing. I watched him fly across the asphalt and land without moving. I thought they'd killed him, too. Then mortars falling from the sky crashed through the pavement around us. Everything was on fire, every movement pain. Simon's helmet rocked upside down at my feet, filled with blood. Half his fucking head was blown off. Now, you tell me. Am I fucked up?"

I waited for her response but it didn't come. She sat in her chair without writing anything down, just listening, and I hated her more with each second that went by. I uncrossed my legs and put both feet on the floor and both hands on my lap, ready to jump up at the opportune second.

She turned to her desk, pulled a thick hardcover book toward her, and opened it. She flipped through the pages, talking quietly, more to herself than to me, about my symptoms: unexplained anger, getting stuck in traumatic memories, feelings of hopelessness. She ran her little ring finger down to the bottom and started spouting off the types of prescription medication I could take to help me with my symptoms.

"Jesus Christ, I could have read the *Physicians' Desk Reference*." I shot up from my chair. "What kind of shit is this? You can't help me. Look at you. You've never been in combat. You've never been in the military. If they cut you in half you still wouldn't pass the height and weight standards." I knew I'd gone too far, but I kept going. "Maybe you shouldn't try counseling war vets until you can keep the goddamn chicken leg out of your mouth."

I wanted to wound her. The pain burnt me, smoked me to the filter, and I needed other people to feel it. I opened the door, walked out through the lobby, stepped through the sliding glass doors, and lit up a cigarette. No one ran after me to yell at me for losing control. No one came out at all. The lack of reaction and my confused state made it possible for me to believe that maybe the little incident hadn't happened, maybe I hadn't even gone in yet, maybe I would never go in. I was a hollow machine with a swarm of bugs flapping their greasy wings in my chest. I looked over to my car to make sure I wasn't sitting in the driver's seat, watching me. For a second I thought I saw myself there. Then I shook my head and thought about going to the emergency room and asking them to drill a hole in my skull to let the demons out.

The hell with it, I thought. I threw my cigarette down and squashed it out with the toe of my shoe. *I need a drink.*

The End of Staff Sergeant Sean Davis

I'm not sure how long I stayed drunk, exactly, but I know it lasted weeks. Sometime in early February, a major from the wounded soldier program called and told me that since I had missed the last month's worth of physical therapy appointments the army had proclaimed me fit for duty and dropped me from full-time status. The paychecks would stop. If I wanted money I would have to go to the drills once a month, and that money was significantly less. It wouldn't quite pay the rent.

The change of status put me back on the battalion's radar. The next day I went back to ignoring Sergeant Stimpson's phone calls. I didn't know what would happen next, but I imagined MPs coming to the house and taking me off in handcuffs for being AWOL.

A few days went by, and I found myself sitting in the dark on the couch in the living room at three in the morning, staring at my giant elephant-shit canvas. The blotches mixed together in bulges, making a bigger form in the middle that I had probably meant to be a giant, disfigured shark. Nothing worked. Life was shit. Hell, in a month I would probably be begging for change on a freeway off-ramp. I shook my head, then finished the last of the cheapest vodka the corner liquor store had. The shit made me cough and my eyes water. When I gathered myself I saw the Christmas tree still in the corner, naked and dry.

Everything was ruined, broken, and wrecked. I wasn't even responsible enough to take down holiday decorations. The rage returned and I jumped from the couch, grabbed the fucking tree by the top, and pulled it out the door to the front yard, the makeshift ornaments flying off in every direction.

The grass was cold and wet from winter dew, but I stood barefoot in only cargo shorts in the middle of our yard, strangling the skeleton of Christmas. I snatched the lighter from my pocket and burned the fucker right there. The tree was so dry it went up in a ball of flame in seconds. The whole neighborhood was illuminated. I stood watching the flames and thought of the Library of Alexandria, Joan of Arc, the monks protesting in Vietnam, and my Humvee.

"Motherfucker!" Andy yelled behind me and disappeared back into the house. Thirty seconds later he jumped down from the porch with a pot of water and threw it onto the base of the fire. I just stood and watched.

"Holy shit, what happened?" Andy covered the flames on the lawn with a blanket he grabbed from the couch.

"Wish I knew," I said.

The little emergency had taken a lot out of me. When we were all sure that the fire was completely out, I went back to my basement and fell asleep. A few hours later, I woke to my cell phone ringing. I saw it was my Blasted Brother Liam Quinn. I picked it up.

"Sean, where the hell have you been? You all right, man? We're worried."

I licked the rough roof of my mouth and smacked my lips. My eyes were swollen and dried out. They didn't want to open. "Living the dream."

"The unit's been trying to get ahold of you," he said.

"Sorry, brother. I've been busy."

He asked if I had listened to any of the messages and told me that they needed me in ASAP to sign some paperwork. I imagined standing blindfolded in front of a firing squad, but I knew I would have to go in sooner or later. There was no use putting it off. I told him I would be down that day.

"Awesome, man. After you get done give me a call. We'll grab a beer at Suds."

I struggled through my daily hangover to shower, shave, and dress. I couldn't find a uniform, so I wore my best set of civilian clothes. The entire hour-and-a-half drive to Corvallis, I visualized a few different scenarios, but with the same result. I knew I was going to be chaptered out, but I didn't know what code. The easiest one to get my head around was AWOL.

I parked on the street, only a couple feet from where I'd parked the very first time I pulled into the armory. The day wasn't so different, either: a little colder, but the same clouds. College kids still kicked by on skateboards or rode their bikes on the sidewalk out front, the strip mall was still busy with people, and the rosebushes by the front door were still dying, but there was one difference I noticed immediately. The monument with the eternal flame had three new, smaller black marble blocks on top of the old ones. I thought my eyes were playing with me. When I walked up to it I saw only one block had names on it—Simon's name and a few other Oregonians who had died during the Iraq and Afghanistan wars—but there was room for many more. The other two were blank.

A cold drizzle fell, and I wanted badly to remember the last sunny day. Maybe it was the day we came back from Texas. Goddamn, I had thunder in my chest that day. Simon and I walked to the pub, and then he went to surprise June. My mind went to Danny, and Baldwin, and Cederman, and Sergeant First Class Schofield, and Lieutenant Caius. They were still fighting in Iraq while I sat on my ass back here, a drunken waste. I'd kept myself from thinking about them for so long that I had let myself slide into being the type of person they wouldn't have let me be. I wasn't the person they knew anymore and the person I had become was someone they wouldn't have liked.

The armory seemed empty, but the blue metal doors were propped open. I walked in and to my right just as I entered was a framed picture of Simon in uniform. It was hanging from a nail driven into the white cinderblock. Next to his were other framed pictures of the three men in our company who had been killed in the war. I heard boots behind me, and Sergeant Stimpson's voice.

"Can I help you?"

Turning to face him was one of the hardest things I had done since coming back.

"Holy shit, Sergeant Davis. I've been trying to get ahold of you." He smiled.

"Hey, Scott. I'm sorry about that, but here I am ready to face the music."

He invited me into his office, the office that fast-talking Danny Addison had run before the war. I sat down on the foldout chair in front of his desk. I was ready for the worst, but Sergeant Stimpson wasn't angry or nervous like I would have thought. Instead, he acted excited and updated me about Bravo Company. I knew most of it. Even living my flophouse life I read the papers, watched the news, and checked MySpace and Facebook, although I couldn't bring myself to correspond with them. I knew all about the battles they had fought in Najaf and Fallujah. Everyone in the state did. *The New York Times*, *Time* magazine, and *The Washington Post* had featured pictures of them taken by an embedded reporter. *The National Enquirer* even used a picture of Dave Schofield on the cover as a stock photo for a story about war widows.

They were a month from coming home and had been taken out of the mission rotation. In a few short weeks they would board a plane at Baghdad International Airport and fly into Fort Lewis, Washington. Their homecoming meant I would see them again, but it also meant I could stop blaming myself for not being there when they needed me.

"I'm sorry, Scott. I'm sorry I didn't answer when you called."

"Don't worry about it. You're here now." He found my folder and opened it.

A chill ran over my face and my spine felt like rolled paper. I expected the worst.

"Everything okay?" he asked.

"Some days are better than others."

He nodded with sympathy. "Well, this will cheer you up," he said, and handed me a couple of papers stapled together.

I searched the paper for the charges, for the letters AWOL, for the date I would be separated from the service. Nothing on the paper made any sense. After a minute or so, Sergeant Stimpson helped me out.

"You're being promoted," he said with a big smile. "Sorry I didn't tell you what it was about, but I wanted to surprise you."

"What?" My nerves caused a superficial little laugh.

"You're going to have your own platoon." He stood up and leaned across the desk to shake my hand. I grabbed it like a man drowning. "Sign those and you're officially Sergeant First Class Davis. You'll be pinned next Friday during first formation at 1700 hours. Then Saturday you'll take your new platoon to the MOUT course out at Rilea."

Since I had been sent back early, I was pretty much the only staff sergeant with combat experience on the promotion list, and when a slot came open they had given it to me. Sergeant Stimpson had covered for me, and God bless him for it, but it made me feel like shit. Not only did he keep me out of trouble, he worked on my promotion. Now I owed him. I owed him enough not to blow this second chance, even though I didn't want it.

Captain Intenso Rides Again

I had made it to the bottom rung of the higher enlisted. Even though I really wanted to see my Blasted Bastard brother again, I knew seeing Liam would end with me blackout drunk on the couch in his basement with his dog. Getting my shit together was an opportunity I didn't want, but I didn't have a choice. Being promoted to this rank with only eleven total years in was extraordinary. Most soldiers go their entire career without being considered for it. When I saw my platoon again I would have achieved something great, even if I didn't feel like I deserved it. I couldn't help but think that first sergeant would be possible in a few more years. Hell, sergeant major of Oregon was possible before I reached my full twenty years.

Unfortunately, this resolve only lasted until the next day, when I found that my self-destructive behavior wasn't something I could just stop whenever I wanted. The bottle wasn't done with me, and just because I believed the promotion would make me a soldier again didn't mean I was capable of being one.

Certain realities sunk in. The army said I was fit for duty, but there was no way I could pass a physical training test at that time. I went out for a jog and my right leg swelled to the point of bursting; my knee ached like someone had stuck it with a spike. I couldn't do push-ups or pull-ups with my fucked-up arm and shoulder, and the more time I spent sober the more I heard the ringing in my ears. Would I be able to carry the weight I had before, physically or mentally? If even the thought of putting on a uniform nauseated me, how would I stand in front of a formation of men and expect to lead them?

The pressure to turn it around was too great. I drank heavily again. At first I called it a celebration. The strays at the Asylum drank to me, the war hero. After a few nights, I zeroed in on a chubby little brunette who loved to paint still lifes of skulls next to her favorite brand of cigarettes. By Thursday night I was searching bottles of bourbon for the courage I would need the next day. The chubby brunette and I took our party to my basement around three in the morning so I could distract myself in another way.

Francisco shook me awake. A single light bulb silhouetted his wild hair. Mortar attack, machine-gun fire, explosions, screaming, the CASH, Texas, *60 Minutes*, Jaime, the Asylum. I couldn't get a grasp on anything, and then there was Francisco standing over me. I sprung up.

"Hey, man, don't you have army today? Are you okay?" Francisco stood with his hands palms out.

I looked down at the empty blankets on the futon.

"She left around noon, dude."

There wasn't any light coming down the stairs. I had slept through the day. "What time is it?"

"A quarter after seven."

"Fuck, fuck, fuck."

I tore around my living space, digging through piles of clothes for a uniform. I found my boots and a few brown T-shirts, but nothing else. The more I moved, the more I realized I was in between the drunk and the hangover. Broken shards of glass sloshed around in my head. My stomach flipped and I sat again, trying not to vomit.

Francisco disappeared up the stairs, leaving me miserable and alone. I looked down at my feet, saw my cell phone, and swallowed hard. Four missed calls from the armory. I plopped down on the bed and thought that all my problems would be solved if the fucking hangover would just kill me. I could say I was sick, but no one would buy it, and I couldn't feign ignorance. There was no use calling without a good excuse, and they would tell by my voice I was still drunk. In the end I decided to sleep for a couple of hours and figure out my next step after I woke up. I set my alarm for six in the morning in the hope of having enough time to drive down to Corvallis before they loaded the buses and moved out to Camp Rilea on the coast.

I woke up a few minutes before my alarm and called the armory right away. A young private with a name I didn't recognize answered the phone. He told me that the buses had already loaded at 0400 hours. The new company commander had left the kid instructions to find me and figure out what the hell was going on.

"What do you want me to tell him, Sergeant?" the kid asked.

"Nothing. I'm on my way."

I sped to Camp Rilea hoping that I wouldn't get pulled over, because there was little doubt I could still be tagged for a DUI. The alcohol oozed from my skin. I cursed myself for the first hour of the drive. Then I laughed at the situation. On my first official day as a platoon sergeant I had missed formation, missed movement, and lost the respect of men I hadn't even met. I was driving impaired at a high rate of speed through mountain curves to go and train men for combat, which was something that had topped my list of things never to do again.

I didn't even have a uniform. The closest thing I could find was a civilian pair of green cargo pants, the side pockets of which I had stuffed with one-shot bottles of Jack Daniel's. I did find one of the brown T-shirts I had worn in Iraq. It had my last name and blood type drawn on it with permanent marker. I also found an old field jacket that Liam had bought for me. They wore them like motorcycle-club jackets. It had my name and rank sewn on it, but it wasn't government issue. I had even run out the door without shaving. I looked like the poster boy for homeless veterans.

When I arrived at Rilea, I flashed my military ID to the guy at the front gate and asked with wild eyes where the soldiers were training. Before he could answer, I drove on through. I remembered the general direction of the MOUT site, but I hadn't been there since the old commander told us we were going to war.

I remembered being honored for having the best squad in the battalion. I saw us up there in front of everyone like it just happened, my squad and me getting medals pinned on our chests in front of four hundred other soldiers. Simon was there too, full of pride. My thoughts swirled and time warped. I became confused about whether or not any of it had happened yet, or had ever happened at all. Wouldn't it be great if there were even the smallest chance I made it all up?

I couldn't catch my breath and this made me dizzy. Cold sweat beaded on my forehead and rolled down my cheek and neck. My chest tightened. My vision narrowed. I pulled over and fumbled in my pocket, cracked the seal on one of the bottles of whiskey and downed it quick. The car idled. I threw my head back on the headrest and stared at the ceiling.

My heart was beating hard, like it hated me; maybe it did. I screamed a whole-body scream, using every muscle, loud and long. I kept screaming until I ran out of air and coughed. My cough turned to a laugh, because now everything was funny. I laughed loud and strong until the laughter faded to sobs.

I sat there until all the windows fogged up, but after a few minutes I remembered what I needed to do and wiped the inside of the windshield with my sleeve. A quarter mile up the road I saw three guys in uniform smoking cigarettes. They had to know what the hell was going on. I stepped out of my car under the same fucking cloud that was always there and headed toward the soldiers. Thank God one of them happened to be Sergeant Jason Hosford, the third Blasted Bastard. He'd gone back to the unit now that the bullet wound in his knee had healed up.

"Jesus Christ, Sean. Are you okay?" He took a step toward me with his arms out, like he expected me to fall over.

I was taken aback by the question. I thought I had gathered myself enough to be presentable. I smiled. "Yeah, man. Did I miss the party? What are you guys doing?"

"Waiting for the PX to open." Jason turned to the other two soldiers. They were both young lower enlisted, a private first class and a specialist. "Head over to the company. I'll be there in a second." After they left he turned to me. "Where the hell is your uniform?"

I shook my head and shrugged. "I've been moving around so much I couldn't find one."

"Well, you can't go to formation like that. What the hell are you doing?"

I was cracking another one-shotter of whiskey. "You want one? I have a couple more."

"It's eight in the morning. Are you okay?" He moved beside me and put his hand on my back. Before I knew it we were walking.

The cold bit through my jacket. "You remember the last time we had a sunny day?"

"It's winter, man. That's how it goes."

I used his razor and he gave me a pair of his BDUs. I was almost a half a foot taller than him and forty pounds heavier, but I made it fit. Jason gave me his Gore-Tex jacket to wear over his BDU top so no one would notice it had his nametag instead of mine. He didn't ask me where I was the night before. Instead, he told me I would be instructing cadets from OSU that day on how to properly clear a house, and that he would do his best to cover for me with the new commander.

"This guy is a quartermaster officer, only here until the guys get back from overseas. I don't know if he'll try to make an example of you or laugh it off."

My reflection in the latrine mirror had aged drastically.

"I definitely shouldn't be used as an example."

An hour later I sat on the front steps of a fake house in the middle of a fake town, smoking a cigarette in the foggy morning and thinking that maybe I could get through this shit. I hadn't been caught so far, and now that I was a platoon sergeant it would almost take an Act of Congress to bust me. I still wanted to pull it together. I owed every noncommissioned officer who'd never made it to this level. Above all, I didn't want to do any disservice to Simon's memory by being an asshole drunk and a horrible soldier.

The MOUT site had a dozen or so houses in the fake village, and each house had a trainer with a task the cadets needed to complete. There were only a limited number of cadets, so it was a good possibility that no one even knew I was late.

After fifteen minutes or so, seven skinny kids in battle dress uniforms walked up with their M4s slung over their shoulders; every single one of them looked like they'd never needed to scrape a razor over their chins. They were from the Oregon State University ROTC program: children who might someday become officers in the army. I stood up and they all fell into rank in front of me. I introduced myself for the first time as Sergeant First Class Davis, my voice rough from screaming, laughing, and crying alone in my car only an hour before. I ordered them to the position of parade rest. They stood there letting the ocean mist spray their faces, ready to learn the soldier's trade.

I let them stand there for a few minutes and then asked, "Do any of you speak Arabic?"

The question confused them. No one answered so I asked again, and they all said no.

"Marhaban," I said. "That's a good greeting. I want you to say that a couple times. Memorize it. If you don't know it at the end of this training, you're going to owe me thirty push-ups."

A kid with freckles spattered across his face and a bad slouch said, "Sergeant, aren't we here to learn how to clear a house? I didn't know language lessons had anything to do with that."

A few of the others laughed at this. These kids hadn't even been through basic training yet. They played at being soldiers and only had an inkling of military etiquette. They didn't know of the punitive measures that came with such an insolent tone, but I'd teach them. This little shit. I was trying to save their lives. I stared him down and walked over to him until I was uncomfortably close. I wasn't going to scream at him. No, he expected that. Instead I whispered in a hoarse, unnerving voice.

"What are you going to say to the people in the house while you're rummaging through their personal belongings wearing a high-powered assault rifle?" I turned down the line to the rest of them. "What do you do if you kick a door off the hinges and find a sixty-year-old woman with terror in her eyes? You're going to shoot her, right? You're all tough guys. Fucking smoke the bitch, right? Why stop there? Waste her daughters in the next room; show those fuckers who's in charge."

None of them dared to move or look at me. The mist grew heavier and turned to rain; the drops thudded on our uniforms and equipment. I turned from them and stared at the horizon for too long. In the corner of my eye I could see them looking to each other.

"Marhaban, goddammit. Remember that. I'm serious, you forget that and you'll owe me. Now stack on that door."

We ran through the textbook way to clear a house several times. I tried hard to not lose my shit, but memories of every house came flooding back. They ran through the front door and I showed them their routes according to the position they stacked in. The one man had to go a certain way, the two man the other, and so on until the breach man pulled up the rear. They flowed through the house repeatedly until the drill started to become muscle memory. After an hour they started making sloppy mistakes. They told me they were tired. I had no patience. I wanted to tear their heads off, jump around, and make sure they knew how important this shit really was.

"You don't think the troops over there are tired? Shit, that's the one constant in combat. That's why we do these drills even when you're exhausted. You train how you fight because your buddy's life depends on you doing your fucking job." And then I went into the day of the ambush, how we hadn't had enough sleep, how the intel was fucked up, how the equipment was substandard, and anything else I could think of. I told them of the heroics of Baldwin and Liam Quinn, and gave them a graphic description of how my good friend was killed. I called them back into formation and asked them to give me the greeting. I made them all do push-ups, then sent them to the other house and lit another cigarette. The whole thing left me exhausted, like I was on continuous ops again.

At lunch the new commander walked over to my fake house. I snapped to attention and saluted. He was older and shorter than

I imagined, and he had a mustache so I disliked him immediately. The curve in his spine told me he was prior service, probably infantry. He waved me down to parade rest. "We missed you last night, Sergeant."

"Sir, I apologize…"

"Sergeant Stimpson already told me you were sick. He also told me you received a Purple Heart from General Petraeus."

"Yes, sir." I hadn't realized at the time it was General Petraeus, but the name sounded familiar. Who knows which general it was; I just agreed.

"I expect good things from you, son. Carry on." With that he walked off.

The Boys Make It Home

I kept doing my best to live up to my promotion, but drills were only one weekend a month. The time between my army weekends, I stayed in the Asylum with drunken artists, potheads, and other assorted minimum-wage kids trying to find a way to get by.

The rain never stopped for more than a day at a time for the rest of the month. The unemployment checks barely covered my living expenses. Without a constant flow of money I wasn't able to buy the alcohol every night. Without the alcohol the people stopped coming as much. The party had ended. I didn't think I'd miss all the chaos and craziness, but without the freaks and misfits I fell into an epic loneliness. Francisco did his best to help me out, but I still isolated myself and put up walls against any real relationship, friend or otherwise. I had a deep need to do the right thing; I just didn't know how. I completely stopped all drugs but the legal ones sent to me by the VA. I abused them too, but that didn't stop me from calling it progress.

One day I sat alone in the living room, surrounded by dying houseplants, trying to decide if I should get a pet or kill myself with half a bottle of Vicodin, when Andy came home. He fell into the door, whipping it open, and laughed, almost falling. At first I thought he was drunk, but when he dragged Jaime in behind him, holding her hand, I knew he was just in love. Both of their faces beamed until they saw me sitting on the couch in the dark. I looked into Jaime's face, and then to Andy, and smiled.

"Hey, guys. How're things?"

Andy stuttered something about them hiking up Multnomah Falls in the rain, and that was why they were dripping all over the carpet. I picked up a book that happened to be on the floor by the couch, a Time-Life book on the paranormal that I had bought at the Goodwill a few days before.

"I was just catching up on some reading."

When I looked down at a random page the two of them moved to the door, making an exaggerated attempt not to get too close to each other. I heard them say their goodbyes on the porch, then whisper in a more familiar tone. A minute later Andy came back inside and flopped down in a chair. We sat there for a couple seconds, me pretending to read about Civil War ghosts and him staring at the wall. Then he leaned over toward the lamp next to him. "You mind if I turn the light on? I can barely see. How are you reading?"

"The bulb's out in that one." I turned the page to a story on chupacabras.

Andy got up, turned the living room light on, and said, "It was her idea not to tell you. I wanted to right away. You know, that's how I am."

I shut the book and looked up at him. "Except for you're not. Not right now."

We looked at each other, and for the briefest moment I was able to use my eyes to communicate my real anger and frustration. How was I still stuck on this girl? Maybe I wasn't, but seeing her happy with someone else pissed me off. I had failed everywhere.

I relaxed and laughed it off. "I'm fucking with you. Seriously, don't worry about it, man. We broke up months ago. I left her. I know people say this all the time, but no hard feelings."

Andy smiled and plopped down in the chair again. "Holy shit, I'm so glad to hear you say that. I felt like such an asshole. Jaime thought for sure this would tear you up."

"What? Shit, come on." I hated the fact that she was right, but tried to hide it by smiling and pretending to read about monster sharks. Now I couldn't kill myself because she'd think I was doing it over her. This pissed me off, and that fact made me realize that I really wasn't stuck on her anymore.

One of our friends was looking for a roommate, and I jumped on the opportunity to miss out on hearing the loud sex between Andy and Jaime from my basement. I packed up my books, my art supplies, and my futon and moved into my own room in an apartment only two miles away from the Asylum, with Mike.

Mike was a pathologist in the morgue at Providence Hospital. He removed diseased organs from corpses in the hope that researchers could find a cure for whatever had just killed the poor son of a bitch. Whenever he got home we would talk about the dead in a way most people wouldn't appreciate. He told me that the weirdest thing about cutting people open was that it always made him hungry. This isn't something that pathologists tell normal people. It was disgusting and he knew it, but it was the truth. Even the vegetarian pathologists craved barbecue after a few months at the hospital. I was amazed that he could do what he did and still exist within society. He did smoke a lot of pot and play games on his computer; I guess we all had ways to escape. Mine was chasing oxycodone with bourbon.

Bravo Company returned on Saint Patrick's Day, 2005. I caught a ride with Liam and we drove north on I-5 under one solid gray cloud to Fort Lewis, Washington. We filled the cab of his pickup truck with nervous laughter. I couldn't talk about anything serious, because in the back of my mind I kept running through scenarios of seeing each of my best friends, these men who had become more family to me than my mother or father.

Liam's parents would meet us there. They still had a son at war: Brian Quinn, a rifleman in Staff Sergeant Tom Cederman's squad. I couldn't wait to see Cederman, my old roommate in Iraq. We hadn't spoken since the day before the ambush.

This homecoming would be the end of a period of my life that had consumed everything else. The boys were coming home, landing at McChord Air Force Base any time now, and they would be paraded to a big hall for the news crews to film their tears of joy at seeing their families again.

I could finally stop reading the papers, watching the news, and living in a constant state of fear that another of us would be hit by an IED, a stray RPG, or a bullet. Bravo Company was back from the war and now we could all go back to the way it was before. These were the thoughts Liam interrupted by telling me some of the guys weren't going to be happy to see him.

I punched him in the shoulder and laughed.

"No, really. I, well, I slept with a couple of their girlfriends," he said.

I don't know why I was surprised. He had the best intentions, but somehow he had accidentally slept with Burkert's fiancée and Danny's girl Clara.

"Jesus, Liam. What the fuck were you thinking?"

"I don't know, man." He looked straight ahead like the road could end any second.

We met up with Liam's parents and went to the giant warehouse. Family members, loved ones, and Vietnam veterans who truly knew the importance of a proper homecoming filled the stands. They roared with applause when the men marched onto the concrete drill floor and stood under an American flag the size of a football field. We looked down on the battalion, over 400 men standing at the position of attention with their eyes straight ahead, disciplined even at a time like this. Each company lined up behind their own guidon, with Bravo Company in the middle.

The governor took the podium and spoke of duty, honor, and sacrifice. He made it a point to tell the crowd he had stood at the funeral of every Oregon soldier killed in the war, and I respected him for that. When the governor finished, the colonel took the stage and congratulated the battalion for successfully completing their mission. He held a moment of silence for the men we had lost. After so many rounds of thunderous applause, there could not have been a man down on the floor who didn't feel like a real goddamn American Hero. I envied them.

At the end of the ceremony, the colonel called for the men who were wounded and sent back early to join the formation. My cheeks flushed. I didn't want to take any of the attention away from the boys, but Liam's parents pulled at our elbows and pushed us to go down. I thanked them but said I wasn't going to go, but then the Vietnam vets sitting around us stood up, clapped, and told us to get down there. These men never received a proper welcome home from their war. We couldn't refuse, so we walked down the aisle of the bleachers and into the back of the big formation.

We walked straight to Second Platoon in the middle of Bravo Company. The men in formation turned their heads to see us, even in the position of attention. Out of nowhere Tom Cederman broke ranks and grabbed me tight. He wrapped his arms around me and we hugged. When he didn't let go I understood how badly he had been affected when Simon died and I was hurt. I thought of the day Cederman came back from the shitter not knowing we were being sent to war, the training at Fort Hood, and sharing a trailer with him in Iraq.

The crowd rose and applauded as we stood there, our arms around each other, fighting tears. He became everything I'd lost in this war and the happiness I felt at finally getting it back. I thought I might never let him go. We finally pulled away from each other, red-faced and sniffling. I looked up into hundreds of faces: our fathers, grandfathers, wives, children, brothers, sisters, extended family, and combat veterans from other wars. With my heart beating through my fingertips I moved slowly to the position of attention. Bravo Company stood under waves of flashing cameras and applause like thunder rolling through a valley. News crews scurried around us to find the best camera angles.

The colonel called us all to attention, and the applause slowed but didn't stop. When he said we were dismissed, the people in the stands poured out onto the drill floor. Every family reunited with their soldier. Men held babies they'd just met. Husbands and wives embraced, ignoring the cameras. Parents beaming with pride hugged their soldier sons and daughters.

Still Taking Orders

I thought all I had to do was keep my shit together long enough for Bravo Company to get home and then everything would be good again, but after the homecoming ceremony everyone went their own way. Now that our war was over, we went back to meeting up only one weekend a month like any other National Guard company. Everyone went from soldiers in combat to civilians trying to reassemble the lives they had left two years ago.

Schofield had been promoted to first sergeant for a unit in some far-off town. Lieutenant Caius moved back to Arizona. The men were all having a hard time reintegrating into society. There was no family anymore. Not only were the two top leaders gone, the company had been rearranged a half dozen times while at war, and new people had arrived. These replacements—who I'd never met—had spent more time in combat with Bravo Company than I had. Everything had been shaken up and new relationships had been formed. Everything had changed and just about everyone was having serious problems with the transition.

Only about a dozen guys showed up to the next drill. When I saw that the new command wasn't really trying to track them down, I left too. Every week that followed, I would hear some horror story about one of them doing too many drugs, drinking too much, getting divorced or arrested. These men were the pillars of my hope that I could turn it around, but their lives were as fucked up as mine, and this was happening all over the state. It got so bad that the VA opened an inpatient PTSD center in Cottage Grove, which would be used by dozens of men from our battalion, including fast-talking Danny Addison.

I thought I could pull myself out of this when they came back, but I was wrong. I drank myself to sleep every night and started the day with three Vicodin. My anger returned and I always left the apartment trashed. I stopped going to Francisco's house because Andy and Jaime were always there, the happy couple, happier than she ever was with me.

One day I finally answered my brother Vince's call and went to his house. He and his wife had just had twins, and he wanted to include me in family dinners. They all started out nice enough with the pleasant talk, but then he asked me about the army, and worse, my art. I drank to punish myself and said hurtful things. The last dinner I showed up to ended with me telling him his daughter looked like a little Hitler because of her hair, a perfect little Hitler. And his son looked like a chubby Mussolini. At the door, drunk as hell, I yelled that I would not eat in the same house as the Axis of Evil and left. One more bridge burned.

You can only chain-smoke and think about suicide for so long. After a while you need to either do it or get off your ass. Or maybe I was just bored. I decided to find a job. The skills I'd learned in the infantry didn't translate so well to civilian employment. I could set up a claymore mine or lead men across an objective, and my shot group was the size of a quarter one hundred fifty meters from the target, but, surprisingly, that didn't impress anyone looking to hire people in the customer service industry. No matter how many times I checked the veteran's box on an application, it never got me an interview. One year of art school didn't help either. In the end I was hired on by a friend of a friend, as a waiter at a seasonal restaurant that floated in the Columbia River between Oregon and Washington.

Mike's friend Don owned the place and opened it from April to October every year. I don't know how Mike and Don met, but I know it had something to do with the morgue. Don practiced law most of the year and thought managing a restaurant on a giant floating deck during the sunny months would be a great escape. It had a grill, a deep fryer, and a full bar complete with colorful umbrellas in every margarita. The satellite radio was always tuned to the Jimmy Buffett station.

I had never waited tables before, but didn't think it would be too difficult. Most of the staff was made up of female college students who had worked there a few seasons. They used me to lift heavy things, reach tall things, and take out the garbage. We pooled tips so I didn't mind. Every once in a while someone would ask me about the military, and between running orders for fish and chips or deep-fried clams I told them how I used to rappel out of helicopters into a hot landing zone, patrol the Green Zone on foot, and kick down doors to search houses.

When I was in public I kept my shit together, but my life wasn't changing. Sometimes I would see something while driving that reminded me of Iraq. After a few minutes this would have me screaming and pounding the steering wheel, not knowing if I was laughing or crying. Police officers with radar guns always freaked the shit out of me. Every morning I told myself I wouldn't drink that night, but every night found me buying another pint of whiskey or a six-pack. The biggest frustration was that I couldn't get past this one year in my life. Every trigger set me back to zero, no matter how much progress I made.

The one-year anniversary of the ambush was around the corner, and I would soon learn that a person's body possesses memories just like the brain. The closer the day loomed, the more my injuries from the ambush ached and the more frequent my nightmares became. I tried to interact socially, but I came off clumsy and vulgar.

I managed to make it to the weekend drills over the summer, but we never did anything but clean weapons and equipment because the command was trying to deal with the flood of incidents. Every weekend someone ended up in the county or city jail. The newspapers ran stories on soldiers coming back and getting arrested for domestic violence, public drunkenness, or drug use. Why was anyone surprised? These men were in country one minute, leveling buildings with indirect fire and pulling triggers on the enemy, and then two days later they were back at home dealing with relationships and regular jobs, trying to fit back into the sitcom life. They went from having power over life and death, playing a role in history, to cashiering at Safeway, rotating tires, or waiting tables.

One morning I was opening the restaurant. I sprayed the goose shit from the docks out front, I rolled up the canopy walls, and then I went to refill a jar of lollipops. The lollipops were free for people waiting for a table. One of the opening-shift duties was to refill the bowl every morning. I grabbed a box of them from the dry storage and for some reason had a hard time opening the damned thing. I fumbled with it for a few seconds, turning it over trying to find a corner or a perforated tab to tear, without success. Suddenly I dug the fingernails of each hand into the box as hard as I could and tore the fucking thing in half, slamming them all down on the deck and sending the suckers flying in every direction. Then I stomped on them, crushing a dozen with the heels of my shoes and screaming. The hate took a long time to get out. When I looked up, there was Don with an armful of frozen fish. We sat down and talked for half an hour. Things I had never realized poured from my mouth. I wasn't okay. The shit I had seen and done had affected me in ways I had never comprehended. I hated that I carried this guilt over Simon's death. What was the point of going on? Don listened to me talk about my fear of starting my life over again. I knew I wanted to go back to school and have a serious relationship with a woman, but I knew my problems were too big to let that happen. He told me I should talk to someone and asked if the va hospital did that sort of thing. I told him I didn't know, but I agreed to find out in order to keep my job.

Einherjar, a painting done by Sean and his brother. The Einherjar are the warriors taken to Valhalla by the Valkyries in Norse mythology.

The Einherjar

The mental hygiene clinic at the VA hospital wasn't the only place in town for a veteran to find help for PTSD. Going up the hill was wrong for me; the dank atmosphere didn't foster healing, and I think I may have threatened the life of a fat Christmas tree who worked there. I found a satellite outpatient office called the Vet Center and made an appointment. The offices were on the bottom floor of a plain-looking four-story office building off Northeast Eighty-Second Avenue, right next to a series of seedy lingerie shops that offered personal viewings and intimate conversations with the models. I didn't expect much.

Within minutes of entering the place, I sat in the office of a woman veteran who had a PhD hanging over her desk. When she introduced herself, she didn't talk about degrees and credentials; instead she told me she did two tours in Vietnam as a nurse at a combat army surgical hospital.

Dr. Rotterdam never brought up my war, she didn't have a folder of information on me, and she didn't make any judgments. I started telling her about stomping on the lollipops and before I knew it I was talking about the explosion at the North Gate, the ambush—all the way back to my time in Haiti. She listened, but she didn't offer me drugs, or a way to meditate, or a breathing exercise. She did ask me if I had any hobbies I loved. We ended the session by agreeing I should get back to creating art.

I drove back to the house feeling empty, but not in the way everyone talks about. All the shit I had carried inside of me was gone, like I forced a cleaning rod through a carbon-filled rifle barrel. It amazed me that just talking to someone who really listened made me feel so much lighter. The pain wasn't gone, and my self-destruction definitely wasn't, either, but I saw a small way out and that made things a little easier.

I planned to set up my easel and buy more supplies, and by the next week I would have a concept sketch done, with brighter colors and balance. This wasn't that big of a deal, but the excitement snowballed. I had done one thing to move toward progress; more seemed possible.

Six hours later my feet were killing me from running from table to kitchen and back. It was one of the hottest days of the year, and the warm weather always brought the crowds to the floating restaurant. The patrons couldn't have been shittier. One of the girls had called off, so I had to bus and wait the tables. Four groups of diners stiffed me, most of them young kids whose outfits and accessories were worth more than my entire wardrobe. Where was all of the excitement and possibility I had felt that morning?

We stopped taking diners at sunset. An hour later I was sitting at the imitation tiki bar with two of the waitresses and the fry cook. Bear fried our food—that's what the girls called him, probably because he was fat and hairy. I never learned his real name, but I did know he had done over a year of jail time somewhere in Washington state. The two waitresses were sweet, pretty things, and I mean the type of pretty that I thought put them out of my league. April had light red hair, cute rectangular glasses, and perpetually bare shoulders. Those shoulders drove me crazy with how soft and smooth they looked. Lindsay killed me with her smile, my God. Even at the busiest and most chaotic times, she always smiled—but not just with her mouth. She had a full-body smile, and that body, holy shit.

I sipped my after-shift drink with Lindsay sitting next to me, April next to her, and Bear on the end. At the end of the night the staff always made fun of the worst customers, and usually I sat and laughed a bit but never joined the conversation. That night I did. Nothing any of us said was funny but we laughed as a way to release frustration. Sometime during the conversation Lindsay turned to me. "Don said you were in the Marines?"

I stopped mid-sip and said, "Army infantry."

"Sorry." She wasn't prepared for the curtness of my response. I guess I wasn't either.

"No, I'm sorry. I respect the Marines, but they're two different branches," I said, trying to sound warmer.

"But you were in Iraq?" Her full attention was on me, something that didn't happen very often.

"Yeah, but not very long. They sent me home after I got blown up." The words sounded wrong after they left my mouth.

"You were blown up? I'm sorry." And she really was.

I paused for a while, noticing how a small touch of strangeness in the way her top lip curved made her that much more beautiful. She had high cheekbones and kindness in her voice.

"You're sorry?" I asked.

"About you getting blown up."

"Oh, well, you didn't do it." The conversation lulled so I tried a smile to bring it back, but April and Bear decided they wanted to go to a pub up the street. I thanked them for inviting me, but I didn't feel like being around a bunch of drunk people I didn't know.

I stopped at the 7-Eleven by my house and bought a six-pack of Widmer Brothers Hefeweizen with my tips from that night. I drank four of them, one right after the other, in the living room. The house was hot as hell so I opened all the windows and the door. An anchorman on the television talked with urgency about Hurricane Katrina cutting across Florida, gaining momentum before it would hit New Orleans. When I popped open the fifth beer I sat and looked at it for a while. I wish I had come to some epiphany about life that changed my behavior and erased my bad habits, but I didn't. Those moments just don't happen for real. Instead, bored with the television news, I set up my easel and painted gesso over my elephant-shit painting until I sat staring at a white canvas.

I drank the sixth beer.

Suddenly, I picked up a pencil and started the rough sketch of an old Norse myth I'd always loved: the fallen soldiers brought to Valhalla by the Valkyrie who waited for the world to end by eating, drinking, fighting, and singing. I worked on that painting until I couldn't keep my eyes open.

After a few hours of sleep, I woke up and started painting on the picture again. I did this during both my days off. The colors, balance, and light logic had to be just right. The big fire reflected on every face. In the background, lurking in the bushes and blending in with the darkness outside the fire, was the giant body of a wild boar.

I painted until an hour before work and showed up with different-colored swipes and blotches on my clothes and skin. Work was tolerable, and my attitude improved. As soon as I was off I would go back to painting.

I still drank beer and wine, but not as much and never to excess. After finishing the Norse piece, I started others. Soon five paintings hung in the living room and one on the easel.

One time, after coming home from a day shift, I found Mike at the house with a friend of his. I hadn't seen him in over a week and hadn't expected him. His friend was a short, bald man about my age with a long goatee. He wore a gray button-up Dickies shirt, black leather biker boots, and a studded belt that held up his worn jeans.

I apologized to Mike for the mess and he smiled; his eyes were slits. "Don't worry about it, man. We were just checking out the art. Kick-ass."

His friend stuck out his hand and every finger had a silver ring on it. He told me his name was Elvis—no shit, Elvis—and he owned a pub in Southeast. "We have art hanging every month. You ever think about putting a show together?"

Before I could answer, Mike clapped his hands. "Hell yeah, man. That's a great idea."

Elvis squatted next to a canvas leaning against the couch. "What's this one?"

I went right into the story. "That's Ajax. Ajax went through the whole Trojan War without a scratch. He was the only one who received no help from the gods, but after it was over he killed himself because the kings gave Achilles's armor to Odysseus."

"That's fucking bad-ass." Elvis stood up and went to another one hanging over the couch. I explained each one, and I don't know if they were genuinely interested or just very stoned, but they listened intently.

"Seriously, man, give me a call and we'll hang this stuff," Elvis said, and handed me his card.

The two of them had stopped by to pick up some weed, and they were off again. I wasn't sure if Elvis was serious or not, but having the paintings appreciated made me feel almost as high as they were. I gave myself two weeks to finish a couple more of them, and then I would see what happened.

I told Dr. Rotterdam about work, my art, and Elvis the pub owner. She was excited for me, but then she asked about my anger issues and nightmares. I still had them, but not as often. Life was hard but getting livable. Then I told her about Simon's theory on holes. How he'd said that everything we do was just to fill a hole—either physically, emotionally, or in some other way. I brought it up because it made sense to me when I was going through my bad times. She paused, chewing on the end of her pen for a couple seconds, and nodded. "True, in a way. But you have to remember the hole is always going to be there, and whatever we surround ourselves with is going to slip inside."

I thought about the dead animals on the side of the road, the violence of war, and the drugs and alcohol. Then I thought of the brotherhood, the kinship, and the good times. Who I was as a person depended on who and what I surrounded myself with. Was this a stupid feel-good moment? I don't know, maybe, but it helped me.

I started to look forward to working with Lindsay at the floating restaurant and watching her glide around the deck in her little sundresses. Whenever she needed something heavy lifted, she called for me, asking for Mr. Muscles. I tried hard to find any way I could to flirt with her, but *everyone* flirted with her. I had no idea if she noticed me more than any of the regulars that hung out at the bar, but then she asked me about all the paint on my clothes and my forearms. I told her what I was working on and that I might have a show coming up.

"An artist and a soldier, huh?" She stood in mock surprise, her hands on her hips.

I nodded with profound goofiness.

"You know, you can ask me out if you want."

I again nodded with profound goofiness.

An hour later, my cell buzzed in my pocket. When I saw it was the armory calling, I waved to Don that I was going on a break and walked to the end of the dock, behind the dry storage room. Danny Addison announced right away that Bravo Company, or what was left of it, would be deploying to Hurricane Katrina rescue operations in New Orleans. He told me we were leaving in seven days. He said I needed to pack my shit and call my squad leaders.

I hung up the phone and watched a couple of ducks fight over some breadcrumbs on the water. I had been feeling on top of the world just a second before. I had finally found a way to chip away at all the problems and I had begun to see that with some work I could get my life back on track. Or I could go on another deployment. On a deployment life is so much easier. You don't have to think about relationships with other people, how to make the rent, or how spend your free time; all you have to worry about is accomplishing the mission and taking care of your men. For a while I had a choice and even before heading to Louisiana was mandatory, I decided to go.

A big part of me wanted to help out, but the real reason I wanted to go was to escape my struggle with the transition back to real life.

I walked back to the restaurant very calmly and told Don that the army was sending me to New Orleans in a couple days and I would need the next couple weeks off. He cocked his head like I had told him a bad joke. I had announced it loud enough for Lindsay to hear. She looked over for a second but didn't react. At the end of my shift that day, Don called me over and gave me three hundred dollars. He said to use it however I thought it would help the most and that he wouldn't let me leave without it. I thanked him. I almost got to my car before deciding to run back and ask Lindsay for her number. She wrote it on a bar napkin and put on lipstick just to make a little kiss at the bottom.

Break Glass in Case of War

In Baghdad I had expected to see blocks of rubble, walls blown off buildings, and all that other end-of-the-world shit, but seeing words in my own language on wrecked signs, smashed pieces of the corporate logos I grew up with spread through the streets, and types of cars I'd driven before up to their windows in putrid water—that was very different. The hurricane had ravaged the landscape, and the devastation in New Orleans reminded me that nature demanded a deep respect. It showed me that man was still a beginner when it came to destruction. The gray clouds and rubble left in the storm's wake had drained all the color from the city. There was only sludge water that looked solid enough to stand on, but that was just an illusion created by the saturated pieces of people's belongings floating around. The flood took everything up to the roofs of the houses. The only way we could get around was via the overpasses and elevated highways.

We were stationed at a Baptist seminary right in the middle of the city, off Gentilly Boulevard, which had inexplicably been untouched by the devastation all around it. The seminary stood on a small piece of elevated land just high enough to have become an island in the sick floodwaters. Being dirty infantryman, we weren't allowed to go inside any of the buildings. We had to set up our cots and mosquito nets under awnings, overhangs, or anything else that blocked the alternating rain and direct sun, depending on the day.

It was strange to be issued the same weapons and live rounds that we'd carried in Iraq while patrolling through an American city. Well, we didn't have the big machine guns, grenades, or claymore mines, but the rifles and individual equipment were the same. I had loved the idea of coming down to help clean up and save lives on a humanitarian mission and thought we would be filling sandbags or wading through the toxic waters to find stranded people.

The day after we arrived I was called into a staff briefing since I was acting platoon leader, and the company commander told me and the other two lieutenants that when New Orleans flooded some inmates might have escaped from three different prisons in

Sean on site after Hurricane Katrina.

the area. One third of the police force was unaccounted for, and the project housing had exploded into riots right before the worst of the storm hit.

Chaos, excitement, disorder, live rounds in oiled chambers: I fucking loved it. My favorite drug flowed through my brain and body again, giving me a spiritual erection five miles long. The CO gave me my area of operations and the rules of engagement. I was ready to take my platoon and get shit done. It was just like war, but better.

We didn't have patrol vehicles because we were in such a hurry to get down there, so we commandeered city buses. None of us knew how to drive something that big, but it didn't matter; whatever we might hit was smashed to shit anyway. I stood at the front of the bus with one leg on the fare-taker like a pirate sailing through the apocalypse. There is no better feeling in this world than leading highly armed men on a mission through a completely ravaged wasteland.

Businesses set up tents at the Superdome to give out hot food to the rescue workers. On the second day, newly promoted Sergeant First Class Danny Addison rolled into the seminary with a busload of Domino's pizzas and Krispy Kreme donuts. We had all the food, blankets, equipment, and working radios we needed because we were in America, not some forgotten patch of desert.

People from all over the country drove down to help, and many of them got in our way, but their hearts were in the right place. People sacrificed in order to help others they didn't know because we were all Americans. *Christ*, I thought, *wouldn't it be great if we all decided we were earthlings instead?*

The temperature was hitting triple digits before noon—still not as hot as Iraq, but the humidity in the South steals a person's strength. Other than that, I was feeling good: barking orders, making decisions, planning missions. I was bigger than the sky that first day, so big I could eat the sun without burning my tongue. My mission was to search the flood-damaged houses to find the bodies of people who'd stayed and prisoners who were hiding from the law inside the evacuated zone.

Second Platoon, Bravo Company, was heading out on another real-world mission. I was playing the part of Lieutenant Caius. Danny Addison was now the platoon sergeant, and a few of the

NCOs from other platoons were my squad leaders. I split the platoon and sent Danny with one half while I took the other.

Our area of operations was Orleans Parish, where the poorest of the poor lived. We patrolled streets with rows of shotgun houses and a few small—maybe one- or two-bedroom—homes. Only ten miles into our first patrol, we found a father and son who'd decided to tough out the storm. They had a corner house with a little bit of property surrounding it that looked to be a junkyard.

Since none of the gas stations in the area worked and the roads were filled with abandoned cars, the two of them drove around gathering supplies in a modified go-kart with a metal shopping basket welded to the back.

They had been out foraging all day when we stopped them, and they were a sight to see: two big-bellied, Southern-grown men with bushy beards, both wearing faded blue overalls and nothing else except brand-new running shoes and head protection. The older man was in his sixties and wore a yellow hard hat with the letters LSU written on it in Sharpie; the son had an old blue football helmet, his beard sticking through the facemask.

I discovered some people live better after the world ends.

They had two dozen microwave dinners, Sterno canned fuel, four packs of white XXXL underwear, five twelve-packs of different sodas, seven pairs of brand-new sunglasses, and three big bottles of top-shelf whiskey. They were going to keep trucking right past us, but I stood in the middle of the road and waved them down. The son took off his helmet and got off his go-kart. I said hello and told them the food probably wasn't any good after not being refrigerated the last couple weeks.

The son stepped up, nervous, like he thought we were going to take what they had gathered or confiscate it. "Yeah, you probably right, but I found the dessert's still good. I give the rest to the dogs. So, we in trouble or what?"

"No, this is your neighborhood. We just want to know if you need anything," I said.

This surprised him. We did walk the streets like a movement to contact, ready for a fight, but our mission was to tell the holdouts to leave the area for their own safety, and I didn't feel like doing that. I didn't feel like following those orders. And that was the first moment I realized something had changed inside me. I thought that if I could go back to the simple life of following orders, accomplishing the mission, and looking after my men, then all the shit that made my life complicated would go away, but it wasn't working.

We gave the two men a couple cases of water from our bus and continued our patrol. A few hours later we were one block into clearing the twenty blocks in our area of operations when Battalion called me. I found that being an acting lieutenant put me on their radar. "Bulldog Six, this is Ghost Six. We have a frago."

There was an amendment to our initial order. "Make sure your guys are not entering houses unless the door is already open." The kid on the radio went on to say that a reporter had shadowed a patrol and saw soldiers kicking down doors and searching American citizens' houses without the consent of the owners. This led to a question of civil rights and a big news story about unnecessary property damage to the flood-ravaged houses.

"Roger, good copy, Ghost Six, but if the dead holdouts don't answer the door when we knock, how are we supposed to find them?" I asked.

"Wait one…" I waited and pictured the lower-ranking enlisted man on the radio getting up to ask my dumb question of the higher-ranking officer drinking coffee. A few seconds went by before a bigger voice came on. "Bulldog Six, this is Ghost Six Actual. Do you have a question with your mission?"

"Well, sir, I understand the spirit of the mission," I said. "I guess I'm having problems with semantics."

"Bulldog Six, Charlie Mike, Ghost Six out."

"So, what should we do, Sergeant?" Dirty Burt asked.

"Knock really hard with your foot."

We knocked really hard with our feet for the rest of the afternoon, and to our surprise most of the doors flew open. And whenever we found an open door we were obligated to follow orders and search the place. The boys fought over who got to knock at each house, but in the end we took turns, including me. The floodwaters had receded in certain neighborhoods, so we were sent in to clear the houses on those streets. Once the house was cleared, we marked the exterior of the house with spray paint that we took from the smashed-up hardware store. I would mark it with our unit number, the date, and whether we had found anything important like a weapon or stolen goods. The flood was all around us, and that stagnant black water smelled incredibly toxic. It sat there without waves or any movement except when the rare broken gas line made it bubble slowly. The water was full of death, sewage, and broken possessions.

I tried very hard to keep my momentum, to keep my enthusiasm from fading, but every single time I splintered a doorframe by kicking a deadbolt I smelled the desert for an instant. There was no one to shoot at us in New Orleans, but that didn't keep my heart from jumping just like it did in Hamtown. I had been affected by the war more than I had thought, and the realization was slowly working its way into my consciousness. The heat, the gear, the memories. Soon my equipment pulled me down, all my war injuries started to ache, and my limp returned for the rest of that day. I pushed all that shit to the side and kept jobbing.

Every house smelled like rich, dark soil cut with the stench of death. Back in my days as an incident responder, I learned that death has a distinct smell. It's a sweet, sickly smell, like blood rotting in veins, with a taste like sucking on a penny. The whole city reeked of it. When we went inside homes after the water went down, that smell became a physical obstacle. The walls in every room were split in half; the top teal, white, or whatever pleasant color someone would pick to live in, the bottom half covered with crusty, shit-brown mud, algae, and microbes that lived by eating the dead and rotting. Objects accumulated by families, little knick-knacks and treasures, became scattered flotsam in the slime on the floor.

I don't think a person could have looked at that damage and not tried to imagine the water rushing through the city through house after house, swallowing the chemicals and toxic liquids in each car; each house, each garage, everything adding to the sludge. The water overtaking men, women, and animals in its inevitable way; the water filling their lungs, killing them and stealing their bodies, the decay adding to the toxicity. Every crack, every small space in a house let the flood in. Nothing was watertight. Now the water had receded, and it left a thick layer of scum on everything that didn't float: flat-screen TVs, chairs, couches, kitchen appliances, beds, and other furniture. Framed pictures of precious moments *did* float, and while the toxic film never completely covered some of them it still clung around the happy face of a child, a couple hugging each other, a grandmother with her granddaughter.

We found big piles of stolen goods inside every fifth house or so. I'd say twenty percent of the people in our patrol area played the looting game. It surprised me to see only one of these houses had stockpiled water or canned food. Everyone else stole piles of Air Jordans and other name-brand shoes, bottles of top-shelf alcohol, cigarette cartons, or dirty magazines.

That night at the seminary I kicked back on my cot, listening to all the bugs buzz and bounce off my mosquito netting while I squeezed a barbequed chicken patty from a plastic MRE pouch. If you looked past the fact that we were patrolling American streets with rifles, and that those streets looked like the aftermath of World War III, you could say it was a successful day. The last thing I did before sleeping on my cot was to brief the captain on our progress. He was pleased, but my body ached and I began to question whether I could do it anymore.

Flying Sharks and Zombie Squirrels

It was close to one hundred degrees and about two in the afternoon. My squad and I stood on an overpass above Highway 10, surrounding a five-foot-long shark carcass. The humidity kept me in a continual coat of sweat. The only relief was the occasional light breeze, but even that always brought the smell of decaying animals. I breathed shallowly through my mouth; a person wasn't meant to get used to those types of smells. Angry flies scattered from the shark's eyes whenever any of us moved. It must have been a thing of beauty, moving through the deep waters of the Gulf of Mexico, nature's killing machine, but at my feet it was just a giant decomposing carcass.

"Holy shit. This thing probably flew twenty miles in the hurricane," Walken said.

"This is a fucking tiger shark," Schaeffer said.

The skin was dry and wrinkled, and the mouth hung to the side, showing teeth black at the base and white at the tips.

"It's a bull shark, there's no doubt about it," Walken said.

"No way, Corporal. Look at the fucking stripes." Schaeffer said, pointing at what he believed to be stripes across its back.

"Bulldog Six, this is Ghost Six. What is your status?" the battalion RTO called over the radio. I had called in a body when we saw the thing from a distance and they wanted an update on the situation.

"Those are scratches," Walken said. "It flew inside the hurricane and all types of shit ran into it."

I squinted to see if they were scratches or stripes, without caring one way or the other. The radio called again, "Bulldog Six, this is Ghost Six, do you have a Delta Bravo, over?" A Delta Bravo was the army's phonetic alphabet for DB, which stood for dead body. I decided they were scratches and wondered why they didn't just say dead body. The city was full of them. It wasn't a secret.

"Sarge, what do you think?" Walken asked me.

I took off my helmet and ran my hand through my soaked hair.

"I don't give a shit what kind of shark it is, let's see what's inside," Dirty Burt said as he pulled out a knife and knelt down next to it. He stabbed it under the mouth and cut it right down to its asshole. Water and stomach contents spilled out like someone had popped a waterbed mattress. We all jumped back several feet so all the shit wouldn't get on our boots.

The stomach contents were mostly fish, but something else popped out, too. At first I thought it was coral, but after I kicked it a bit I realized it was a deer antler.

"Bulldog Six, this is Ghost Six, we need a sitrep, over," the radio called again. Sitrep was short for situation report.

"Sergeant, are you going to answer them?" Walken asked me.

I heard him but kept staring at the shark, thinking, *Everything moves toward its end.*

"I wonder where the other antler is," Dirty Burt laughed.

"Sergeant, Battalion really wants to get ahold of us," Walken repeated.

I unclipped the hand-mic from my webgear and answered, "Roger, Ghost Six, we have a single Delta Bravo." I gave them the eight-digit grid coordinate.

"Bulldog Six, we need a description of the body, over."

"Sure, it is approximately five foot three, one hundred and twenty pounds, blue in color with what appear to be scratches on its back," I said.

"I told you. This is a fucking bull shark," Walken said.

"Roger, Bulldog Six, Charlie Mike, out."

The next morning we were ahead of schedule, so we pulled an extra mission. The captain needed us to clear the projects. Because the waters had recently receded enough to get to them, the escaped prisoners might be hiding there. I took my half of the platoon and headed out.

When we arrived, it was obvious that the flood had only given one of the five buildings back; the other four were still covered up to the first-floor windows. There was no way we would set foot in those fetid waters. The other rescue workers had told us stories of seeing animals drinking it in the morning and dying the same night, so wading shoulder-deep in the shit to clear out government housing for the poorest of the poverty-stricken wasn't an option.

One of the young privates from my platoon threw a rock into the middle of an oil rainbow floating about fifty feet in. The splash invited more rocks, and in a few minutes a half-dozen of the soldiers were trying to hit the circle-blotch of colors. The sound startled a few dogs and got them barking. I looked down the street on both sides of us, but didn't see where the hell they were until one of my squad leaders pointed up at the project balconies. There they were: American bulldogs, Rottweilers, and Doberman pinschers of all sizes paced back and forth on the balconies, starving, dying of thirst. I stared up at what had to be a hundred dying dogs while their yelps, whines, and cries filled the streets and bounced off every wall.

"Christ, we better call this in." I fumbled for the radio.

The dogs had been left in the apartments by their masters. My platoon sliced into the plastic pouches of all the MREs we carried, and we did our best to toss them to the animals we could reach. The cries wouldn't stop. I had to walk away for a while, find a place to sit in the shade, and try as hard as I could not to think of the men with their guts blown out at North Gate.

Two hours later, I stood in the sun on what would have been a very unremarkable street corner while the rest of the squad took a break in the shade of a house on the other side. I stared at a black man in his fifties hanging upside down from a telephone pole. He was the first person we'd found this way, but it wasn't an uncommon sight throughout the city. In one of the briefings, the captain had told us about the upside-down dead people. The initial responders buzzed around on their motorboats trying to find the live people. At first, whenever they found a dead one, they recovered the body, but soon there were too many to recover so they tied the people to telephone poles, sometimes with the corpse's belt or shoestrings, and called in their grid coordinates for the body retrieval team. The body retrieval team was overworked and couldn't get to all of the grid coordinates before the water went down. The scene didn't seem to affect the boys at all, but I stared at this man. Before I was blown up I probably wouldn't have cared either, but now I did. No one could ever guess they would end up in that way. Was that it? I don't know.

Behind me the boys argued. Corporal Craig Walken yelled at one of the men in his team. "There's no such thing as zombie squirrels!"

I walked over to the shade and pulled out a cigarette.

"Look, right there, that fucking squirrel chewed through his own fucking cheek." Private Schaeffer pointed.

Sure enough, there was a squirrel with a big hole in his right cheek, standing on his hind legs, staring at us without fear.

"You don't know what's in this fucking water," Private Schaeffer said.

A lot of dead shit was in the water. I looked back at the man hanging from the telephone pole. His skin wasn't brown anymore; it had turned the color of ash and it didn't reflect the sun. The bloat stretched his clothes, and all his weight rested on the side of his head, his spine shaped like a C.

"You watch too much television. They've been in the trees this whole time. They're not undead; they're fucking starving. Watch." Walken pulled a PowerBar from his right cargo pocket, peeled it open, and threw some to the squirrel. The squirrel jumped to catch it in the air. It bounced off and rolled a ways down the street. Another squirrel pounced on it. The two squirrels fought.

"See, see! I never saw two squirrels fight like that—they're fucking zombies," Schaeffer said.

I took off my helmet, ran my hand through my sweat-drenched hair, and arched my back. My equipment felt twice as heavy as it had the day before. I called Battalion Command over the radio and told them about the body. There was two minutes of radio silence and then they told me to Charlie Mike.

A week later, Battalion sent us to search an extremely poor section of Orleans Parish called Indian Village. Every street was named after a Native American tribe that had lived in the area before we pushed them west. Naming a ghetto after them must have seemed like some sort of tribute at one time. Those houses had such thin walls I doubted they had any insulation. Most of them were old shotgun houses no wider than two front doors side by side; others weren't anything more than built-up shacks. All of them had been half-filled with floodwaters.

We kicked the doors in. Around noon we found a wild-eyed woman wearing a dingy floral-patterned housedress three sizes too big hiding in her bathtub behind the shower curtain. She scared the shit out of Walken. He almost shot her, but instead brought her out to the front to talk to me. She loudly informed me that her name was Mimi. She said, "I was conceived in this house, I was born in this house, I lived in this house my whole life, and I will die in this house."

I asked her why she had hidden from us.

"Look at you. If you were me, you'd hide too."

I looked at the squad, standing with the same combat load we carried in Iraq, listening to her.

"You think you boys would be carrying guns if Beverly Hills flooded?"

I asked her what she'd been living on and if she needed anything. She told me that every day, in the afternoon, she would go around and find the things she needed, so she was fine, except she may need more insulin in a week or so. She'd had type 1 diabetes since her teens.

"Mimi, insulin needs to be refrigerated or it won't work," I told her.

This started her on a rant about how much weight she'd lost since the flood, and how sometimes she would just pass out and sleep for hours. I knew this meant her body was breaking down from the lack of insulin. She was lucky she hadn't fallen into a coma.

"I'm sorry, Mimi, but you're going to have to come with us." Immediately, I knew those were the wrong words. I should have explained that I only wanted her to be looked over by a doctor and taken care of. I should have said she'd be dead in a couple days if she didn't come with us.

Her frightened eyes looked from one soldier to the next like a cornered animal, and she started screaming for us to leave. I called in the situation on the battalion net, and Captain Charbonneau was on the other end. Within fifteen minutes he arrived with some of the headquarters platoon, an ambulance, and a news crew. I introduced them to Mimi. The medical personnel worked on her while the captain gave an exclusive interview about how his company had saved another life. Officers were still the same, no matter the deployment. I told my squad to load up, and we slipped off to the next sector.

Private Schaeffer drove our dented and dinged bus through the abandoned cars and fallen trees to the neighborhood around Pontchartrain Park. The guys in back joked about Mimi, imitating her voice: "I was conceived in this house, I was born in this house…" The vibration of my cell phone surprised me. It wasn't something that happened a lot while on patrol. I flipped it open to see a text from Jaime.

The best thing happened, I am now engaged to be Mrs. Andy Hoffman.

I had no idea why she would send this to me, but then I saw it was a mass text, probably to everyone in her phone. I knew they were getting along, and Andy was a nice enough guy, but marriage? The news didn't piss me off, but I couldn't help but remember some moments. She was my first beautiful thing. But there would be others. I stared out the window. The setting sun reflected off the oils on the water, coloring the sides of the houses with blues, yellows, and greens.

Franklin Avenue was our western limit, and we cleared all the houses on the way to Peoples Avenue, our eastern limit. In this way we zigzagged south through the middle-class neighborhoods. These houses were nicer than the others. They had yards, extra rooms, handsome siding, and thick doors, and many of the windows had been boarded up by the owners before the evacuation.

Twilight came, and I decided we would clear one more street before heading back to the seminary. My turn to knock came up, and it took three good kicks to break the deadbolt. The smell of death hit me hard before the door had swung all the way open. I clicked on the flashlight mounted to the barrel of my rifle. The narrow beam cut through the dark into the living room, and I saw a body, naked except for boxer shorts, on the mattress of a pullout couch.

"We got someone," I said.

I covered my nose with my left sleeve and stepped into the room. The squad flowed in behind me. The beams of our four flashlights moved over the scene. A man lay on a bare, striped mattress, a revolver in his right hand, resting on a blood-crusted pillow with the left half of his head missing. On his right thigh was a single piece of lined notebook paper. I stepped a few feet closer to inspect the paper. It had his name, social security number, and birthday written in a shaky hand, and it had been plastic-wrapped around his leg to waterproof it and fix it there.

One of the privates cussed, ran outside, and emptied his guts off the porch. A couple more of the men did the same. I didn't move, only breathed shallowly through my mouth to avoid the smell, but I could still taste it in my lungs. My hands started tingling like they were asleep, then my feet. Little sparks flew around at the edge of my vision. I turned around and told everyone to clear out.

When I called it in, the battle captain told me that since this man didn't die from the flood it was a big deal. He instructed us to stay until the police came. Someone pulled out a deck of cards and the guys played a game, smoked cigarettes, and bullshitted. I walked to the street and called Jaime, let it ring once, and then hung up and called Andy instead. I congratulated him and told him I'd help throw his bachelor party.

We didn't get back until after eleven at night. I was drained, mentally and physically. We all filed by a box of MREs and picked one up. While we sat on our cots digging the plastic spoons into the main meal pouches, I glanced from man to man trying to see if this shit affected them as much as it affected me, but they laughed and joked. The men who didn't puke at the suicide's house made fun of the men who did. An hour later most everyone was asleep, and half were snoring.

I couldn't sleep, but I wasn't awake. I was somewhere in between, dreaming up memories of all the dead people I'd seen: the couple burned alive in the white car at North Gate; a chest blown out across loose sand; bodies in Haiti dumped into the bay at Port-au-Prince; the broken man dying at my feet in his own shit and blood; and Simon, hunched over in the truck, fully engulfed in flames. The last memory woke me up suddenly, and I didn't want to close my eyes again, afraid the images would be trapped in my head if I did. At times I was afraid to even blink. I don't know how long I stared at the ceiling, listening to the buzz of crickets, before finally going to sleep.

I drifted into another dream, where I saw myself sitting with the suicide man at his kitchen table. The deafening sounds of the hurricane pounded at the walls of his house and I felt the absolute terror I imagined he felt. The wind screamed like a jet engine and pulled at the corners of the plywood nailed over the windows. The candles had all blown out and refused to be lit again. We sat paralyzed by fear in the dark except when the lightning flashed, making our faces deathly white and reflecting off the black floodwaters pouring in and swirling around our feet. His revolver lay on the table between us. The dream ended when I reached for it.

I didn't shave or change clothes the next morning before heading to the daily briefing. The captain gave me a sector to clear and told us about the other rescue teams in the area. We were the only ones still looking for dead bodies, but there were at least a dozen civilian teams to help the animals. They had collected most of the dogs from the projects, had even found a couple rabbits and a Komodo dragon. On my way back to my platoon, the command sergeant major called me over. He was a broad-chested career man with a ranger tab and the professional leadership style to make everyone want to do their best.

"Sergeant Davis." I felt him inspecting every whisker on my chin. "Are you feeling all right?"

"Yes, Sergeant Major." I stood at parade rest.

"Good. I wanted to tell you you're doing a hell of a job," he said. "I read the report about the insulin-dependent diabetic. That's what we're here for—to save lives."

I thanked him.

He straightened his patrol cap and said, "As you may have heard, my oldest boy got his commission and, well, you know these young lieutenants. They have big ideas, and without a good platoon sergeant to show them the ropes, well, they can make mistakes."

"Yes, Sergeant Major."

"I want you to be his platoon sergeant, you know, to train him up. Don't take any shit from him," he said with a smile.

I tried hard not to show my surprise. Again, I thought I was fucking up and about ready to get thrown out. "Thank you, Sergeant Major. I would be honored."

We stood looking at each other for a couple seconds. "Well, that's it. I know he'll be in good hands." I knew he wanted me to say something, but I couldn't thank him. I didn't want to lie to him. There was no way I was going to return to the old unit and be a platoon sergeant. I was done. Maybe I didn't know it until right then, but the infantryman inside me was gone.

I turned to return to my platoon, but he stopped me. "Sergeant Davis."

"Sergeant Major?"

"Make sure you drag a razor across that face before you head out today."

"Yes, Sergeant Major."

Whole

On November 11, 2011, I'm wearing a black suit and tie, holding my two-year-old daughter in my arms, and looking into the bright blue sky. The clouds are gone, at least for the day. A couple of meadowlarks take turns chasing each other across the treetops in the distance. City noises are distant and I'm at peace. I take a deep breath of that Pacific Northwest air to see if I can taste the trees. It's ten in the morning and thousands of people line the streets of Albany, Oregon, waiting for the Veterans Day parade to start. I stand in front of an old five-ton truck with a banner zip-tied to the side that reads, "Grand Marshalls, Presidential Unit Citation Recipients, Battle of Fallujah, Iraq, November 2004, 2nd Platoon, Bravo Company, 2/162."

My wife and Simon's mother stand with me by this truck in a staging area for the parade. High school kids dressed in their band uniforms gather behind us, with shiny buttons, tall hats with chin straps, and bright green stripes running down their pant legs. They text or play games on their phones or talk and laugh with each other. Ahead of us, four Boy Scouts decide their positions for the march, holding a banner announcing who we are. Floats from locally owned businesses, vintage cars, and different types of clubs run down the street in both directions. A veterans' motorcycle club is up front, and I think I saw horses at the end when we passed it all to find our position.

This parade, they say, is the biggest Veterans Day parade west of the Mississippi.

The PUC, or Presidential Unit Citation, is the same award given to the men who killed Osama bin Laden; 101st Airborne Division won it for the invasion of Normandy. It's a big fucking deal. The Pentagon awarded the PUC to my platoon for their amazing feats in the Battle of Najaf, months after I had been sent home, but Schofield and the rest of the men invited me down anyway.

Most of us have stayed in touch and gotten together when we can, and it seemed like the more time that passed the more sacred our war experience became, and the more we cherished each other and our relationships. But it was a rough road. A few tried to commit suicide, a few were arrested, a few disappeared completely. Lieutenant Caius was promoted a few times and sent to be on the staff of the US consulate in Kazakhstan; Quinn fully recovered and joined Special Forces. A bunch of the guys left the military but went back as contractors, doing the same job and getting paid four times as much. We all cope in different ways. Maybe someday we will get together again, like in that painting of the Vikings in Valhalla I did years ago. Maybe someday we will...

But today the sky is blue and I'm standing on a corner with my wife at my side, my two-year-old daughter squirming in my arms. Tom Cederman, the man I shared a trailer with in Iraq, waves and throws a play salute at the Boy Scouts. A smile spreads across my face before he even sees me. Patterson is behind him, holding hands with his wife. Then I see Melvin and Addison. I hand my daughter to Simon's mother so I can hug the friends I haven't seen in months, or, in some cases, years.

Simon's mother lost her only child and I blamed myself, but I still reached out to her. Seeing her or talking to her was painful when I first started to get my shit together, but I didn't let that stop me from calling her on holidays or his birthday. In my mind I was keeping a promise to him. Sometimes our conversation would last only a couple of seconds, but I kept calling, then started going to her house, then began inviting her into my life. Now she plays the role of matriarch in my small family. Unfortunately, Simon's father wasn't interested in talking to me. The one time I met the man, he wouldn't shake my hand. I understand why.

My father died from his thirty-year suicide by drugs and alcohol a few years after I returned from Katrina and left the military. He stayed alive long enough to see me graduate with my bachelor's degree, but not my master's. I was okay with that because he was proud of me, and that was all I had really wanted since those times growing up in the Cascade Mountains.

After I married Kell and we bought our house in Northeast Portland, my mother moved in with us for a while, but she left again, saying she really wasn't the grandmother type. She left a hole, but one that Simon's mother filled. My children have a grandmother, and I have a family with her and these men.

So my family and I climb up the tailgate and onto the five-ton truck, the first one I've been on since training in Texas. Not all the boys from the platoon are here; Corporal Walken dropped off the radar after Katrina, but I did hear he was married and had a little girl. Mechaiah O'Brian disappeared soon after returning from Iraq and getting arrested for drug possession, but the good news is that I found him this year — on Facebook of all places. He's on the dean's list at a university in Portland and looks to be in a solid relationship with a man he loves. None of us had any idea Mechaiah was gay and none of us would have cared. He turned out to be one of the best soldiers I've ever served with, and I only hope that I didn't do anything to make him think he couldn't tell me. I will reach out to him soon. I hope to be good friends again.

Schofield, Cederman, Melvin, Patterson, fast-talking Danny Addison, and myself all smile to the waving crowd with our wives and children around us. Simon's mother sits beside me and I put my arm around her. My two-year-old daughter sits on her lap and throws candy to the crowd. Laughing children run alongside the truck and stop to pick up the Jolly Ranchers and fun-sized candy bars before going back to their families. Elderly men and women sit in foldout chairs holding small American flags stapled to sticks. My daughter's eyes light up at seeing so many people, and she calls Simon's mom Nana and points. Every minute or so they laugh and smile at each other.

Baldwin couldn't make it. He's out of town with his new wife. The army awarded him the Silver Star for saving my life that day, and they made a goddamn action figure out of him. Really — I have a couple. He's about four inches tall, in full desert camo, flak vest, and ammo pouches just like he used to wear them, and he's holding a shotgun. When I visit him and his wife, we have a beer or two and I make fun of them. I tell him he never carried the shotgun, I did. I laugh at the fact that he's also a video game character in the official army video game.

I wave and smile at people holding signs thanking me for my service, but this isn't a happily-ever-after. The nightmares don't go away. The physical injuries caused some permanent damage; the emotional injuries, too. The war changed me in many ways, but I did get through the toughest times. There were many times I didn't think I would. Art and words saved me. They did. The artist inside me did what the soldier couldn't. The artist found a new purpose and something to live for. When the Veterans Association told me they'd help me go to school, I attacked it like I would any other mission, and in five years had my master's degree in fine arts.

The truck moves at five miles an hour, and sharpshooting Tom Cederman leans over to ask me how my life's been. I tell him about how my brother and I have an art show coming up. My day job pays the bills, but our last series of paintings sold for at least two hundred dollars apiece in only a few months. We sold a couple for six hundred dollars. I told him how I'd had a few stories published in some literary magazines, and I was close to finishing my Iraq memoir. And as I'm saying this to him, I see Dirty Burt behind the crowd on the curb, walking along with the truck. He's skinny like he was during the war, but not a healthy type of skinny. His cheeks and chin are sharp and his eyes sockets are deeper and darker. The clothes he's wearing are dirty and two sizes too big. Meth. I'd heard that he'd kicked it, but maybe not.

We all yell at him to get on the truck and something flashes across his face. Pride, maybe, but it only lasts until he realizes the crowd is looking at him, too. The attention unnerves him and he just shakes his head and stops walking.

When he first returned from the war, Burt nosedived like many of us, but he really shot to rock bottom with the help of alcohol and nasty drugs. Schofield told me that the last time he'd seen Burt was when he talked the county sheriff into releasing him after he was arrested for bare-knuckle fighting. He fought for money after last call outside some tavern. The last anyone heard, he was married and expecting his second child.

The truck keeps moving and he grows smaller, but I can still see that unnecessary, self-inflicted shame in his eyes. I don't know if he'll get through this and that scares the hell out of me. Too many of us came back empty inside, with a need to self-destruct. He is the real reason I wrote this book. I don't think the world needs another war story about a squad of men who fought against all odds and won, who rallied against near-impossible obstacles until the tear-jerking end, whose story could easily be made into a Hollywood blockbuster. Maybe if I write a book exposing my faults and how vulnerable, confused, and scared-as-shit I was throughout this time in my life, it can help someone like Burt. Maybe it can help someone like Simon's mom. Maybe it can help a servicemember's sister, mother, or father. If more people could see that the men and women who fought in this war weren't invincible heroes but real people with fears, faults, and hopes, then they might understand the problems those service members have after coming back. If I write a book and hold nothing back, showing others it's possible to get through the drunken nights of unexplainable rage or impossible sadness, then maybe I can help someone out there.

Off in the distance, the army band, with their big percussion and brass section, plays something beautiful but just a bit out of tune. I laugh. My two-year-old daughter hugs Simon's mom tight and says, "Nana, more candy." Nana looks over at me. I smile and nod, and for the moment I'm whole.

Terminology:
All Those Things a Person Needs to Know to Be a Good Infantry Soldier

Think of the infantry as a giant, mean Russian doll with a bunch of smaller mean Russian dolls inside, all of them equipped with shoulder-fired, air-cooled, magazine-fed semi-automatic weaponry. There are four soldiers to a team and two teams to a squad. Three line squads and one weapons squad make a platoon. Three line platoons and one headquarters platoon make a company. Three line companies and one headquarters company make a battalion. Team–Squad–Platoon–Company–Battalion. A battalion has roughly 350–1,000 soldiers in it.

Line infantry squads are what Steven Spielberg makes all the cool movies about. Each squad has one squad leader, which every Hollywood leading man would give his left nut to play (while making a million times more money pretending to do it than the man who is getting shot at with real bullets). There are also two team leaders, two light machine gunners, two grenadiers, one rifleman, and one designated sharpshooter. The infantry line squad is the mallet that the US Army uses to beat its weary drum. Squad leaders and team leaders carry M4 rifles (you've seen one in every major war movie in the past five or ten years), machine gunners carry M249 Squad Automatic Weapons (SAW) with chain-linked ammo (spits lots of bullets, but these are smaller than the ones in a heavy machine gun). Grenadiers carry M203s, which are M4 rifles with grenade launchers under the barrel (think the final scene in *Scarface*), and the designated marksman carries an M14 semi-automatic. The M14 looks like the M1 (think *Saving Private Ryan*) but with a twenty-round magazine. These men know everything about each other. They know each other's family members, their favorite sayings, their dreams, their hopes; they even know where the birthmarks are on each other's girlfriends.

Weapons squads carry two heavy machine guns: the M240s, which took the place of the M60s (think *Rambo*), and—if they could get their hands on it—the M2 .50 caliber machine gun that could easily shoot a VW Bug in half quicker than you can say, "Holy shit—you just shot that car in half." Weapons squad is historically filled with the bulkiest, craziest, and smartest soldiers. They are the ones who keep the enemies shitting their pants instead of shooting at the line squads.

An infantry line company has three line squads and a weapons squad. The members of a good infantry line company are closer to each other than you are to your family. The members of a great infantry line company are closer to each other than you are to your genitalia. One great infantry line company could fend off the armies of Xerxes, Alexander, and Genghis Khan—if you gave them enough ammo and Class iv (building materials) to dig a proper defensive perimeter. This is not an exaggeration.

A battalion is made up of three or four line companies and one headquarters company. The headquarters companies exist for logistic and administrative purposes. These units plan attacks, wash clothes, deliver mail, and get the line units their beans and bullets. Historically, they are led by majors, captains, and master sergeants, but populated by pogues (fat-bodies that the line companies threw out) and broke-dicks (Joes who hurt themselves in training—or complain that they did in order to get out of training) and sometimes the very smartest soldiers (because officers don't know as much about computers or radios as the younger "Nintendo-Nofriendo" generation). If a soldier is too bad at his job or too good at his job, he ends up in a headquarters company.

Rank structure for enlisted men:
  E stands for enlisted.
    E1 & E2: Both are private ranks with little difference between the two; their tears could fill an ocean.
    E3: PFC, or Private First Class—a private who has suddenly become self-aware.
    E4: Specialist—a glorified private who gets put in charge every once in a while.
    E4: Corporal—more than a specialist but less than a sergeant, and whenever you find a shit detail, they are in charge. They are the lowest-ranking noncommissioned officer (NCO). They get paid the same as a specialist, but have to do more to earn it.
    E5: SGT, Sergeant or Buck Sergeant—the blossom from an unjustified arrogance. A newly promoted buck sergeant feels he could fix the world if given a loud enough bullhorn.

E6: SSG, or Staff Sergeant—proper rank for a squad leader and the best position in the military. The SSG has just enough rank to afford a bit of independence, but not enough to attend staff meetings. The higher-ups believe him capable of leading a squad in combat but incapable of understanding PowerPoint. This illusion is kept up by both sides, giving the SSG the ability to avoid bureaucratic bullshit and the officers a false sense of superiority.

E7: SFC, or Sergeant First Class—proper rank for a platoon sergeant. He leads thirty-plus men and has to deal with the platoon leader, the company commander, and the whining of all the enlisted men in his platoon. SFCs always get the best lines in military movies. They are the ones portrayed as sons of bitches with hearts of gold. They kick around and cuss at their own men while chewing a cigar in one scene, and then secretly sacrifice for them in the next.

E8: First Sergeant—highest-ranking NCO in a company. They are very elusive and rarely seen in the wild due to staff meetings and battalion briefings. These war-hardened warriors gave up their authority to lead missions in order to be a conduit between the enlisted and the officers. Their duties include translating information coming from the officers to a language the enlisted will understand, filtering bullshit, and ensuring their soldiers receive cots and MREs when possible. A first sergeant's one outlet is torturing privates with horribly tedious details.

E9: Sergeant Major—the highest-ranking NCO in the battalion, and usually a badass who killed fifteen guys with his KA-BAR and one with his can opener during the last war. Remember two things about a sergeant major: only speak when spoken to and STAY OFF HIS GRASS. Sergeants major are extremely territorial and will inevitably find the most trafficked patch of grass in the unit to call his so when a new private walks on the grass all the fury of a twenty-plus-year career can be unleashed.

Rank structure for Officers:
O stands for officer and they are of a higher class. The lowest officer, the platoon leader, technically outranks the most senior NCO in the military, but everyone knows that if a second lieutenant tried to order around a higher enlisted he'd be wearing his ass for a hat.

O1 & O2: Both lieutenant ranks with little difference between them. They will act like they lead the platoon while following their platoon sergeant's "suggestions," although a good lieutenant will plan missions and really look out for the well-being of his men.

O3: Captain, Commander, or CO (Commanding Officer)—leads the company. Given just enough rope to tie a noose and throw it over a low branch. He's the guy who usually dies going into the second act in all the good war movies.

O4: Major—has almost a serious enough rank to write a credible war book that may someday be turned into a movie starring someone like Mel Gibson. They spend their time compiling reports and briefing each other while doing little actual work. If they are injured in wartime, it's a good bet they tripped over or fell off of something.

O5: Lieutenant Colonel—almost a full-bird colonel, but still only an oak leaf. Battalion commanders start out as LTCS and then get their bird if they stay out of trouble, although the pressure of being in this situation can turn an otherwise competent man completely insane in about seven weeks' time. I say this because I saw it happen.

O6: Colonel—like a tenured professor. This man can do little wrong. He is insulated from the troops and, on today's modern battlefield, the danger as well, except for the exceptional ones. Colonels are to be avoided at all times, unless you have the same last name. Then they are to go immediately in front of you in the chow line. Other than that an infantryman has little need for one.

During my time in the infantry there were no women. It is the only job in any of the armed forces that females aren't permitted to do, now that the navy has begrudgingly given them slots on submarines. The military gave us no official reasoning for this, leaving it up to the soldiers to assume that a penis was vital for combat. I feel it is inevitable that infantry will be coed, but it hasn't happened yet.

Acknowledgments

This book wouldn't have happened without the support, help, and friendship of a great many people. This list includes but is not limited to the following:

Team Davis—Kelly, Cody, Cora, and Jackie Juniper

Keith and Vince Davis for being the best brothers a guy could have

Jackie and Sheila Herman for being so supportive

Karen Hilsendager for being a mother to me and a grandmother to my kids

Mike Magnuson for being a worthy and generous mentor

Kase, Mary, and Lucas Johnstun

Craig Leslie

Miah Washburn for helping me help returning veterans

The Rogue Cell Crew for helping me as a returned veteran

Joe Thomas Baca III, Kyle Smetana, and Jarrett Brown for the asylum days

Jason Allen for the late night winter editing sessions

Jonathan Stark

Tom and Karin Davenport

Michael Coan

Mike Geyer

Kyle Crawshaw

Katya Amato for learning all those dead languages

Pete Salerno, Chris Kent, Toph Bailey, John Ashford, Dave Williams, Kris Haney, Shane and Brian Ward, Matt Zedwick, Matt McCreery, Joe Hogland, Peter Brady, Cliff Matier, Jason Winslow, Chris Johnson, John Willingham, Tommy Houston, Keith Dow, Shad Thomas, Tim Marr, and all the men of Bravo Company.

Ooligan Press

Ooligan Press takes its name from a Native American word for the common smelt or candlefish. A vibrant and integral part of Portland's publishing community, Ooligan operates within the Department of English at Portland State University. Ooligan Press is staffed by students pursuing master's degrees in an apprenticeship program under the guidance of a core faculty of publishing professionals.

Project Managers
- Laurel Boruck
- Mary Breaden
- Emily Gravlin
- Kait Heacock
- Whitney Smyth

Editing
- Sarah Currin-Moles (manager)
- Lacey Friedly (manager)
- Drew Lazzara (manager)
- Jonathan Stark (manager)
- Jennifer Tibbet (manager)
- Gino Cerruti
- Marco España
- Gina Fox
- Rebekah Hunt
- Tara Lehmann
- Kathryn Osterndorff
- Lo Pirie
- Courtney Pondelick
- Whitney Smyth
- Katey Trnka
- Geoff Wallace
- Travis Willmore

Design
- Riley Kennysmith (manager)
- Lorna Nakell (manager)
- Paul Dudley
- Gina Fox

Marketing & Promotions
- Laurel Boruck (manager)
- Adam Salazar (manager)
- Sarah Currin-Moles
- Marco España
- Sarah Hale
- Lauren Hudgins
- Ariana Marquis
- Sabrina Parys
- Mary Presnell
- David Quinton
- Katy Roberts
- Tiffany Shelton
- Brian Tibbetts
- Ariana Vives

Digital
- Kai Belladone (manager)
- Mary Presnell
- Camille Watts

Colophon

The Wax Bullet War is set in Palatino LT Std, which is based on Hermann Zapf's 1950 Palatino for the Stempl foundry. Titles are set in League Gothic, from The League of Moveable Type.